BRITISH ENGL

ENGLISH FINNISH

THEME-BASED DICTIONARY

Contains over 9000 commonly used words

T&P BOOKS PUBLISHING

Theme-based dictionary British English-Finnish - 9000 words
British English collection

By Andrey Taranov

T&P Books vocabularies are intended for helping you learn, memorize and review foreign words. The dictionary is divided into themes, covering all major spheres of everyday activities, business, science, culture, etc.

The process of learning words using T&P Books' theme-based dictionaries gives you the following advantages:

- Correctly grouped source information predetermines success at subsequent stages of word memorization
- Availability of words derived from the same root allowing memorization of word units (rather than separate words)
- Small units of words facilitate the process of establishing associative links needed for consolidation of vocabulary
- Level of language knowledge can be estimated by the number of learned words

T&P Books Publishing
www.tpbooks.com

ISBN: 978-1-78400-023-3

This book is also available in E-book formats.
Please visit www.tpbooks.com or the major online bookstores.

FINNISH THEME-BASED DICTIONARY
British English collection

T&P Books vocabularies are intended to help you learn, memorize, and review foreign words. The vocabulary contains over 9000 commonly used words arranged thematically.

- Vocabulary contains the most commonly used words
- Recommended as an addition to any language course
- Meets the needs of beginners and advanced learners of foreign languages
- Convenient for daily use, revision sessions, and self-testing activities
- Allows you to assess your vocabulary

Special features of the vocabulary

- Words are organized according to their meaning, not alphabetically
- Words are presented in three columns to facilitate the reviewing and self-testing processes
- Words in groups are divided into small blocks to facilitate the learning process
- The vocabulary offers a convenient and simple transcription of each foreign word

The vocabulary has 256 topics including:

Basic Concepts, Numbers, Colors, Months, Seasons, Units of Measurement, Clothing & Accessories, Food & Nutrition, Restaurant, Family Members, Relatives, Character, Feelings, Emotions, Diseases, City, Town, Sightseeing, Shopping, Money, House, Home, Office, Working in the Office, Import & Export, Marketing, Job Search, Sports, Education, Computer, Internet, Tools, Nature, Countries, Nationalities and more ...

TABLE OF CONTENTS

PRONUNCIATION GUIDE

Letter	Finnish example	T&P phonetics alphabet	English example
A a	Avara	[ɑ]	shorter than in park, card
B b	Bussi	[b]	baby, book
C c	C-rappu	[s]	city, boss
D d	Kadulla	[d]	day, doctor
E e	Pelto	[e]	elm, medal
F f	Filmi	[f]	face, food
G g	Jooga	[g]	game, gold
H h	Hattu	[h]	home, have
I i	Piha	[i]	shorter than in feet
J j	Juna	[j]	yes, New York
K k	Katu	[k]	clock, kiss
L l	Lapio	[l]	lace, people
M m	Muna	[m]	magic, milk
N n	Nainen	[n]	name, normal
O o	Kova	[o]	pod, John
P p	Papin	[p]	pencil, private
R r	Ruoka	[r]	rice, radio
S s	Suosio	[s]	city, boss
T t	Tapa	[t]	tourist, trip
U u	Uni	[u]	book
V v	Vaaka	[ʋ]	vase, winter
Y y	Tyttö	[y]	fuel, tuna
Z z	Fazer	[ʦ]	cats, tsetse fly
Ä ä	Älä	[æ]	chess, man
Ö ö	Pöllö	[ø]	eternal, church

Diphthongs

ää	Ihmetyttää	[æ:]	longer than in brand
öö	Miljardööri	[ø:]	first, thirsty
aa	Notaari	[a:]	calf, palm
ii	Poliisi	[i:]	feet, meter
oo	Koomikko	[o:]	fall, bomb
uu	Nojapuut	[u:]	pool, room
yy	Flyygeli	[y:]	longer than fuel

ABBREVIATIONS used in the dictionary

ab.	-	about
adj	-	adjective
adv	-	adverb
anim.	-	animate
as adj	-	attributive noun used as adjective
e.g.	-	for example
etc.	-	et cetera
fam.	-	familiar
fem.	-	feminine
form.	-	formal
inanim.	-	inanimate
masc.	-	masculine
math	-	mathematics
mil.	-	military
n	-	noun
pl	-	plural
pron.	-	pronoun
sb	-	somebody
sing.	-	singular
sth	-	something
v aux	-	auxiliary verb
vi	-	intransitive verb
vi, vt	-	intransitive, transitive verb
vt	-	transitive verb

BASIC CONCEPTS

Basic concepts. Part 1

1. Pronouns

I, me	**minä**	[miɲæ]
you	**sinä**	[siɲæ]
he	**hän**	[ɦæn]
she	**hän**	[ɦæn]
it	**se**	[se]
we	**me**	[me]
you (to a group)	**te**	[te]
they	**he**	[he]

2. Greetings. Salutations. Farewells

Hello! (fam.)	**Hei!**	[hej]
Hello! (form.)	**Hei!**	[hej]
Good morning!	**Hyvää huomenta!**	[hyʋæ: huomentɑ]
Good afternoon!	**Hyvää päivää!**	[hyʋæ: pæjʋæ:]
Good evening!	**Hyvää iltaa!**	[hyʋæ: iltɑ:]
to say hello	**tervehtiä**	[terʋehtiæ]
Hi! (hello)	**Moi!**	[moj]
greeting (n)	**terve**	[terʋe]
to greet (vt)	**tervehtiä**	[terʋehtiæ]
How are you?	**Mitä kuuluu?**	[mitæ ku:lu:]
What's new?	**Mitä on uutta?**	[mitæ on u:ttɑ]
Bye-Bye! Goodbye!	**Näkemiin!**	[ɲækemi:in]
See you soon!	**Pikaisiin näkemiin!**	[pikɑjsi:in ɲækemi:in]
Farewell!	**Hyvästi!**	[hyʋæsti]
to say goodbye	**hyvästellä**	[hyʋæsteʎæ]
Cheers!	**Hei hei!**	[hej hej]
Thank you! Cheers!	**Kiitos!**	[ki:itos]
Thank you very much!	**Paljon kiitoksia!**	[pɑlʰøn ki:itoksiɑ]
My pleasure!	**Ole hyvä**	[ole hyʋæ]
Don't mention it!	**Ei kestä kiittää**	[ej kestæ ki:ittæ:]
It was nothing	**Ei kestä**	[ej kestæ]
Excuse me!	**Anteeksi!**	[ɑnte:ksi]
to excuse (forgive)	**antaa anteeksi**	[ɑntɑ: ɑnte:ksi]
to apologize (vi)	**pyytää anteeksi**	[py:tæ: ɑnte:ksi]

My apologies	**Pyydän anteeksi**	[py:dæn ante:ksi]
I'm sorry!	**Anteeksi!**	[ante:ksi]
to forgive (vt)	**antaa anteeksi**	[anta: ante:ksi]
please (adv)	**ole hyvä**	[ole hyʋæ]
Don't forget!	**Älkää unohtako!**	[ælkæ: unohtako]
Certainly!	**Tietysti!**	[tietysti]
Of course not!	**Eipä tietenkään!**	[ejpæ tieteŋkæ:n]
Okay! (I agree)	**Olen samaa mieltä!**	[olen sama: mieltæ]
That's enough!	**Riittää!**	[ri:ittæ:]

3. How to address

mister, sir	**Herra**	[herra]
madam	**Rouva**	[rouʋa]
miss	**Neiti**	[nejti]
young man	**Nuori mies**	[nuorimies]
young man (little boy)	**Poika**	[pojka]
miss (little girl)	**Tyttö**	[tyttø]

4. Cardinal numbers. Part 1

0 zero	**nolla**	[nolla]
1 one	**yksi**	[yksi]
2 two	**kaksi**	[kaksi]
3 three	**kolme**	[kolme]
4 four	**neljä**	[nel^{h}jæ]
5 five	**viisi**	[ʋi:isi]
6 six	**kuusi**	[ku:si]
7 seven	**seitsemän**	[sejʦemæn]
8 eight	**kahdeksan**	[kahdeksan]
9 nine	**yhdeksän**	[yhdeksæn]
10 ten	**kymmenen**	[kymmenen]
11 eleven	**yksitoista**	[yksi tojsta]
12 twelve	**kaksitoista**	[kaksi tojsta]
13 thirteen	**kolmetoista**	[kolme tojsta]
14 fourteen	**neljätoista**	[nel^{h}jæ tojsta]
15 fifteen	**viisitoista**	[ʋi:isi tojsta]
16 sixteen	**kuusitoista**	[ku:si tojsta]
17 seventeen	**seitsemäntoista**	[sejʦemæn tojsta]
18 eighteen	**kahdeksantoista**	[kahdeksan tojsta]
19 nineteen	**yhdeksäntoista**	[yhdeksæn tojsta]
20 twenty	**kaksikymmentä**	[kaksi kymmentæ]
21 twenty-one	**kaksikymmentäyksi**	[kaksi kymmentæ yksi]
22 twenty-two	**kaksikymmentäkaksi**	[kaksi kymmentæ kaksi]
23 twenty-three	**kaksikymmentäkolme**	[kaksi kymmentæ kolme]
30 thirty	**kolmekymmentä**	[kolme kymmentæ]
31 thirty-one	**kolmekymmentäyksi**	[kolme kymmentæ yksi]

32 thirty-two	**kolmekymmentäkaksi**	[kolme kymmentæ kaksi]
33 thirty-three	**kolmekymmentäkolme**	[kolme kymmentæ kolme]
40 forty	**neljäkymmentä**	[nel^{h}jæ kymmentæ]
41 forty-one	**neljäkymmentäyksi**	[nel^{h}jæ kymmentæ yksi]
42 forty-two	**neljäkymmentäkaksi**	[nel^{h}jæ kymmentæ kaksi]
43 forty-three	**neljäkymmentäkolme**	[nel^{h}jæ kymmentæ kolme]
50 fifty	**viisikymmentä**	[ʋi:isi kymmentæ]
51 fifty-one	**viisikymmentäyksi**	[ʋi:isi kymmentæ yksi]
52 fifty-two	**viisikymmentäkaksi**	[ʋi:isi kymmentæ kaksi]
53 fifty-three	**viisikymmentäkolme**	[ʋi:isi kymmentæ kolme]
60 sixty	**kuusikymmentä**	[ku:si kymmentæ]
61 sixty-one	**kuusikymmentäyksi**	[ku:si kymmentæ yksi]
62 sixty-two	**kuusikymmentäkaksi**	[ku:si kymmentæ kaksi]
63 sixty-three	**kuusikymmentäkolme**	[ku:si kymmentæ kolme]
70 seventy	**seitsemänkymmentä**	[sejʦemæn kymmentæ]
71 seventy-one	**seitsemänkymmentäyksi**	[sejʦemæn kymmentæ yksi]
72 seventy-two	**seitsemänkymmentäkaksi**	[sejʦemæn kymmentæ kaksi]
73 seventy-three	**seitsemänkymmentäkolme**	[sejʦemæn kymmentæ kolme]
80 eighty	**kahdeksankymmentä**	[kahdeksan kymmentæ]
81 eighty-one	**kahdeksankymmentäyksi**	[kahdeksan kymmentæ yksi]
82 eighty-two	**kahdeksankymmentäkaksi**	[kahdeksan kymmentæ kaksi]
83 eighty-three	**kahdeksankymmentäkolme**	[kahdeksan kymmentæ kolme]
90 ninety	**yhdeksänkymmentä**	[yhdeksæn kymmentæ]
91 ninety-one	**yhdeksänkymmentäyksi**	[yhdeksæn kymmentæ yksi]
92 ninety-two	**yhdeksänkymmentäkaksi**	[yhdeksæn kymmentæ kaksi]
93 ninety-three	**yhdeksänkymmentäkolme**	[yhdeksæn kymmentæ kolme]

5. Cardinal numbers. Part 2

100 one hundred	**sata**	[sata]
200 two hundred	**kaksisataa**	[kaksi sata:]
300 three hundred	**kolmesataa**	[kolme sata:]
400 four hundred	**neljäsataa**	[nel^{h}jæ sata:]
500 five hundred	**viisisataa**	[ʋi:isi sata:]
600 six hundred	**kuusisataa**	[ku:si sata:]
700 seven hundred	**seitsemänsataa**	[sejʦemæn sata:]
800 eight hundred	**kahdeksansataa**	[kahdeksan sata:]
900 nine hundred	**yhdeksänsataa**	[yhdeksæn sata:]
1000 one thousand	**tuhat**	[tuhat]
2000 two thousand	**kaksituhatta**	[kaksi tuhatta]
3000 three thousand	**kolmetuhatta**	[kolme tuhatta]
10000 ten thousand	**kymmenentuhatta**	[kymmenen tuhatta]
one hundred thousand	**satatuhatta**	[sata tuhatta]
million	**miljoona**	[mil^{h}ø:na]
billion	**miljardi**	[mil^{h}jardi]

6. Ordinal numbers

first (adj)	**ensimmäinen**	[ensimmæjnen]
second (adj)	**toinen**	[tojnen]
third (adj)	**kolmas**	[kolmɑs]
fourth (adj)	**neljäs**	[nel^{h}jæs]
fifth (adj)	**viides**	[ʋi:ides]
sixth (adj)	**kuudes**	[ku:des]
seventh (adj)	**seitsemäs**	[sejʦemæs]
eighth (adj)	**kahdeksas**	[kɑhdeksɑs]
ninth (adj)	**yhdeksäs**	[yhdeksæs]
tenth (adj)	**kymmenes**	[kymmenes]

7. Numbers. Fractions

fraction	**murtoluku**	[murtoluku]
one half	**puolet**	[puolet]
one third	**kolmannes**	[kolmɑŋes]
one quarter	**neljännes**	[nel^{h}jæŋes]
one eighth	**kahdeksannes**	[kɑhdeksɑŋes]
one tenth	**kymmenennes**	[kymmeneŋes]
two thirds	**kaksi kolmasosaa**	[kɑksi kolmɑsosɑ:]
three quarters	**kolme neljäsosaa**	[kolme nel^{h}jæsosɑ:]

8. Numbers. Basic operations

subtraction	**vähennyslasku**	[ʋæheŋys lɑsku]
to subtract (vi, vt)	**vähentää**	[ʋæhentæ:]
division	**jako**	[jɑko]
to divide (vt)	**jakaa**	[jɑkɑ:]
addition	**yhteenlasku**	[yhte:nlɑsku]
to add up (vt)	**laskea yhteen**	[lɑskeɑ yhte:n]
to add (vi)	**lisätä**	[lisætæ]
multiplication	**kertolasku**	[kertolɑsku]
to multiply (vt)	**kertoa**	[kertoɑ]

9. Numbers. Miscellaneous

digit, figure	**numero**	[numero]
number	**luku**	[luku]
numeral	**lukusana**	[lukusɑnɑ]
minus	**miinus**	[mi:inus]
plus	**plus**	[plus]
formula	**kaava**	[kɑ:ʋɑ]
calculation	**laskenta**	[lɑskentɑ]
to count (vt)	**laskea**	[lɑskeɑ]

to count up	**laskea**	[laskea]
to compare (vt)	**verrata**	[ʋerrata]
How much?	**Kuinka paljon?**	[kuiŋka palʰon]
How many?	**Kuinka monta?**	[kuiŋka monta]
sum, total	**summa**	[summa]
result	**tulos**	[tulos]
remainder	**jäännös**	[jæ:ŋøs]
a few ...	**muutama**	[mu:tama]
few, little (adv)	**vähän**	[ʋæɦæn]
the rest	**muu**	[mu:]
one and a half	**puolitoista**	[puolitojsta]
dozen	**tusina**	[tusina]
in half (adv)	**kahtia**	[kahtia]
equally (evenly)	**tasan**	[tasan]
half	**puoli**	[puoli]
time (three ~s)	**kerta**	[kerta]

10. The most important verbs. Part 1

to advise (vt)	**neuvoa**	[neuʋoa]
to agree (say yes)	**suostua**	[suostua]
to answer (vi, vt)	**vastata**	[ʋastata]
to apologize (vi)	**pyytää anteeksi**	[py:tæ: ante:ksi]
to arrive (vi)	**saapua**	[sa:pua]
to ask (~ oneself)	**kysyä**	[kysyæ]
to ask (~ sb to do sth)	**pyytää**	[py:tæ:]
to be (vi)	**olla**	[olla]
to be afraid	**pelätä**	[peʎætæ]
to be hungry	**minulla on nälkä**	[minulla on ɲælkæ]
to be interested in ...	**kiinnostua**	[ki:iŋostua]
to be needed	**tarvitsee**	[tarʋitse:]
to be surprised	**ihmetellä**	[ihmeteʎæ]
to be thirsty	**minulla on jano**	[minulla on æno]
to begin (vt)	**alkaa**	[alka:]
to belong to ...	**kuulua**	[ku:lua]
to boast (vi)	**kehua**	[kehua]
to break (split into pieces)	**rikkoa**	[rikkoa]
to call (for help)	**kutsua**	[kutsua]
can (v aux)	**voida**	[ʋojda]
to catch (vt)	**ottaa kiinni**	[otta: ki:iŋi]
to change (vt)	**muuttaa**	[mu:tta:]
to choose (select)	**valita**	[ʋalita]
to come down	**laskeutua**	[laskeutua]
to come in (enter)	**tulla sisään**	[tulla sisæ:n]
to compare (vt)	**verrata**	[ʋerrata]
to complain (vi, vt)	**valittaa**	[ʋalitta:]

to confuse (mix up)	**sotkea**	[sotkeɑ]
to continue (vt)	**jatkaa**	[jɑtkɑ:]
to control (vt)	**tarkastaa**	[tɑrkɑstɑ:]
to cook (dinner)	**laittaa**	[lɑjttɑ:]
to cost (vt)	**maksaa**	[mɑksɑ:]
to count (add up)	**laskea**	[lɑskeɑ]
to count on …	**luottaa**	[luottɑ:]
to create (vt)	**luoda**	[luodɑ]
to cry (weep)	**itkeä**	[itkeæ]

11. The most important verbs. Part 2

to deceive (vi, vt)	**pettää**	[pettæ:]
to decorate (tree, street)	**koristaa**	[koristɑ:]
to defend (a country, etc.)	**puolustaa**	[puolustɑ:]
to demand (request firmly)	**vaatia**	[ʋɑ:tiɑ]
to dig (vt)	**kaivaa**	[kɑjʋɑ:]
to discuss (vt)	**käsitellä**	[kæsiteʎæ]
to do (vt)	**tehdä**	[tehdæ]
to doubt (have doubts)	**epäillä**	[epæjʎæ]
to drop (let fall)	**pudottaa**	[pudottɑ:]
to exist (vi)	**olla olemassa**	[ollɑ olemɑssɑ]
to expect (foresee)	**nähdä ennakolta**	[ɲæhdæ eŋɑkoltɑ]
to explain (vt)	**selittää**	[selittæ:]
to fall (vi)	**kaatua**	[kɑ:tuɑ]
to fancy (vt)	**pitää**	[pitæ:]
to find (vt)	**löytää**	[løytæ:]
to finish (vt)	**lopettaa**	[lopettɑ:]
to fly (vi)	**lentää**	[lentæ:]
to follow … (come after)	**seurata**	[seurɑtɑ]
to forget (vi, vt)	**unohtaa**	[unohtɑ:]
to forgive (vt)	**antaa anteeksi**	[ɑntɑ: ɑnte:ksi]
to give (vt)	**antaa**	[ɑntɑ:]
to give a hint	**vihjata**	[ʋih^{h}jɑtɑ]
to go (on foot)	**mennä**	[meŋæ]
to go for a swim	**kylpeä**	[kylpeæ]
to go out (from …)	**poistua**	[pojstuɑ]
to guess right	**arvata**	[ɑrʋɑtɑ]
to have (vt)	**omistaa**	[omistɑ:]
to have breakfast	**syödä aamiaista**	[syødæ ɑ:miɑjstɑ]
to have dinner	**illastaa**	[illɑstɑ:]
to have lunch	**syödä päivällistä**	[syødæ pæjʋællistæ]
to hear (vt)	**kuulla**	[ku:llɑ]
to help (vt)	**auttaa**	[ɑuttɑ:]
to hide (vt)	**piilotella**	[pi:ilotellɑ]
to hope (vi, vt)	**toivoa**	[tojʋoɑ]

to hunt (vi, vt)	**metsästää**	[metsæstæ:]
to hurry (vi)	**kiirehtiä**	[ki:irehtiæ]

12. The most important verbs. Part 3

to inform (vt)	**tiedottaa**	[tiedotta:]
to insist (vi, vt)	**pysyä kannassaan**	[pysyæ kaŋassa:n]
to insult (vt)	**loukata**	[loukata]
to invite (vt)	**kutsua**	[kutsua]
to joke (vi)	**laskea leikkiä**	[laskea lejkkiæ]
to keep (vt)	**säilyttää**	[sæjlyttæ:]
to keep silent	**olla vaiti**	[olla ʋajti]
to kill (vt)	**murhata**	[murhata]
to know (sb)	**tuntea**	[tuntea]
to know (sth)	**tietää**	[tietæ:]
to laugh (vi)	**nauraa**	[naura:]
to liberate (city, etc.)	**vapauttaa**	[ʋapautta:]
to look for ... (search)	**etsiä**	[etsiæ]
to love (sb)	**rakastaa**	[rakasta:]
to make a mistake	**erehtyä**	[erehtyæ]
to manage, to run	**johtaa**	[øhta:]
to mean (signify)	**merkitä**	[merkitæ]
to mention (talk about)	**mainita**	[majnita]
to miss (school, etc.)	**olla poissa**	[olla pojssa]
to notice (see)	**huomata**	[huomata]
to object (vi, vt)	**väittää vastaan**	[ʋæjttæ: ʋasta:n]
to observe (see)	**seurata**	[seurata]
to open (vt)	**avata**	[aʋata]
to order (meal, etc.)	**tilata**	[tilata]
to order (mil.)	**käskeä**	[kæskeæ]
to own (possess)	**omistaa**	[omista:]
to participate (vi)	**osallistua**	[osallistua]
to pay (vi, vt)	**maksaa**	[maksa:]
to permit (vt)	**antaa lupa**	[anta: lupa]
to plan (vt)	**suunnitella**	[su:ŋitella]
to play (children)	**leikkiä**	[lejkkiæ]
to pray (vi, vt)	**rukoilla**	[rukojlla]
to prefer (vt)	**katsoa parhaaksi**	[katsoa parha:ksi]
to promise (vt)	**luvata**	[luʋata]
to pronounce (vt)	**lausua**	[lausua]
to propose (vt)	**ehdottaa**	[ehdotta:]
to punish (vt)	**rangaista**	[raŋajsta]
to read (vi, vt)	**lukea**	[lukea]
to recommend (vt)	**suositella**	[suositella]
to refuse (vi, vt)	**kieltäytyä**	[kæltæytyæ]
to regret (be sorry)	**sääliä**	[sæ:liæ]
to rent (sth from sb)	**vuokrata**	[ʋuokrata]

to repeat (say again)	**toistaa**	[tojsta:]
to reserve, to book	**reservoida**	[reseruojda]
to run (vi)	**juosta**	[juosta]

13. The most important verbs. Part 4

to save (rescue)	**pelastaa**	[pelasta:]
to say (~ thank you)	**sanoa**	[sanoa]
to scold (vt)	**haukkua**	[haukkua]
to see (vt)	**nähdä**	[ɲæhdæ]
to sell (vt)	**myydä**	[my:dæ]
to send (vt)	**lähettää**	[ʎæhettæ:]
to shoot (vi)	**ampua**	[ampua]
to shout (vi)	**huutaa**	[hu:ta:]
to show (vt)	**näyttää**	[ɲæyttæ:]
to sign (document)	**allekirjoittaa**	[allekirʰojtta:]
to sit down (vi)	**istua**	[istua]
to smile (vi)	**hymyillä**	[hymyjʎæ]
to speak (vi, vt)	**keskustella**	[keskustella]
to steal (money, etc.)	**varastaa**	[uarasta:]
to stop (cease)	**lakata**	[lakata]
to stop (for pause, etc.)	**pysähtyä**	[pysæhtyæ]
to study (vt)	**oppia**	[oppia]
to swim (vi)	**uida**	[ujda]
to take (vt)	**ottaa**	[otta:]
to think (vi, vt)	**ajatella**	[ajatella]
to threaten (vt)	**uhata**	[uhata]
to touch (by hands)	**koskettaa**	[kosketta:]
to translate (vt)	**kääntää**	[kæ:ntæ:]
to trust (vt)	**luottaa**	[luotta:]
to try (attempt)	**koettaa**	[koetta:]
to turn (~ to the left)	**kääntää**	[kæ:ntæ:]
to underestimate (vt)	**aliarvioida**	[aliaruiojda]
to understand (vt)	**ymmärtää**	[ymmærtæ:]
to unite (vt)	**yhdistää**	[yhdistæ:]
to wait (vt)	**odottaa**	[odotta:]
to want (wish, desire)	**haluta**	[haluta]
to warn (vt)	**varoittaa**	[uarojtta:]
to work (vi)	**työskennellä**	[tyøskeŋeʎæ]
to write (vt)	**kirjoittaa**	[kirʰojtta:]
to write down	**kirjoittaa muistiin**	[kirʰojtta: mujsti:in]

14. Colours

colour	**väri**	[uæri]
shade (tint)	**vivahdus**	[uiuahdus]
hue	**värisävy**	[uæri sæuy]

rainbow	**sateenkaari**	[sate:n ka:ri]
white (adj)	**valkoinen**	[ʋalkojnen]
black (adj)	**musta**	[musta]
grey (adj)	**harmaa**	[harma:]
green (adj)	**vihreä**	[ʋihreæ]
yellow (adj)	**keltainen**	[keltajnen]
red (adj)	**punainen**	[punajnen]
blue (adj)	**sininen**	[sininen]
light blue (adj)	**vaaleansininen**	[ʋa:lean sininen]
pink (adj)	**vaaleanpunainen**	[ʋa:lean punajnen]
orange (adj)	**oranssi**	[oranssi]
violet (adj)	**violetti**	[ʋioletti]
brown (adj)	**ruskea**	[ruskea]
golden (adj)	**kultainen**	[kultajnen]
silvery (adj)	**hopeinen**	[hopejnen]
beige (adj)	**beige**	[be:ge]
cream (adj)	**kermanvärinen**	[kerman ʋærinen]
turquoise (adj)	**turkoosi**	[turko:si]
cherry red (adj)	**kirsikanpunainen**	[kirsikan punajnen]
lilac (adj)	**sinipunainen**	[sini punajnen]
crimson (adj)	**karmiininpunainen**	[karmi:inen punajnen]
light (adj)	**vaalea**	[ʋa:lea]
dark (adj)	**tumma**	[tumma]
bright (adj)	**kirkas**	[kirkas]
coloured (pencils)	**väri-**	[ʋæri]
colour (e.g. ~ film)	**värillinen**	[ʋærillinen]
black-and-white (adj)	**mustavalkoinen**	[musta ʋalkojnen]
plain (one colour)	**yksivärinen**	[yksiʋærinen]
multicoloured (adj)	**erivärinen**	[eriʋærinen]

15. Questions

Who?	**Kuka?**	[kuka]
What?	**Mikä?**	[mikæ]
Where? (at, in)	**Missä?**	[missæ]
Where (to)?	**Mihin?**	[mihin]
Where ... from?	**Mistä?**	[mistæ]
When?	**Milloin?**	[millojn]
Why? (aim)	**Mitä varten?**	[mitæ ʋarten]
Why? (reason)	**Miksi?**	[miksi]
What for?	**Minkä vuoksi?**	[miŋkæ ʋuoksi]
How? (in what way)	**Miten?**	[miten]
What? (which?)	**Millainen?**	[millajnen]
Which?	**Mikä?**	[mikæ]
To whom?	**Kenelle?**	[kenelle]
About whom?	**Kenestä?**	[kenestæ]

About what?	**Mistä?**	[mistæ]
With whom?	**Kenen kanssa?**	[kenen kanssa]
How many?	**Kuinka monta?**	[kuiŋka monta]
How much?	**Kuinka paljon?**	[kuiŋka palʰon]
Whose?	**Kenen?**	[kenen]

16. Prepositions

with (accompanied by)	**kanssa**	[kanssa]
without	**ilman**	[ilman]
to (indicating direction)	**...ssa/ssä**	[ssa] / [ssæ]
about (talking ~ ...)	**...sta, ...stä**	[sta], [stæ]
before (in time)	**ennen**	[eŋen]
in front of ...	**edessä**	[edessæ]
under (beneath, below)	**alla**	[alla]
above (over)	**yllä**	[yʎæ]
on (atop)	**päällä**	[pæ:ʎæ]
from (off, out of)	**...sta, ...stä**	[sta], [stæ]
of (made from)	**...sta, ...stä**	[sta], [stæ]
in (e.g. ~ ten minutes)	**päästä**	[pæ:stæ]
over (across the top of)	**yli**	[yli]

17. Function words. Adverbs. Part 1

Where? (at, in)	**Missä?**	[missæ]
here (adv)	**täällä**	[tæ:ʎæ]
there (adv)	**siellä**	[sieʎæ]
somewhere (to be)	**jossain**	[øssajn]
nowhere (not anywhere)	**ei missään**	[ej missæ:n]
by (near, beside)	**vieressä**	[ʋæressæ]
by the window	**ikkunan vieressä**	[ikkunan ʋæressæ]
Where (to)?	**Mihin?**	[mihin]
here (e.g. come ~!)	**tänne**	[tæŋe]
there (e.g. to go ~)	**tuonne**	[tuoŋe]
from here (adv)	**täältä**	[tæ:ltæ]
from there (adv)	**sieltä**	[sieltæ]
close (adv)	**lähellä**	[ʎæheʎæ]
far (adv)	**kaukana**	[kaukana]
near (e.g. ~ Paris)	**luona**	[luona]
nearby (adv)	**vieressä**	[ʋæressæ]
not far (adv)	**lähelle**	[ʎæhelle]
left (adj)	**vasen**	[ʋasen]
on the left	**vasemmalla**	[ʋasemmalla]

to the left	**vasemmalle**	[ʋasemalle]
right (adj)	**oikea**	[ojkea]
on the right	**oikealla**	[ojkealla]
to the right	**oikealle**	[ojkealle]
in front (adv)	**edessä**	[edessæ]
front (as adj)	**etumainen**	[etumajnen]
ahead (in space)	**eteenpäin**	[ete:npæjn]
behind (adv)	**takana**	[takana]
from behind	**takaa**	[taka:]
back (towards the rear)	**takaisin**	[takajsin]
middle	**keskikohta**	[keskikohta]
in the middle	**keskellä**	[keskeʎæ]
at the side	**sivulta**	[siʋulta]
everywhere (adv)	**kaikkialla**	[kajkkialla]
around (in all directions)	**ympärillä**	[ympæriʎæ]
from inside	**sisäpuolelta**	[sisæ puolelta]
somewhere (to go)	**jonnekin**	[øŋekin]
straight (directly)	**suoraan**	[suora:n]
back (e.g. come ~)	**takaisin**	[takajsin]
from anywhere	**jostakin**	[østakin]
from somewhere	**jostakin**	[østakin]
firstly (adv)	**ensiksi**	[ensiksi]
secondly (adv)	**toiseksi**	[tojseksi]
thirdly (adv)	**kolmanneksi**	[kolmaŋeksi]
suddenly (adv)	**äkkiä**	[ækkiæ]
at first (adv)	**alussa**	[alussa]
for the first time	**ensi kerran**	[ensi kerran]
long before ...	**kauan ennen kuin**	[kauan eŋen kuin]
anew (over again)	**uudestaan**	[u:desta:n]
for good (adv)	**pysyvästi**	[pysyʋæsti]
never (adv)	**ei koskaan**	[ej koska:n]
again (adv)	**taas**	[ta:s]
now (adv)	**nyt**	[nyt]
often (adv)	**usein**	[usejn]
then (adv)	**silloin**	[silloin]
urgently (quickly)	**pikaisesti**	[pikajsesti]
usually (adv)	**tavallisesti**	[taʋallisesti]
by the way, ...	**muuten**	[mu:ten]
possible (that is ~)	**ehkä**	[ehkæ]
probably (adv)	**todennäköisesti**	[toden ɲækøjsesti]
maybe (adv)	**voi olla**	[ʋoj olla]
besides ...	**lisäksi**	[lisæksi]
that's why ...	**siksi**	[siksi]
in spite of ...	**huolimatta**	[huolimatta]
thanks to ...	**avulla**	[aʋulla]
what (pron.)	**mikä**	[mikæ]

that	**että**	[ettæ]
something	**jokin**	[økin]
anything (something)	**jotakin**	[øtakin]
nothing	**ei mitään**	[ej mitæ:n]
who (pron.)	**kuka**	[kuka]
someone	**joku**	[øku]
somebody	**joku**	[øku]
nobody	**ei kukaan**	[ej kuka:n]
nowhere (a voyage to ~)	**ei mihinkään**	[ej mihiŋkæ:n]
nobody's	**ei kenenkään**	[ej keneŋkæ:n]
somebody's	**jonkun**	[øŋkun]
so (I'm ~ glad)	**niin**	[ni:in]
also (as well)	**myös**	[myøs]
too (as well)	**myös**	[myøs]

18. Function words. Adverbs. Part 2

Why?	**Miksi?**	[miksi]
for some reason	**jostain syystä**	[østajn sy:stæ]
because ...	**koska**	[koska]
for some purpose	**jonkin vuoksi**	[øŋkin ʋuoksi]
and	**ja**	[ja]
or	**tai**	[taj]
but	**mutta**	[mutta]
for (e.g. ~ me)	**varten**	[ʋarten]
too (excessively)	**liian**	[li:ian]
only (exclusively)	**vain**	[ʋajn]
exactly (adv)	**tarkasti**	[tarkasti]
about (more or less)	**noin**	[nojn]
approximately (adv)	**likimäärin**	[likimæ:rin]
approximate (adj)	**likimääräinen**	[likimæ:ræjnen]
almost (adv)	**melkein**	[melkejn]
the rest	**muu**	[mu:]
each (adj)	**joka**	[øka]
any (no matter which)	**jokainen**	[økajnen]
many, much (a lot of)	**paljon**	[palʰøn]
many people	**monet**	[monet]
all (everyone)	**kaikki**	[kajkki]
in exchange for ...	**korvauksena**	[korʋauksena]
in exchange (adv)	**sijaan**	[sija:n]
by hand (made)	**käsin**	[kæsin]
hardly (negative opinion)	**tuskin**	[tuskin]
probably (adv)	**varmaan**	[ʋarma:n]
on purpose (adv)	**tahallaan**	[tahalla:n]
by accident (adv)	**sattumalta**	[sattumalta]

very (adv)	**erittäin**	[erittæjn]
for example (adv)	**esimerkiksi**	[esimerkiksi]
between	**välillä**	[ʋæliʎæ]
among	**keskellä**	[keskeʎæ]
so much (such a lot)	**niin paljon**	[ni:in pɑlʰøn]
especially (adv)	**erikoisesti**	[erikojsesti]

Basic concepts. Part 2

19. Weekdays

Monday	**maanantai**	[mɑ:nɑntɑj]
Tuesday	**tiistai**	[ti:istɑj]
Wednesday	**keskiviikko**	[keskiʋi:ikko]
Thursday	**torstai**	[torstɑj]
Friday	**perjantai**	[perʰjɑntɑj]
Saturday	**lauantai**	[lɑuɑntɑj]
Sunday	**sunnuntai**	[suŋuntɑj]
today (adv)	**tänään**	[tænæ:n]
tomorrow (adv)	**huomenna**	[huomeŋɑ]
the day after tomorrow	**ylihuomenna**	[ylihuomeŋɑ]
yesterday (adv)	**eilen**	[ejlen]
the day before yesterday	**toissapäivänä**	[tojssɑ pæjʋæɲæ]
day	**päivä**	[pæjʋæ]
working day	**työpäivä**	[tyøpæjʋæ]
public holiday	**juhlapäivä**	[juhlɑpæjʋæ]
day off	**vapaapäivä**	[ʋɑpɑ:pæjʋæ]
weekend	**viikonloppu**	[ʋi:ikon loppu]
all day long	**koko päivän**	[koko pæjʋæn]
next day (adv)	**ensi päivänä**	[ensi pæjʋæɲæ]
two days ago	**kaksi päivää sitten**	[kɑksi pæjʋæ: sitten]
the day before	**aattona**	[ɑ:ttonɑ]
daily (adj)	**jokapäiväinen**	[økɑ pæjʋæjnen]
every day (adv)	**joka päivä**	[økɑ pæjʋæ]
week	**viikko**	[ʋi:ikko]
last week (adv)	**viime viikolla**	[ʋi:ime ʋi:ikollɑ]
next week (adv)	**ensi viikolla**	[ensi ʋi:ikollɑ]
weekly (adj)	**jokaviikkoinen**	[økɑʋi:ikkojnen]
every week (adv)	**joka viikko**	[økɑ ʋi:ikko]
twice a week	**kaksi kertaa viikossa**	[kɑksi kertɑ: ʋi:ikossɑ]
every Tuesday	**joka tiistai**	[økɑ ti:istɑj]

20. Hours. Day and night

morning	**aamu**	[ɑ:mu]
in the morning	**aamulla**	[ɑ:mullɑ]
noon, midday	**puolipäivä**	[puolipæjʋæ]
in the afternoon	**iltapäivällä**	[iltɑ pæjʋæʎæ]
evening	**ilta**	[iltɑ]
in the evening	**illalla**	[illɑllɑ]

night	**yö**	[yø]
at night	**yöllä**	[yøʎæ]
midnight	**puoliyö**	[puoli yø]
second	**sekunti**	[sekunti]
minute	**minuutti**	[minu:tti]
hour	**tunti**	[tunti]
half an hour	**puoli tuntia**	[puoli tuntiɑ]
quarter of an hour	**vartti**	[ʋɑrtti]
fifteen minutes	**viisitoista minuuttia**	[ʋi:isitojstɑ minu:ttiɑ]
24 hours	**vuorokausi**	[ʋuoro kɑusi]
sunrise	**auringonnousu**	[ɑuriŋon nousu]
dawn	**sarastus**	[sɑrɑstus]
early morning	**varhainen aamu**	[ʋɑrhɑjnen ɑ:mu]
sunset	**auringonlasku**	[ɑuriŋon lɑsku]
early in the morning	**aamulla aikaisin**	[ɑ:mullɑ ɑjkɑjsin]
this morning	**tänä aamuna**	[tæɲæ ɑ:munɑ]
tomorrow morning	**ensi aamuna**	[ensi ɑ:munɑ]
this afternoon	**tänä päivänä**	[tæɲæ pæjʋæɲæ]
in the afternoon	**iltapäivällä**	[iltɑ pæjʋæʎæ]
tomorrow afternoon	**huomisiltapäivällä**	[huomis iltɑ pæjʋæʎæ]
tonight (this evening)	**tänä iltana**	[tæɲæ iltɑnɑ]
tomorrow night	**ensi iltana**	[ensi iltɑnɑ]
at 3 o'clock sharp	**tasan kolmelta**	[tɑsɑn kolmeltɑ]
about 4 o'clock	**noin neljältä**	[nojn nel^{h}æltæ]
by 12 o'clock	**kahdentoista mennessä**	[kɑhdentojstɑ menessæ]
in 20 minutes	**kahdenkymmenen minuutin kuluttua**	[kɑhdeŋkymmenen minu:tin kuluttuɑ]
in an hour	**tunnin kuluttua**	[tuŋin kuluttuɑ]
on time (adv)	**ajoissa**	[ɑøjssɑ]
a quarter to ...	**varttia vaille**	[ʋɑrttiɑ ʋɑjlle]
within an hour	**tunnin kuluessa**	[tuŋin kuluessɑ]
every 15 minutes	**viidentoista minuutin välein**	[ʋi:iden tojstɑ minu:tin ʋælejn]
round the clock	**ympäri vuorokauden**	[ympæri ʋuoro kɑuden]

21. Months. Seasons

January	**tammikuu**	[tɑmmiku:]
February	**helmikuu**	[helmiku:]
March	**maaliskuu**	[mɑ:lisku:]
April	**huhtikuu**	[huhtiku:]
May	**toukokuu**	[toukoku:]
June	**kesäkuu**	[kesæku:]
July	**heinäkuu**	[hejɲæku:]
August	**elokuu**	[eloku:]

September	**syyskuu**	[sy:sku:]
October	**lokakuu**	[lokaku:]
November	**marraskuu**	[marrasku:]
December	**joulukuu**	[øuluku:]
spring	**kevät**	[keʋæt]
in spring	**keväällä**	[keʋæ:ʎæ]
spring (as adj)	**keväinen**	[keʋæjnen]
summer	**kesä**	[kesæ]
in summer	**kesällä**	[kesæʎæ]
summer (as adj)	**kesäinen**	[kesæjnen]
autumn	**syksy**	[syksy]
in autumn	**syksyllä**	[syksyʎæ]
autumn (as adj)	**syksyinen**	[syksyjnen]
winter	**talvi**	[talʋi]
in winter	**talvella**	[talʋella]
winter (as adj)	**talvinen**	[talʋinen]
month	**kuukausi**	[ku:kausi]
this month	**tässä kuukaudessa**	[tæssæ ku:kaudessa]
next month	**ensi kuukaudessa**	[ensi ku:kaudessa]
last month	**viime kuukaudessa**	[ʋi:ime ku:kaudessa]
a month ago	**kuukausi sitten**	[ku:kausi sitten]
in a month	**kuukauden kuluttua**	[ku:kauden kuluttua]
in two months	**kahden kuukauden kuluttua**	[kahden ku:kauden kuluttua]
a whole month	**koko kuukauden**	[koko ku:kauden]
all month long	**koko kuukauden**	[koko ku:kauden]
monthly (~ magazine)	**kuukautinen**	[ku:kautinen]
monthly (adv)	**kuukausittain**	[ku:kausittajn]
every month	**joka kuukausi**	[øka ku:kausi]
twice a month	**kaksi kertaa kuukaudessa**	[kaksi kerta: ku:kaudessa]
year	**vuosi**	[ʋuosi]
this year	**tänä vuonna**	[tæɲæ ʋuoŋa]
next year	**ensi vuonna**	[ensi ʋuoŋa]
last year	**viime vuonna**	[ʋi:ime ʋuoŋa]
a year ago	**vuosi sitten**	[ʋuosi sitten]
in a year	**vuoden kuluttua**	[ʋuoden kuluttua]
in two years	**kahden vuoden kuluttua**	[kahden ʋuoden kuluttua]
a whole year	**koko vuoden**	[koko ʋuoden]
all year long	**koko vuoden**	[koko ʋuoden]
every year	**joka vuosi**	[øka ʋuosi]
annual (adj)	**vuosittainen**	[ʋuosittajnen]
annually (adv)	**vuosittain**	[ʋuosittajn]
4 times a year	**neljä kertaa vuodessa**	[nel^{h}jæ kerta: ʋuodessa]
date (e.g. today's ~)	**päivä**	[pæjʋæ]
date (e.g. ~ of birth)	**päivämäärä**	[pæjʋæmæ:ræ]

calendar	**kalenteri**	[kalenteri]
half a year	**puoli vuotta**	[puoli ʋuotta]
six months	**vuosipuolisko**	[ʋuosi puolisko]
season (summer, etc.)	**kausi**	[kausi]
century	**vuosisata**	[ʋuosisata]

22. Time. Miscellaneous

time	**aika**	[ajka]
instant (n)	**tuokio**	[tuokio]
moment	**hetki**	[hetki]
instant (adj)	**hetkellinen**	[hetkellinen]
period (length of time)	**ajanjakso**	[ajan^hjakso]
life	**elämä**	[eʎæmæ]
eternity	**ikuisuus**	[ikujsu:s]
epoch	**kausi**	[kausi]
era	**ajanlasku**	[ajanlasku]
cycle	**jakso**	[jakso]
period	**vaihe**	[ʋajhe]
term (short-~)	**määräaika**	[mæ:ræajka]
the future	**tulevaisuus**	[tuleʋajsu:s]
future (as adj)	**ensi**	[ensi]
next time	**ensi kerralla**	[ensi kerralla]
the past	**menneisyys**	[meŋejsy:s]
past (recent)	**viime**	[ʋi:ime]
last time	**viime kerralla**	[ʋi:ime kerralla]
later (adv)	**myöhemmin**	[myøhemmin]
after	**jälkeenpäin**	[jælke:npæjn]
nowadays (adv)	**nykyään**	[nykyæ:n]
now (adv)	**nyt**	[nyt]
immediately (adv)	**heti**	[heti]
soon (adv)	**kohta**	[kohta]
in advance (beforehand)	**ennakolta**	[eŋakolta]
a long time ago	**kauan**	[kauan]
recently (adv)	**äskettäin**	[æskettæjn]
destiny	**kohtalo**	[kohtalo]
memories (childhood ~)	**muisto**	[mujsto]
archives	**arkisto**	[arkisto]
during ...	**aikana**	[ajkana]
long, a long time (adv)	**kauan**	[kauan]
not long (adv)	**vähän aikaa**	[ʋæɦæn ajka:]
early (in the morning)	**aikaisin**	[ajkajsin]
late (not early)	**myöhään**	[myøhæ:n]
forever (for good)	**ainiaaksi**	[ajnia:ksi]
to start (begin)	**aloittaa**	[alojtta:]
to postpone (vt)	**siirtää**	[si:irtæ:]
at the same time	**samanaikaisesti**	[saman ajkajsesti]

permanently (adv)	**alituisesti**	[alitujsesti]
constant (noise, pain)	**vakinainen**	[ʋakinajnen]
temporary (adj)	**väliaikainen**	[ʋæli ajkajnen]
sometimes (adv)	**joskus**	[øskus]
rarely (adv)	**harvoin**	[harʋojn]
often (adv)	**usein**	[usejn]

23. Opposites

rich (adj)	**rikas**	[rikas]
poor (adj)	**köyhä**	[køyɦæ]
ill, sick (adj)	**sairas**	[sajras]
healthy (adj)	**terve**	[terʋe]
big (adj)	**iso**	[iso]
small (adj)	**pieni**	[pæni]
quickly (adv)	**nopeasti**	[nopeasti]
slowly (adv)	**hitaasti**	[hita:sti]
fast (adj)	**nopea**	[nopea]
slow (adj)	**hidas**	[hidas]
cheerful (adj)	**iloinen**	[ilojnen]
sad (adj)	**surullinen**	[surullinen]
together (adv)	**yhdessä**	[yhdessæ]
separately (adv)	**erikseen**	[erikse:n]
aloud (to read)	**ääneen**	[æ:ne:n]
silently (to oneself)	**itsekseen**	[itsekse:n]
tall (adj)	**korkea**	[korkea]
low (adj)	**matala**	[matala]
deep (adj)	**syvä**	[syʋæ]
shallow (adj)	**matala**	[matala]
yes	**kyllä**	[kyʎæ]
no	**ei**	[ej]
distant (in space)	**kaukainen**	[kaukajnen]
nearby (adj)	**läheinen**	[ʎæhejnen]
far (adv)	**kaukana**	[kaukana]
nearby (adv)	**vierellä**	[ʋiereʎæ]
long (adj)	**pitkä**	[pitkæ]
short (adj)	**lyhyt**	[lyhyt]
good (kindhearted)	**hyvä**	[hyʋæ]
evil (adj)	**vihainen**	[ʋihajnen]

married (adj)	**naimisissa oleva**	[nɑjmisissɑ oleʋɑ]
single (adj)	**naimaton**	[nɑjmɑton]
to forbid (vt)	**kieltää**	[kjeltæ:]
to permit (vt)	**antaa lupa**	[ɑntɑ: lupɑ]
end	**loppu**	[loppu]
beginning	**alku**	[ɑlku]
left (adj)	**vasen**	[ʋɑsen]
right (adj)	**oikea**	[ojkeɑ]
first (adj)	**ensimmäinen**	[ensimmæjnen]
last (adj)	**viimeinen**	[ʋi:imejnen]
crime	**rikos**	[rikos]
punishment	**rangaistus**	[rɑŋɑjstus]
to order (vt)	**käskeä**	[kæskeæ]
to obey (vi, vt)	**alistua**	[ɑlistuɑ]
straight (adj)	**suora**	[suorɑ]
curved (adj)	**käyrä**	[kæyræ]
heaven	**paratiisi**	[pɑrɑti:isi]
hell	**helvetti**	[helʋetti]
to be born	**syntyä**	[syntyæ]
to die (vi)	**kuolla**	[kuollɑ]
strong (adj)	**voimakas**	[ʋojmɑkɑs]
weak (adj)	**heikko**	[hejkko]
old (adj)	**vanha**	[ʋɑnhɑ]
young (adj)	**nuori**	[nuori]
old (adj)	**vanha**	[ʋɑnhɑ]
new (adj)	**uusi**	[u:si]
hard (adj)	**kova**	[koʋɑ]
soft (adj)	**pehmeä**	[pehmeæ]
warm (adj)	**lämmin**	[ʎæmmin]
cold (adj)	**kylmä**	[kylmæ]
fat (adj)	**lihava**	[lihɑʋɑ]
slim (adj)	**laiha**	[lɑjhɑ]
narrow (adj)	**kapea**	[kɑpeæ]
wide (adj)	**leveä**	[leʋeæ]
good (adj)	**hyvä**	[hyʋæ]
bad (adj)	**huono**	[huono]
brave (adj)	**rohkea**	[rohkeɑ]
cowardly (adj)	**pelkurimainen**	[pelkurimɑjnen]

24. Lines and shapes

square	**neliö**	[neliø]
square (as adj)	**neliömäinen**	[neliømæjnen]
circle	**ympyrä**	[ympyræ]
round (adj)	**pyöreä**	[pyøreæ]
triangle	**kolmio**	[kolmio]
triangular (adj)	**kolmikulmainen**	[kolmi kulmajnen]
oval	**soikio**	[sojkio]
oval (as adj)	**soikea**	[sojkea]
rectangle	**suorakulmio**	[suorakulmio]
rectangular (adj)	**suorakulmainen**	[suorakulmajnen]
pyramid	**pyramidi**	[pyramidi]
rhombus	**vinoneliö**	[ʋino neliø]
trapezium	**trapetsi**	[trapetsi]
cube	**kuutio**	[ku:tio]
prism	**prisma**	[prisma]
circumference	**ympyrä**	[ympyræ]
sphere	**pallo**	[pallo]
globe (sphere)	**pallo**	[pallo]
diameter	**halkaisija**	[halkajsija]
radius	**säde**	[sæde]
perimeter	**ympärysmitta**	[ympærys mittæ]
centre	**keskus**	[keskus]
horizontal (adj)	**vaakasuora**	[ʋa:ka suora]
vertical (adj)	**pystysuora**	[pysty suora]
parallel (n)	**leveyspiiri**	[leʋeyspi:iri]
parallel (as adj)	**yhdensuuntainen**	[yhden su:ntajnen]
line	**viiva**	[ʋi:iʋa]
stroke	**viiva**	[ʋi:iʋa]
straight line	**suora**	[suora]
curve (curved line)	**käyrä**	[kæyræ]
thin (line, etc.)	**ohut**	[ohut]
contour (outline)	**ääriviivat**	[æ:ri ʋi:iʋat]
intersection	**leikkauskohta**	[lejkkaus kohta]
right angle	**suora kulma**	[suora kulma]
segment	**segmentti**	[segmentti]
sector	**sektori**	[sektori]
side (of triangle)	**puoli**	[puoli]
angle	**kulma**	[kulma]

25. Units of measurement

weight	**paino**	[pajno]
length	**pituus**	[pitu:s]
width	**leveys**	[leʋeys]
height	**korkeus**	[korkeus]

depth	**syvyys**	[syʊy:s]
volume	**tilavuus**	[tilɑʊu:s]
area	**pinta-ala**	[pintɑ ɑlɑ]
gram	**gramma**	[grɑmmɑ]
milligram	**milligramma**	[milligrɑmmɑ]
kilogram	**kilo**	[kilo]
ton	**tonni**	[toŋi]
pound	**punta**	[puntɑ]
ounce	**unssi**	[unssi]
metre	**metri**	[metri]
millimetre	**millimetri**	[millimetri]
centimetre	**senttimetri**	[senttimetri]
kilometre	**kilometri**	[kilometri]
mile	**peninkulma**	[penin kulmɑ]
inch	**tuuma**	[tu:mɑ]
foot	**jalka**	[jɑlkɑ]
yard	**jaardi**	[jɑ:rdi]
square metre	**neliömetri**	[neliø metri]
hectare	**hehtaari**	[hehtɑ:ri]
litre	**litra**	[litrɑ]
degree	**aste**	[ɑste]
volt	**voltti**	[ʊoltti]
ampere	**ampeeri**	[ɑmpe:ri]
horsepower	**hevosvoima**	[heʊosʊojmɑ]
quantity	**määrä**	[mæ:ræ]
a little bit of ...	**vähän**	[ʊæɦæn]
half	**puoli**	[puoli]
dozen	**tusina**	[tusinɑ]
piece (item)	**kappale**	[kɑppɑle]
size	**koko**	[koko]
scale (map ~)	**mittakaava**	[mittɑkɑ:ʊɑ]
minimum (adj)	**minimaalinen**	[minimɑ:linen]
the smallest (adj)	**pienin**	[pienin]
medium (adj)	**keskimmäinen**	[keskimmæjnen]
maximum (adj)	**maksimaalinen**	[mɑksimɑ:linen]
the largest (adj)	**suurin**	[su:rin]

26. Containers

jar (glass)	**lasitölkki**	[lɑsitølkki]
tin, can	**peltitölkki**	[peltitølkki]
bucket	**sanko**	[sɑŋko]
barrel	**tynnyri**	[tyŋyri]
basin (for washing)	**vati**	[ʊɑti]
tank (for liquid, gas)	**säiliö**	[sæjliø]

hip flask	**kenttäpullo**	[kenttæ pullo]
jerrycan	**kanisteri**	[kanisteri]
cistern (tank)	**säiliö**	[sæjliø]
mug	**tuoppi**	[tuoppi]
cup (of coffee, etc.)	**kuppi**	[kuppi]
saucer	**teevati**	[te:ʋati]
glass (tumbler)	**lasi**	[lasi]
glass (~ of vine)	**malja**	[malʰja]
stew pot	**kattila**	[kattila]
bottle (~ of wine)	**pullo**	[pullo]
neck (of the bottle)	**pullonkaula**	[pulloŋkaula]
carafe	**karahvi**	[karahʋi]
jug (earthenware)	**kannu**	[kaŋu]
vessel (container)	**astia**	[astia]
pot (crock)	**ruukku**	[ru:kku]
vase	**maljakko**	[malʰjakko]
bottle (~ of perfume)	**pullo**	[pullo]
vial, small bottle	**pullonen**	[pullonen]
tube (of toothpaste)	**tuubi**	[tu:bi]
sack (bag)	**säkki**	[sækki]
bag (paper ~, plastic ~)	**kassi**	[kassi]
packet (of cigarettes, etc.)	**paketti**	[paketti]
box (e.g. shoebox)	**laatikko**	[la:tikko]
crate	**laatikko**	[la:tikko]
basket	**kori**	[kori]

27. Materials

material	**aine**	[ajne]
wood	**puu**	[pu:]
wooden (adj)	**puinen**	[pujnen]
glass (n)	**lasi**	[lasi]
glass (as adj)	**lasinen**	[lasinen]
stone (n)	**kivi**	[kiʋi]
stone (as adj)	**kivinen**	[kiʋinen]
plastic (n)	**muovi**	[muoʋi]
plastic (as adj)	**muovinen**	[muoʋinen]
rubber (n)	**kumi**	[kumi]
rubber (as adj)	**kuminen**	[kuminen]
material, fabric (n)	**kangas**	[kaŋas]
fabric (as adj)	**kankaasta**	[kaŋka:sta]
paper (n)	**paperi**	[paperi]
paper (as adj)	**paperinen**	[paperinen]

cardboard (n)	**kartonki**	[kartoŋki]
cardboard (as adj)	**kartonki**	[kartoŋki]
polythene	**polyetyleeni**	[polyetyle:ni]
cellophane	**kelmu**	[kelmu]
plywood	**vaneri**	[ʋaneri]
porcelain (n)	**posliini**	[posli:ini]
porcelain (as adj)	**posliininen**	[posli:ininen]
clay (n)	**savi**	[saʋi]
clay (as adj)	**savi-**	[saʋi]
ceramics (n)	**keramiikka**	[kerami:ikka]
ceramic (as adj)	**keraaminen**	[kera:minen]

28. Metals

metal (n)	**metalli**	[metalli]
metal (as adj)	**metallinen**	[metallinen]
alloy (n)	**seos**	[seos]
gold (n)	**kulta**	[kulta]
gold, golden (adj)	**kultainen**	[kultajnen]
silver (n)	**hopea**	[hopea]
silver (as adj)	**hopeinen**	[hopejnen]
iron (n)	**rauta**	[rauta]
iron (adj), made of iron	**rautainen**	[rautajnen]
steel (n)	**teräs**	[teræs]
steel (as adj)	**teräksinen**	[teræksinen]
copper (n)	**kupari**	[kupari]
copper (as adj)	**kuparinen**	[kuparinen]
aluminium (n)	**alumiini**	[alumi:ini]
aluminium (as adj)	**alumiini-**	[alumi:ini]
bronze (n)	**pronssi**	[pronssi]
bronze (as adj)	**pronssinen**	[pronssinen]
brass	**messinki**	[messiŋki]
nickel	**nikkeli**	[nikkeli]
platinum	**platina**	[platina]
mercury	**elohopea**	[elo hopea]
tin	**tina**	[tina]
lead	**lyijy**	[lyiy]
zinc	**sinkki**	[siŋkki]

HUMAN BEING

Human being. The body

29. Humans. Basic concepts

human being	**ihminen**	[ihminen]
man (adult male)	**mies**	[mies]
woman	**nainen**	[nɑjnen]
child	**lapsi**	[lɑpsi]
girl	**tyttö**	[tyttø]
boy	**poika**	[pojkɑ]
teenager	**teini-ikäinen**	[tejni ikæjnen]
old man	**vanhus**	[ʋɑnhus]
old woman	**eukko**	[eukko]

30. Human anatomy

organism	**elimistö**	[elimistø]
heart	**sydän**	[sydæn]
blood	**veri**	[ʋeri]
artery	**valtimo**	[ʋɑltimo]
vein	**laskimo**	[lɑskimo]
brain	**aivot**	[ɑjʋot]
nerve	**hermo**	[hermo]
nerves	**hermot**	[hermot]
vertebra	**nikama**	[nikɑmɑ]
spine	**selkäranka**	[selkærɑŋkɑ]
stomach (organ)	**mahalaukku**	[mɑhɑ lɑukku]
intestines, bowel	**suolisto**	[suolisto]
intestine (e.g. large ~)	**suoli**	[suoli]
liver	**maksa**	[mɑksɑ]
kidney	**munuainen**	[munuɑjnen]
bone	**luu**	[lu:]
skeleton	**luuranko**	[lu:rɑŋko]
rib	**kylkiluu**	[kylkilu:]
skull	**pääkallo**	[pæ:kɑllo]
muscle	**lihas**	[lihɑs]
biceps	**hauislihas**	[hɑujslihɑs]
triceps	**kolmipäinen olkalihas**	[kolmipæjnen olkɑlihɑs]
tendon	**jänne**	[jæŋe]
joint	**nivel**	[niʋel]

lungs	**keuhkot**	[keuhkot]
genitals	**sukupuolielimet**	[sukupuoli elimet]
skin	**iho**	[iho]

31. Head

head	**pää**	[pæ:]
face	**kasvot**	[kasʋot]
nose	**nenä**	[neɲæ]
mouth	**suu**	[su:]
eye	**silmä**	[silmæ]
eyes	**silmät**	[silmæt]
pupil	**silmäterä**	[silmæteræ]
eyebrow	**kulmakarva**	[kulmakarʋa]
eyelash	**ripsi**	[ripsi]
eyelid	**silmäluomi**	[silmæluomi]
tongue	**kieli**	[kieli]
tooth	**hammas**	[hammas]
lips	**huulet**	[hu:let]
cheekbones	**poskipäät**	[poski:pæ:t]
gum	**ien**	[ien]
palate	**kitalaki**	[kitalaki]
nostrils	**sieraimet**	[sierajmet]
chin	**leuka**	[leuka]
jaw	**leukaluu**	[leukalu:]
cheek	**poski**	[poski]
forehead	**otsa**	[otsa]
temple	**ohimo**	[ohimo]
ear	**korva**	[korʋa]
back of the head	**niska**	[niska]
neck	**kaula**	[kaula]
throat	**kurkku**	[kurkku]
hair	**hiukset**	[hiukset]
hairstyle	**kampaus**	[kampaus]
haircut	**kampaus**	[kampaus]
wig	**tekotukka**	[teko tukka]
moustache	**viikset**	[ʋi:ikset]
beard	**parta**	[parta]
to have (a beard, etc.)	**hänellä on parta**	[ɦæneʎæ on parta]
plait	**letti**	[letti]
sideboards	**poskiparta**	[poskiparta]
red-haired (adj)	**punatukkainen**	[puna tukkajnen]
grey (hair)	**harmaatukkainen**	[harma:tukkajnen]
bald (adj)	**kaljupäinen**	[kalʲjupæjnen]
bald patch	**kalju**	[kalʲju]
ponytail	**poninhäntä**	[poninɦæntæ]
fringe	**otsatukka**	[otsatukka]

32. Human body

hand	**käsi**	[kæsi]
arm	**käsivarsi**	[kæsiʋɑrssi]
toe	**varvas**	[ʋɑrʋɑs]
thumb	**peukalo**	[peukɑlo]
little finger	**pikkusormi**	[pikkusormi]
nail	**kynsi**	[kynsi]
fist	**nyrkki**	[nyrkki]
palm	**kämmen**	[kæmmen]
wrist	**ranne**	[rɑŋe]
forearm	**kyynärvarsi**	[ky:ɲærʋɑrsi]
elbow	**kyynärpää**	[ky:ɲærpæ:]
shoulder	**hartia**	[hɑrtiɑ]
leg	**jalka**	[jɑlkɑ]
foot	**jalkaterä**	[jɑlkɑteræ]
knee	**polvi**	[polʋi]
calf (part of leg)	**pohje**	[pohʰje]
hip	**reisi**	[rejsi]
heel	**kantapää**	[kɑntɑpæ:]
body	**vartalo**	[ʋɑrtɑlo]
stomach	**maha**	[mɑhɑ]
chest	**rinta**	[rintɑ]
breast	**povi**	[poʋi]
flank	**kylki**	[kylki]
back	**selkä**	[selkæ]
lower back	**ristiselkä**	[ristiselkæ]
waist	**vyötärö**	[ʋyøtærø]
navel	**napa**	[nɑpɑ]
buttocks	**pakarat**	[pɑkɑrɑt]
bottom	**takapuoli**	[tɑkɑpuoli]
beauty mark	**luomi**	[luomi]
tattoo	**tatuointi**	[tɑtuojnti]
scar	**arpi**	[ɑrpi]

Clothing & Accessories

33. Outerwear. Coats

clothes	**vaatteet**	[ʋɑ:tte:t]
outer clothing	**päällysvaatteet**	[pæ:llys ʋɑ:tte:t]
winter clothing	**talvivaatteet**	[tɑlʋi ʋɑ:tte:t]
overcoat	**takki**	[tɑkki]
fur coat	**turkki**	[turkki]
fur jacket	**puoliturkki**	[puoli turkki]
down coat	**untuvatakki**	[untuʋɑtɑkki]
jacket (e.g. leather ~)	**takki**	[tɑkki]
raincoat	**sadetakki**	[sɑdetɑkki]
waterproof (adj)	**vedenpitävä**	[ʋedenpitæʋæ]

34. Men's & women's clothing

shirt	**paita**	[pɑjtɑ]
trousers	**housut**	[housut]
jeans	**farkut**	[fɑrkut]
jacket (of man's suit)	**takki**	[tɑkki]
suit	**puku**	[puku]
dress (frock)	**leninki**	[leniŋki]
skirt	**hame**	[hɑme]
blouse	**pusero**	[pusero]
knitted jacket	**villapusero**	[ʋillɑpusero]
jacket (of woman's suit)	**jakku**	[jɑkku]
T-shirt	**T-paita**	[tepɑjtɑ]
shorts (short trousers)	**sortsit**	[sortsit]
tracksuit	**urheilupuku**	[urhejlupuku]
bathrobe	**froteinen aamutakki**	[frotejnen ɑ:mutɑkki]
pyjamas	**pyjama**	[pyjɑmɑ]
sweater	**villapaita**	[ʋillɑpɑjtɑ]
pullover	**neulepusero**	[neule pusero]
waistcoat	**liivi**	[li:iʋi]
tailcoat	**frakki**	[frɑkki]
dinner suit	**smokki**	[smokki]
uniform	**univormu**	[uniʋormu]
workwear	**työvaatteet**	[tyøʋɑ:tte:t]
boiler suit	**haalari**	[hɑ:lɑri]
coat (e.g. doctor's ~)	**lääkärintakki**	[læ:kærin tɑkki]

35. Clothing. Underwear

underwear	**alusvaatteet**	[alusʋa:tte:t]
vest (singlet)	**aluspaita**	[aluspajta]
socks	**sukat**	[sukat]
nightgown	**pyjama**	[pyjama]
bra	**rintaliivit**	[rintali:iʋit]
knee highs	**polvisukat**	[polʋisukat]
tights	**sukkahousut**	[sukkahousut]
stockings	**sukat**	[sukat]
swimsuit, bikini	**uimapuku**	[ujmapuku]

36. Headwear

hat	**hattu**	[hattu]
trilby hat	**fedora-hattu**	[fedora hattu]
baseball cap	**lippalakki**	[lippalakki]
flatcap	**lakki**	[lakki]
beret	**baskeri**	[baskeri]
hood	**huppu**	[huppu]
panama hat	**panama**	[panama]
knitted hat	**pipo**	[pipo]
headscarf	**huivi**	[huiʋi]
women's hat	**hattu**	[hattu]
hard hat	**kypärä**	[kypæræ]
forage cap	**suikka**	[suikka]
helmet	**kypärä**	[kypæræ]
bowler	**knalli**	[knalli]
top hat	**silinterihattu**	[silinteri hattu]

37. Footwear

footwear	**jalkineet**	[jalkine:t]
ankle boots	**varsikengät**	[ʋarsikeŋæt]
shoes (low-heeled ~)	**kengät**	[keŋæt]
boots (cowboy ~)	**saappaat**	[sa:ppa:t]
slippers	**tossut**	[tossut]
trainers	**lenkkitossut**	[leŋkkitossut]
plimsolls, pumps	**lenkkarit**	[leŋkkarit]
sandals	**sandaalit**	[sanda:lit]
cobbler	**suutari**	[su:tari]
heel	**korko**	[korko]
pair (of shoes)	**pari**	[pari]
shoelace	**nauhat**	[nauhat]

to lace up (vt)	**sitoa kengännauhat**	[sitoa keɲæŋauhat]
shoehorn	**kenkälusikka**	[keŋkælusikka]
shoe polish	**kenkävoide**	[keŋkæʋojde]

38. Textile. Fabrics

cotton (n)	**puuvilla**	[pu:ʋila]
cotton (as adj)	**puuvillasta**	[pu:ʋillasta]
flax (n)	**pellava**	[pellaʋa]
flax (as adj)	**pellavasta**	[pellaʋasta]
silk (n)	**silkki**	[silkki]
silk (as adj)	**silkkinen**	[silkkinen]
wool (n)	**villa**	[ʋilla]
woollen (adj)	**villainen**	[ʋillajnen]
velvet	**sametti**	[sametti]
suede	**säämiskä**	[sæ:miskæ]
corduroy	**sametti**	[sametti]
nylon (n)	**nailon**	[najlon]
nylon (as adj)	**nailonista**	[najlonista]
polyester (n)	**polyesteri**	[polyesteri]
polyester (as adj)	**polyesterinen**	[polyesterinen]
leather (n)	**nahka**	[nahka]
leather (as adj)	**nahkainen**	[nahkajnen]
fur (n)	**turkis**	[turkis]
fur (e.g. ~ coat)	**turkis-**	[turkis]

39. Personal accessories

gloves	**käsineet**	[kæsine:t]
mittens	**lapaset**	[lapaset]
scarf (long)	**kaulaliina**	[kaulali:ina]
glasses	**silmälasit**	[silmælasit]
frame (eyeglass ~)	**kehys**	[kehys]
umbrella	**sateenvarjo**	[sate:nʋarø]
walking stick	**kävelykeppi**	[kæʋelykeppi]
hairbrush	**hiusharja**	[hiushar^{h}ja]
fan	**viuhka**	[ʋiuhka]
tie (necktie)	**solmio**	[solmio]
bow tie	**rusetti**	[rusetti]
braces	**henkselit**	[heŋkselit]
handkerchief	**nenäliina**	[neɲæ li:ina]
comb	**kampa**	[kampa]
hair slide	**hiussolki**	[hiussolki]
hairpin	**hiusneula**	[hiusneula]
buckle	**solki**	[solki]

belt	**vyö**	[ʋyø]
shoulder strap	**hihna**	[hihnɑ]
bag (handbag)	**laukku**	[lɑukku]
handbag	**käsilaukku**	[kæsilɑukku]
rucksack	**reppu**	[reppu]

40. Clothing. Miscellaneous

fashion	**muoti**	[muoti]
in vogue (adj)	**muodikas**	[muodikɑs]
fashion designer	**mallisuunnittelija**	[mɑlli su:ŋittelijɑ]
collar	**kaulus**	[kɑulus]
pocket	**tasku**	[tɑsku]
pocket (as adj)	**tasku-**	[tɑsku]
sleeve	**hiha**	[hihɑ]
hanging loop	**silmukka**	[silmukkɑ]
flies (on trousers)	**halkio**	[hɑlkio]
zip (fastener)	**vetoketju**	[ʋetoketʲju]
fastener	**kiinnitin**	[ki:iŋitin]
button	**nappi**	[nɑppi]
buttonhole	**napinläpi**	[nɑpinʎæpi]
to come off (ab. button)	**irtautua**	[irtɑutuɑ]
to sew (vi, vt)	**ommella**	[ommellɑ]
to embroider (vi, vt)	**kirjoa**	[kirʰøɑ]
embroidery	**kirjonta**	[kirʰøntɑ]
sewing needle	**neula**	[neulɑ]
thread	**lanka**	[lɑŋkɑ]
seam	**sauma**	[sɑumɑ]
to get dirty (vi)	**tahraantua**	[tɑhrɑ:ntuɑ]
stain (mark, spot)	**tahra**	[tɑhrɑ]
to crease, crumple (vi)	**rypistyä**	[rypistyæ]
to tear (vt)	**repiä**	[repiæ]
clothes moth	**koi**	[koj]

41. Personal care. Cosmetics

toothpaste	**hammastahna**	[hɑmmɑs tɑhnɑ]
toothbrush	**hammasharja**	[hɑmmɑs hɑrʰjɑ]
to clean one's teeth	**harjata hampaita**	[hɑrʰjɑtɑ hɑmpɑjtɑ]
razor	**partaveitsi**	[pɑrtɑʋejʦi]
shaving cream	**partavaahdoke**	[pɑrtɑʋɑ:hdoke]
to shave (vi)	**ajaa partansa**	[ɑjɑ: pɑrtɑnsɑ]
soap	**saippua**	[sɑjppuɑ]
shampoo	**sampoo**	[sɑmpo:]
scissors	**sakset**	[sɑkset]

nail file	**kynsiviila**	[kynsiʋi:ila]
nail clippers	**kynsileikkuri**	[kynsilejkkuri]
tweezers	**pinsetit**	[pinsetit]
cosmetics	**meikki**	[mejkki]
face pack	**naamio**	[nɑ:mio]
manicure	**kynsienhoito**	[kynsienhojto]
to have a manicure	**hoitaa kynsiä**	[hojtɑ: kynsiæ]
pedicure	**jalkojenhoito**	[jɑlkojenhojto]
make-up bag	**meikkipussi**	[mejkkipussi]
face powder	**puuteri**	[pu:teri]
powder compact	**puuterirasia**	[pu:terirɑsiɑ]
blusher	**poskipuna**	[poskipunɑ]
perfume (bottled)	**parfyymi**	[pɑrfy:mi]
toilet water	**hajuvesi**	[hɑjuʋesi]
lotion	**kasvovesi**	[kɑsʋoʋesi]
cologne	**kölninvesi**	[kølʋinʋesi]
eyeshadow	**luomiväri**	[luomiʋæri]
eyeliner	**rajauskynä**	[rɑjɑuskyɲæ]
mascara	**ripsiväri**	[ripsiʋæri]
lipstick	**huulipuna**	[hu:lipunɑ]
nail polish	**kynsilakka**	[kynsilɑkkɑ]
hair spray	**hiuslakka**	[hiuslɑkkɑ]
deodorant	**deodorantti**	[deodorɑntti]
cream	**voide**	[ʋojde]
face cream	**kasvovoide**	[kɑsʋoʋojde]
hand cream	**käsivoide**	[kæsiʋojde]
anti-wrinkle cream	**ryppyvoide**	[ryppyʋojde]
day (as adj)	**päivä-**	[pæjʋæ]
night (as adj)	**yöllinen**	[yøllinen]
tampon	**tamponi**	[tɑmponi]
toilet paper	**vessapaperi**	[ʋessɑpɑperi]
hair dryer	**hiustenkuivain**	[hiusten kujʋɑjn]

42. Jewellery

jewellery	**korut**	[korut]
precious (e.g. ~ stone)	**kallisarvoinen**	[kɑllisɑrʋojnen]
hallmark	**tarkastusleimaus**	[tɑrkɑstus lejmɑus]
ring	**sormus**	[sormus]
wedding ring	**vihkisormus**	[ʋihkisormus]
bracelet	**rannerengas**	[rɑŋereŋɑs]
earrings	**korvarenkaat**	[korʋɑreŋkɑ:t]
necklace (~ of pearls)	**kaulakoru**	[kɑulɑkoru]
crown	**kruunu**	[kru:nu]
bead necklace	**helmet**	[helmet]

diamond	**timantti**	[timantti]
emerald	**smaragdi**	[smaragdi]
ruby	**rubiini**	[rubi:ini]
sapphire	**safiiri**	[safi:iri]
pearl	**helmet**	[helmet]
amber	**meripihka**	[meri pihka]

43. Watches. Clocks

watch (wristwatch)	**rannekello**	[raŋekello]
dial	**numerotaulu**	[numerotaulu]
hand (of clock, watch)	**osoitin**	[osojtin]
metal bracelet	**rannerengas**	[raŋereŋas]
watch strap	**hihna**	[hihna]
battery	**paristo**	[paristo]
to be flat (battery)	**olla kulunut loppuun**	[olla kulunut loppu:n]
to change a battery	**vaihtaa paristo**	[ʋajhta: paristo]
to run fast	**edistää**	[edistæ:]
to run slow	**jätättää**	[ætættæ:]
wall clock	**seinäkello**	[sejnækello]
hourglass	**tiimalasi**	[ti:imalasi]
sundial	**aurinkokello**	[auriŋko kello]
alarm clock	**herätyskello**	[herætys kello]
watchmaker	**kelloseppä**	[kelloseppæ]
to repair (vt)	**korjata**	[korʰjata]

Food. Nutricion

44. Food

meat	**liha**	[liha]
chicken	**kana**	[kana]
young chicken	**kananpoika**	[kanan pojka]
duck	**ankka**	[aŋkka]
goose	**hanhi**	[hanhi]
game	**riista**	[ri:ista]
turkey	**kalkkuna**	[kalkkuna]
pork	**sianliha**	[sian liha]
veal	**vasikanliha**	[ʋasikan liha]
lamb	**lampaanliha**	[lampa:n liha]
beef	**naudanliha**	[naudan liha]
rabbit	**kaniini**	[kani:ini]
sausage (salami, etc.)	**makkara**	[makkara]
vienna sausage	**nakki**	[nakki]
bacon	**pekoni**	[pekoni]
ham	**kinkku**	[kiŋkku]
gammon (ham)	**kinkku**	[kiŋkku]
pâté	**tahna**	[tahna]
liver	**maksa**	[maksa]
lard	**silava**	[silaʋa]
mince	**jauheliha**	[jauheliha]
tongue	**kieli**	[kieli]
egg	**muna**	[muna]
eggs	**munat**	[munat]
egg white	**valkuainen**	[ʋalkuajnen]
egg yolk	**keltuainen**	[keltuajnen]
fish	**kala**	[kala]
seafood	**äyriäiset**	[æuriæjset]
caviar	**kaviaari**	[kaʋia:ri]
crab	**kuningasrapu**	[kuniŋasrapu]
prawn	**katkarapu**	[katkarapu]
oyster	**osteri**	[osteri]
spiny lobster	**langusti**	[laŋusti]
octopus	**meritursas**	[meritursas]
squid	**kalmari**	[kalmari]
sturgeon	**sampi**	[sampi]
salmon	**lohi**	[lohi]
halibut	**pallas**	[pallas]
cod	**turska**	[turska]

mackerel	**makrilli**	[makrilli]
tuna	**tonnikala**	[toŋikala]
eel	**ankerias**	[aŋkerias]
trout	**lohi**	[lohi]
sardine	**sardiini**	[sardi:ini]
pike	**hauki**	[hauki]
herring	**silli**	[silli]
bread	**leipä**	[lejpæ]
cheese	**juusto**	[ju:sto]
sugar	**sokeri**	[sokeri]
salt	**suola**	[suola]
rice	**riisi**	[ri:isi]
pasta	**makaronit**	[makaronit]
noodles	**nuudeli**	[nu:deli]
butter	**voi**	[ʋoj]
vegetable oil	**kasviöljy**	[kasʋi øl^{h}y]
sunflower oil	**auringonkukkaöljy**	[auriŋon kukka øl^{h}y]
margarine	**margariini**	[margari:ini]
olives	**oliivit**	[oli:iʋit]
olive oil	**oliiviöljy**	[oli:iʋi øl^{h}y]
milk	**maito**	[majto]
condensed milk	**maitotiiviste**	[majto ti:iʋiste]
yogurt	**jogurtti**	[øgurtti]
sour cream	**hapankerma**	[hapan kerma]
cream (of milk)	**kerma**	[kerma]
mayonnaise	**majoneesi**	[maøne:si]
buttercream	**kreemi**	[kre:mi]
groats	**suurimot**	[su:rimot]
flour	**jauhot**	[jauhot]
tinned food	**säilykkeet**	[sæjlykke:t]
cornflakes	**maissimurot**	[majssi murot]
honey	**hunaja**	[hunaja]
jam	**hillo**	[hillo]
chewing gum	**purukumi**	[purukumi]

45. Drinks

water	**vesi**	[ʋesi]
drinking water	**juomavesi**	[juomaʋesi]
mineral water	**kivennäisvesi**	[kiʋeŋæjs ʋesi]
still (adj)	**ilman hiilihappoa**	[ilman hi:ili happoa]
carbonated (adj)	**hiilihappovettä**	[hi:ili happoʋetta]
sparkling (adj)	**hiilihappoinen**	[hi:ili happojnen]
ice	**jää**	[jæ:]

with ice	**jään kanssa**	[jæ:n kanssa]
non-alcoholic (adj)	**alkoholiton**	[alkoholiton]
soft drink	**alkoholiton juoma**	[alkoholiton juoma]
cool soft drink	**virvoitusjuoma**	[ʋirʋojtus juoma]
lemonade	**limonaati**	[limona:ti]
spirits	**alkoholijuomat**	[alkoholi juomat]
wine	**viini**	[ʋi:ini]
white wine	**valkoviini**	[ʋalko ʋi:ini]
red wine	**punaviini**	[puna ʋi:ini]
liqueur	**likööri**	[likø:ri]
champagne	**samppanja**	[samppan^{h}ja]
vermouth	**vermutti**	[ʋermutti]
whisky	**viski**	[ʋiski]
vodka	**viina**	[ʋi:ina]
gin	**gini**	[gini]
cognac	**konjakki**	[kon^{h}jakki]
rum	**rommi**	[rommi]
coffee	**kahvi**	[kahʋi]
black coffee	**musta kahvi**	[musta kahʋi]
white coffee	**maitokahvi**	[majto kahʋi]
cappuccino	**kahvi kerman kera**	[kahʋi kerman kera]
instant coffee	**murukahvi**	[muru kahʋi]
milk	**maito**	[majto]
cocktail	**cocktail**	[koktejl]
milk shake	**pirtelö**	[pirtelø]
juice	**mehu**	[mehu]
tomato juice	**tomaattimehu**	[toma:tti mehu]
orange juice	**appelsiinimehu**	[appelsi:ini mehu]
freshly squeezed juice	**tuoremehu**	[tuore mehu]
beer	**olut**	[olut]
lager	**vaalea olut**	[ʋa:lea olut]
bitter	**tumma olut**	[tumma olut]
tea	**tee**	[te:]
black tea	**musta tee**	[musta te:]
green tea	**vihreä tee**	[ʋihreæ te:]

46. Vegetables

vegetables	**vihannekset**	[ʋihaŋekset]
greens	**kasvikset**	[kasʋikset]
tomato	**tomaatti**	[toma:tti]
cucumber	**kurkku**	[kurkku]
carrot	**porkkana**	[porkkana]
potato	**peruna**	[peruna]
onion	**sipuli**	[sipuli]

garlic	**valkosipuli**	[ʋalko sipuli]
cabbage	**kaali**	[kɑ:li]
cauliflower	**kukkakaali**	[kukkɑkɑ:li]
Brussels sprouts	**brysselinkaali**	[brysseliŋkɑ:li]
broccoli	**brokkolikaali**	[brokkoli kɑ:li]
beetroot	**punajuuri**	[punɑju:ri]
aubergine	**munakoiso**	[munɑkojso]
marrow	**kesäkurpitsa**	[kesækurpitsɑ]
pumpkin	**kurpitsa**	[kurpitsɑ]
turnip	**nauris**	[nɑuris]
parsley	**persilja**	[persil^{h}æ]
dill	**tilli**	[tilli]
lettuce	**salaatti**	[sɑlɑ:tti]
celery	**selleri**	[selleri]
asparagus	**parsa**	[pɑrsɑ]
spinach	**pinaatti**	[pinɑ:tti]
pea	**herne**	[herne]
beans	**pavut**	[pɑʋut]
maize	**maissi**	[mɑjssi]
kidney bean	**pavut**	[pɑʋut]
bell pepper	**paprika**	[pɑprikɑ]
radish	**retiisi**	[reti:isi]
artichoke	**artisokka**	[ɑrtisokkɑ]

47. Fruits. Nuts

fruit	**hedelmä**	[hedelmæ]
apple	**omena**	[omenɑ]
pear	**päärynä**	[pæ:ryɲæ]
lemon	**sitruuna**	[sitru:nɑ]
orange	**appelsiini**	[ɑppelsi:ini]
strawberry	**mansikka**	[mɑnsikkɑ]
tangerine	**mandariini**	[mɑndɑri:ini]
plum	**luumu**	[lu:mu]
peach	**persikka**	[persikkɑ]
apricot	**aprikoosi**	[ɑpriko:si]
raspberry	**vadelma**	[ʋɑdelmɑ]
pineapple	**ananas**	[ɑnɑnɑs]
banana	**banaani**	[bɑnɑ:ni]
watermelon	**vesimeloni**	[ʋesi meloni]
grape	**viinirypäleet**	[ʋi:inirypæle:t]
sour cherry	**hapankirsikka**	[hɑpɑn kirsikkɑ]
sweet cherry	**linnunkirsikka**	[liŋun kirsikkɑ]
melon	**meloni**	[meloni]
grapefruit	**greippi**	[grejppi]
avocado	**avokado**	[ɑʋokɑdo]
papaya	**papaija**	[pɑpɑijɑ]

mango	**mango**	[maŋo]
pomegranate	**granaattiomena**	[grana:tti omena]
redcurrant	**punaherukka**	[punaherukka]
blackcurrant	**mustaherukka**	[mustaherukka]
gooseberry	**karviaiset**	[karʋiajset]
bilberry	**mustikka**	[mustikka]
blackberry	**vatukka**	[ʋatukka]
raisin	**rusinat**	[rusinat]
fig	**viikuna**	[ʋi:ikuna]
date	**taateli**	[ta:teli]
peanut	**maapähkinä**	[ma:pæhkiɲæ]
almond	**manteli**	[manteli]
walnut	**saksanpähkinä**	[saksan pæhkiɲæ]
hazelnut	**hasselpähkinä**	[hassel pæhkiɲæ]
coconut	**kookospähkinä**	[ko:kos pæhkiɲæ]
pistachios	**pistaasi**	[pista:si]

48. Bread. Sweets

confectionery (pastry)	**makeiset**	[makejs et]
bread	**leipä**	[lejpæ]
biscuits	**keksit**	[keksit]
chocolate (n)	**suklaa**	[sukla:]
chocolate (as adj)	**suklaa-**	[sukla:]
sweet	**karamelli**	[karamelli]
cake (e.g. cupcake)	**leivos**	[lejʋos]
cake (e.g. birthday ~)	**kakku**	[kakku]
pie (e.g. apple ~)	**piirakka**	[pi:irakka]
filling (for cake, pie)	**täyte**	[tæyte]
whole fruit jam	**hillo**	[hillo]
marmalade	**marmeladi**	[marmeladi]
waffle	**vohvelit**	[ʋohʋelit]
ice-cream	**jäätelö**	[jæ:telø]

49. Cooked dishes

course, dish	**ruoka**	[ruoka]
cuisine	**keittiö**	[kejttiø]
recipe	**resepti**	[resepti]
portion	**annos**	[aŋos]
salad	**salaatti**	[sala:tti]
soup	**keitto**	[kejtto]
clear soup (broth)	**liemi**	[liemi]
sandwich (bread)	**voileipä**	[ʋoj lejpæ]

fried eggs	**paistettu muna**	[pajstettu muna]
cutlet	**kotletti**	[kotletti]
hamburger (beefburger)	**hampurilainen**	[hampurilajnen]
beefsteak	**pihvi**	[pihʋi]
roast meat	**paisti**	[pajsti]
garnish	**lisäke**	[lisæke]
spaghetti	**spagetti**	[spagetti]
mash	**perunasose**	[peruna sose]
pizza	**pizza**	[pitsa]
porridge (oatmeal, etc.)	**puuro**	[pu:ro]
omelette	**munakas**	[munakas]
boiled (e.g. ~ beef)	**keitetty**	[kejtetty]
smoked (adj)	**savustettu**	[saʋustettu]
fried (adj)	**paistettu**	[pajstettu]
dried (adj)	**kuivattu**	[kujʋattu]
frozen (adj)	**jäädytetty**	[jæ:dytetty]
pickled (adj)	**marinoitu**	[marinojtu]
sweet (sugary)	**makea**	[makea]
salty (adj)	**suolainen**	[suolajnen]
cold (adj)	**kylmä**	[kylmæ]
hot (adj)	**kuuma**	[ku:ma]
bitter (adj)	**karvas**	[karʋas]
tasty (adj)	**maukas**	[maukas]
to cook (in boiling water)	**keittää**	[kejttæ:]
to cook (dinner)	**laittaa ruokaa**	[lajtta: ruoka:]
to fry (vt)	**paistaa**	[pajsta:]
to heat up (food)	**lämmittää**	[ʎæmmittæ:]
to salt (vt)	**suolata**	[suolata]
to pepper (vt)	**pippuroida**	[pippurojda]
to grate (vt)	**raastaa**	[ra:sta:]
peel (n)	**kuori**	[kuori]
to peel (vt)	**kuoria**	[kuoria]

50. Spices

salt	**suola**	[suola]
salty (adj)	**suolainen**	[suolajnen]
to salt (vt)	**suolata**	[suolata]
black pepper	**musta pippuri**	[musta pippuri]
red pepper	**kuuma pippuri**	[ku:ma pippuri]
mustard	**sinappi**	[sinappi]
horseradish	**piparjuuri**	[pipar^h ju:ri]
condiment	**höyste**	[høyste]
spice	**mauste**	[mauste]
sauce	**kastike**	[kastike]
vinegar	**etikka**	[etikka]
anise	**anis**	[anis]

basil	**basilika**	[basilika]
cloves	**neilikka**	[nejlikka]
ginger	**inkivääri**	[iŋkiυæ:ri]
coriander	**korianteri**	[korianteri]
cinnamon	**kaneli**	[kaneli]
sesame	**seesami**	[se:sami]
bay leaf	**laakerinlehti**	[la:kerin lehti]
paprika	**paprika**	[paprika]
caraway	**kumina**	[kumina]
saffron	**sahrami**	[sahrami]

51. Meals

food	**ruoka**	[ruoka]
to eat (vi, vt)	**syödä**	[syødæ]
breakfast	**aamiainen**	[a:miajnen]
to have breakfast	**syödä aamiaista**	[syødæ a:miajsta]
lunch	**päivällinen**	[pæjυællinen]
to have lunch	**syödä päivällistä**	[syødæ pæjυællistæ]
dinner	**illallinen**	[illallinen]
to have dinner	**illastaa**	[illasta:]
appetite	**ruokahalu**	[ruokahalu]
Enjoy your meal!	**Hyvää ruokahalua!**	[hyυæ: ruokahalua]
to open (~ a bottle)	**avata**	[aυata]
to spill (liquid)	**kaataa**	[ka:ta:]
to spill out (vi)	**kaatua**	[ka:tua]
to boil (vi)	**kiehua**	[kiehua]
to boil (vt)	**keittää**	[kejttæ:]
boiled (~ water)	**keitetty**	[kejtetty]
to chill (vt)	**jäähdyttää**	[jæ:hdyttæ:]
to chill (vi)	**jäähtyä**	[jæ:htyæ]
taste, flavour	**maku**	[maku]
aftertaste	**sivumaku**	[siυumaku]
to be on a diet	**olla dieetillä**	[olla die:tiʎæ]
diet	**dieetti**	[die:ti]
vitamin	**vitamiini**	[υitami:ini]
calorie	**kalori**	[kalori]
vegetarian (n)	**kasvissyöjä**	[kasυissyøjæ]
vegetarian (adj)	**kasvis-**	[kasυis]
fats (nutrient)	**rasvat**	[rasυat]
proteins	**valkuaisaineet**	[υalku ajsajne:t]
carbohydrates	**hiilihydraatit**	[hi:ili hydra:tit]
slice (of lemon, ham)	**viipale**	[υi:ipale]
piece (of cake, pie)	**pala**	[pala]
crumb (of bread)	**muru**	[muru]

52. Table setting

spoon	**lusikka**	[lusikka]
knife	**veitsi**	[ʋejʦi]
fork	**haarukka**	[ha:rukka]
cup (of coffee)	**kuppi**	[kuppi]
plate (dinner ~)	**lautanen**	[lautanen]
saucer	**teevati**	[te:ʋati]
serviette	**lautasliina**	[lautasli:ina]
toothpick	**hammastikku**	[hammas tikku]

53. Restaurant

restaurant	**ravintola**	[raʋintola]
coffee bar	**kahvila**	[kahʋila]
pub, bar	**baari**	[ba:ri]
tearoom	**teehuone**	[te: huone]
waiter	**tarjoilija**	[tarʰøjlija]
waitress	**tarjoilijatar**	[tarʰøjlijatar]
barman	**baarimestari**	[ba:rimestari]
menu	**ruokalista**	[ruoka lista]
wine list	**viinilista**	[ʋi:ini lista]
to book a table	**varata pöytä**	[ʋarata pøytæ]
course, dish	**ruoka**	[ruoka]
to order (meal)	**tilata**	[tilata]
to make an order	**tilata**	[tilata]
aperitif	**aperitiivi**	[aperiti:iʋi]
starter	**alkupalat**	[alkupalat]
dessert, sweet	**jälkiruoka**	[jælkiruoka]
bill	**lasku**	[lasku]
to pay the bill	**maksaa lasku**	[maksa: lasku]
to give change	**antaa rahasta takaisin**	[anta: rahasta takajsin]
tip	**juomaraha**	[juomaraha]

Family, relatives and friends

54. Personal information. Forms

name, first name	**nimi**	[nimi]
family name	**sukunimi**	[sukunimi]
date of birth	**syntymäpäivä**	[syntymæ pæjʊæ]
place of birth	**syntymäpaikka**	[syntymæ pɑjkkɑ]
nationality	**kansallisuus**	[kɑnsɑllisu:s]
place of residence	**asuinpaikka**	[ɑsujnpɑjkkɑ]
country	**maa**	[mɑ:]
profession (occupation)	**ammatti**	[ɑmmɑtti]
gender, sex	**sukupuoli**	[sukupuoli]
height	**pituus**	[pitu:s]
weight	**paino**	[pɑjno]

55. Family members. Relatives

mother	**äiti**	[æjti]
father	**isä**	[isæ]
son	**poika**	[pojkɑ]
daughter	**tytär**	[tytær]
younger daughter	**nuorempi tytär**	[nuorempi tytær]
younger son	**nuorempi poika**	[nuorempi pojkɑ]
eldest daughter	**vanhempi tytär**	[ʊɑnhempi tytær]
eldest son	**vanhempi poika**	[ʊɑnhempi pojkɑ]
brother	**veli**	[ʊeli]
sister	**sisar**	[sisɑr]
cousin (masc.)	**serkku**	[serkku]
cousin (fem.)	**serkku**	[serkku]
mummy	**äiti**	[æjti]
dad, daddy	**isä**	[isæ]
parents	**vanhemmat**	[ʊɑnhemmɑt]
child	**lapsi**	[lɑpsi]
children	**lapset**	[lɑpset]
grandmother	**isoäiti**	[isoæjti]
grandfather	**isoisä**	[isoisæ]
grandson	**lapsenlapsi**	[lɑpsenlɑpsi]
granddaughter	**lapsenlapsi**	[lɑpsenlɑpsi]
grandchildren	**lastenlapset**	[lɑsten lɑpset]
uncle	**setä**	[setæ]
aunt	**täti**	[tæti]

nephew	**veljenpoika**	[ʋeʎæn pojka]
niece	**sisarenpoika**	[sisaren pojka]
mother-in-law	**anoppi**	[anoppi]
father-in-law	**appi**	[appi]
son-in-law	**vävy**	[ʋæʋy]
stepmother	**äitipuoli**	[æjtipuoli]
stepfather	**isäpuoli**	[isæpuoli]
infant	**rintalapsi**	[rintalapsi]
baby (infant)	**vauva**	[ʋauʋa]
little boy, kid	**pienokainen**	[pienokajnen]
wife	**vaimo**	[ʋajmo]
husband	**mies**	[mies]
spouse (husband)	**aviomies**	[aʋiomies]
spouse (wife)	**aviovaimo**	[aʋioʋajmo]
married (masc.)	**naimisissa oleva**	[najmisissa oleʋa]
married (fem.)	**naimisissa oleva**	[najmisissa oleʋa]
single (unmarried)	**naimaton**	[najmaton]
bachelor	**poikamies**	[pojkamies]
divorced (masc.)	**eronnut**	[eroŋut]
widow	**leski**	[leski]
widower	**leski**	[leski]
relative	**sukulainen**	[sukulajnen]
close relative	**lähisukulainen**	[ʎæhi sukulajnen]
distant relative	**kaukainen sukulainen**	[kaukajnen sukulajnen]
relatives	**omanlaiset**	[omanlajset]
orphan (boy or girl)	**orpo**	[orpo]
guardian (of minor)	**holhooja**	[holho:ja]
to adopt (a boy)	**ottaa pojaksi**	[otta: pojaksi]
to adopt (a girl)	**ottaa tyttäreksi**	[otta: tyttæreksi]

56. Friends. Colleagues

friend (masc.)	**ystävä**	[ystæʋæ]
friend (fem.)	**ystävätär**	[ystæʋætær]
friendship	**ystävyys**	[ystæʋy:s]
to be friends	**olla ystäviä keskenään**	[olla ystæʋiæ keskenæ:n]
pal (masc.)	**kaveri**	[kaʋeri]
pal (fem.)	**kaveri**	[kaʋeri]
partner	**partneri**	[partneri]
chief (boss)	**esimies**	[esimies]
superior	**päällikkö**	[pæ:likkø]
subordinate	**alainen**	[alajnen]
colleague	**virkatoveri**	[ʋirka toʋeri]
acquaintance (person)	**tuttava**	[tuttaʋa]
fellow traveller	**matkakumppani**	[matka kumppani]

classmate	**luokkatoveri**	[luokka toʋeri]
neighbour (masc.)	**naapuri**	[nɑ:puri]
neighbour (fem.)	**naapuri**	[nɑ:puri]
neighbours	**naapurit**	[nɑ:purit]

57. Man. Woman

woman	**nainen**	[nɑjnen]
girl (young woman)	**neiti**	[nejti]
bride	**morsian**	[morsiɑn]
beautiful (adj)	**kaunis**	[kɑunis]
tall (adj)	**pitkä**	[pitkæ]
slender (adj)	**solakka**	[solɑkkɑ]
short (adj)	**pienikokoinen**	[pienikokojnen]
blonde (n)	**vaaleaverikkö**	[ʋɑ:leɑ ʋerikkø]
brunette (n)	**tummaverikkö**	[tummɑ ʋerikkø]
ladies' (adj)	**naisten**	[nɑjsten]
virgin (girl)	**impi**	[impi]
pregnant (adj)	**raskaana oleva**	[rɑskɑ:nɑ oleʋɑ]
man (adult male)	**mies**	[mies]
blonde haired man	**vaaleaverinen mies**	[ʋɑ:leɑʋerinenmies]
dark haired man	**tummaverinen mies**	[tummɑʋerinenmies]
tall (adj)	**korkea**	[korkeɑ]
short (adj)	**pienikokoinen**	[pienikokojnen]
rude (rough)	**karkea**	[kɑrkeɑ]
stocky (adj)	**tanakka**	[tɑnɑkkɑ]
robust (adj)	**vahva**	[ʋɑhʋɑ]
strong (adj)	**voimakas**	[ʋojmɑkɑs]
strength	**voima**	[ʋojmɑ]
stout, fat (adj)	**lihava**	[lihɑʋɑ]
swarthy (adj)	**tummaihoinen**	[tummɑihojnen]
well-built (adj)	**solakka**	[solɑkkɑ]
elegant (adj)	**tyylikäs**	[ty:likæs]

58. Age

age	**ikä**	[ikæ]
youth (young age)	**nuoruus**	[nuoru:s]
young (adj)	**nuori**	[nuori]
younger (adj)	**nuorempi**	[nuorempi]
older (adj)	**vanhempi**	[ʋɑnhempi]
young man	**nuorukainen**	[nuorukɑjnen]
teenager	**teini-ikäinen**	[tejni ikæjnen]
guy, fellow	**poika**	[pojkɑ]

old man	**vanhus**	[ʋanhus]
old woman	**eukko**	[eukko]
adult	**aikuinen**	[ajkujnen]
middle-aged (adj)	**keski-ikäinen**	[keski ikæjnen]
elderly (adj)	**iäkäs**	[jækæs]
old (adj)	**vanha**	[ʋanha]
retirement	**eläke**	[eʎæke]
to retire (from job)	**jäädä eläkkeelle**	[jæ:dæ eʎække:lle]
pensioner	**eläkeläinen**	[eʎækeʎæjnen]

59. Children

child	**lapsi**	[lapsi]
children	**lapset**	[lapset]
twins	**kaksoset**	[kaksoset]
cradle	**kätkyt, kehto**	[kætkyt], [kehto]
rattle	**helistin**	[helistin]
nappy	**vaippa**	[ʋajppa]
dummy, comforter	**tutti**	[tutti]
pram	**lastenvaunut**	[lasten ʋaunut]
nursery	**lastentarha**	[lasten tarha]
babysitter	**lastenhoitaja**	[lasten hojtaja]
childhood	**lapsuus**	[lapsu:s]
doll	**nukke**	[nukke]
toy	**lelu**	[lelu]
construction set	**rakennussarja**	[rakeŋus sarʰja]
well-bred (adj)	**hyvin kasvatettu**	[hyʋin kasʋatettu]
ill-bred (adj)	**kasvattamaton**	[kasʋattamaton]
spoilt (adj)	**lellitelty**	[lellitelty]
to be naughty	**peuhata**	[peuhata]
mischievous (adj)	**vallaton**	[ʋallaton]
mischievousness	**vallattomuus**	[ʋallattomu:s]
mischievous child	**veitikka**	[ʋejtikka]
obedient (adj)	**kiltti**	[kiltti]
disobedient (adj)	**tottelematon**	[tottelematon]
docile (adj)	**järkevä**	[jærkeʋæ]
clever (intelligent)	**älykäs**	[ælykæs]
child prodigy	**ihmelapsi**	[ihmelapsi]

60. Married couples. Family life

to kiss (vt)	**suudella**	[su:della]
to kiss (vi)	**suudella toisiaan**	[su:della tojsia:n]

family (n)	**perhe**	[perhe]
family (as adj)	**perheellinen**	[perhe:llinen]
couple	**pariskunta**	[pariskunta]
marriage (state)	**avioliitto**	[aʋioli:itto]
hearth (home)	**kotiliesi**	[kotiliesi]
dynasty	**hallitsijasuku**	[hallitsija suku]
date	**tapaaminen**	[tapa:minen]
kiss	**suudelma**	[su:delma]
love (for sb)	**rakkaus**	[rakkaus]
to love (sb)	**rakastaa**	[rakasta:]
beloved	**rakas**	[rakas]
tenderness	**hellyys**	[helly:s]
tender (affectionate)	**hellä**	[heʎæ]
faithfulness	**uskollisuus**	[uskollisu:s]
faithful (adj)	**uskollinen**	[uskollinen]
care (attention)	**huoli**	[huoli]
caring (~ father)	**huolehtivainen**	[huolehtiʋajnen]
newlyweds	**nuoripari**	[nuori pari]
honeymoon	**kuherruskuukausi**	[kuherrus ku: kausi]
to get married (ab. woman)	**mennä naimisiin**	[meŋæ na:jmisi:in]
to get married (ab. man)	**mennä naimisiin**	[meŋæ na:jmisi:in]
wedding	**häät**	[hæ:t]
golden wedding	**kultahäät**	[kultahæ:t]
anniversary	**vuosipäivä**	[ʋuosipæjʋæ]
lover (masc.)	**rakastaja**	[rakastaja]
mistress	**rakastajatar**	[rakastajatar]
adultery	**petos**	[petos]
to commit adultery	**pettää**	[pettæ:]
jealous (adj)	**mustasukkainen**	[musta sukkajnen]
to be jealous	**olla mustasukkainen**	[olla musta sukkajnen]
divorce	**ero**	[ero]
to divorce (vi)	**erota**	[erota]
to quarrel (vi)	**riidellä**	[ri:ideʎæ]
to be reconciled	**tehdä sovinto**	[tehdæ soʋinto]
together (adv)	**yhdessä**	[yhdessæ]
sex	**seksi**	[seksi]
happiness	**onni**	[oŋi]
happy (adj)	**onnellinen**	[oŋellinen]
misfortune (accident)	**onnettomuus**	[oŋettomu:s]
unhappy (adj)	**onneton**	[oŋeton]

Character. Feelings. Emotions

61. Feelings. Emotions

feeling (emotion)	**tunne**	[tuŋe]
feelings	**tunteet**	[tunte:t]
to feel (vt)	**tuntea**	[tunteɑ]
hunger	**nälkä**	[ɲælkæ]
to be hungry	**olla nälkä**	[ollɑ ɲælkæ]
thirst	**jano**	[jɑno]
to be thirsty	**olla jano**	[ollɑ æno]
sleepiness	**uneliaisuus**	[uneliɑjsu:s]
to feel sleepy	**haluta nukkua**	[hɑlutɑ nukkuɑ]
tiredness	**väsymys**	[ʋæsymys]
tired (adj)	**väsynyt**	[ʋæsynyt]
to get tired	**väsyä**	[ʋæsyæ]
mood (humour)	**mieli**	[mieli]
boredom	**ikävä**	[ikæʋæ]
to be bored	**ikävöidä**	[ikæʋøjdæ]
seclusion	**yksinäisyys**	[yksiɲæjsy:s]
to seclude oneself	**eristäytyä**	[eristæytyæ]
to worry (make anxious)	**huolestuttaa**	[huolestuttɑ:]
to be worried	**olla huolissaan**	[ollɑ huolissɑ:n]
worrying (n)	**levottomuus**	[leʋottomu:s]
anxiety	**huolestus**	[huolestus]
preoccupied (adj)	**huolestunut**	[huolestunut]
to be nervous	**hermostua**	[hermostuɑ]
to panic (vi)	**olla paniikissa**	[ollɑ pɑni:ikissɑ]
hope	**toivo**	[tojʋo]
to hope (vi, vt)	**toivoa**	[tojʋoɑ]
certainty	**varmuus**	[ʋɑrmu:s]
certain, sure (adj)	**varma**	[ʋɑrmɑ]
uncertainty	**epävarmuus**	[epæʋɑrmu:s]
uncertain (adj)	**epävarma**	[epæʋɑrmɑ]
drunk (adj)	**juopunut**	[juopunut]
sober (adj)	**selvä**	[selʋæ]
weak (adj)	**heikko**	[hejkko]
happy (adj)	**onnellinen**	[oŋellinen]
to scare (vt)	**pelottaa**	[pelottɑ:]
fury (madness)	**raivo**	[rɑjʋo]
rage (fury)	**raivo**	[rɑjʋo]
depression	**masennus**	[mɑseŋus]
discomfort	**epämukavuus**	[epæmukɑʋu:s]

comfort	**mukavuudet**	[mukaʋu:det]
to regret (be sorry)	**sääliä**	[sæ:liæ]
regret	**sääli**	[sæ:li]
bad luck	**huono onni**	[huono oŋi]
sadness	**mielipaha**	[mieli paha]
shame (feeling)	**häpeä**	[ɦæpeæ]
merriment, fun	**ilo**	[ilo]
enthusiasm	**into**	[into]
enthusiast	**intoilija**	[intoilija]
to show enthusiasm	**osoittaa innostus**	[osojtta: iŋostus]

62. Character. Personality

character	**luonne**	[luoŋe]
character flaw	**vajaus**	[ʋajaus]
mind, reason	**järki**	[jærki]
conscience	**omatunto**	[omatunto]
habit (custom)	**tottumus**	[tottumus]
ability	**kyky**	[kyky]
can (e.g. ~ swim)	**osata**	[osata]
patient (adj)	**kärsivällinen**	[kærsiʋællinen]
impatient (adj)	**kärsimätön**	[kærsimætøn]
curious (inquisitive)	**utelias**	[utelias]
curiosity	**uteliaisuus**	[uteliajsu:s]
modesty	**vaatimattomuus**	[ʋa:timattomu:s]
modest (adj)	**vaatimaton**	[ʋa:timaton]
immodest (adj)	**epähieno**	[epæhieno]
laziness	**laiskuus**	[lajsku:s]
lazy (adj)	**laiska**	[lajska]
lazy person (masc.)	**laiskuri**	[lajskuri]
cunning (n)	**viekkaus**	[ʋiekkaus]
cunning (as adj)	**viekas**	[ʋiekas]
distrust	**epäluottamus**	[epæluottamus]
distrustful (adj)	**epäluuloinen**	[epælu:lojnen]
generosity	**anteliaisuus**	[anteliajsu:s]
generous (adj)	**antelias**	[antelias]
talented (adj)	**lahjakas**	[lah^{h}jakas]
talent	**lahja**	[lah^{h}ja]
courageous (adj)	**rohkea**	[rohkea]
courage	**rohkeus**	[rohkeus]
honest (adj)	**rehellinen**	[rehellinen]
honesty	**rehellisyys**	[rehellisy:s]
careful (cautious)	**varovainen**	[ʋaroʋajnen]
courageous (adj)	**uljas**	[ul^{h}jas]
serious (adj)	**vakava**	[ʋakaʋa]

strict (severe, stern)	**ankara**	[aŋkara]
decisive (adj)	**päättävä**	[pæ:ttæʋæ]
indecisive (adj)	**epävarma**	[epæʋarma]
shy, timid (adj)	**arka**	[arka]
shyness, timidity	**arkuus**	[arku:s]
confidence (trust)	**luottamus**	[luottamus]
to believe (trust)	**uskoa**	[uskoa]
trusting (naïve)	**luottavainen**	[luottaʋajnen]
sincerely (adv)	**vilpittömästi**	[ʋilpittømæsti]
sincere (adj)	**vilpitön**	[ʋilpitøn]
sincerity	**vilpittömyys**	[ʋilpittømy:s]
open (person)	**avoin**	[aʋojn]
calm (adj)	**rauhallinen**	[rauhallinen]
frank (sincere)	**avomielinen**	[aʋomielinen]
naïve (adj)	**lapsellinen**	[lapsellinen]
absent-minded (adj)	**hajamielinen**	[hajamielinen]
funny (amusing)	**hauska**	[hauska]
greed	**ahneus**	[ahneus]
greedy (adj)	**ahne**	[ahne]
stingy (adj)	**kitsas**	[kitsas]
evil (adj)	**vihainen**	[ʋihajnen]
stubborn (adj)	**itsepäinen**	[itsepæjnen]
unpleasant (adj)	**epämiellyttävä**	[epæmiellyttæʋæ]
selfish person (masc.)	**egoisti**	[egoisti]
selfish (adj)	**egoistinen**	[egoistinen]
coward	**pelkuri**	[pelkuri]
cowardly (adj)	**pelkurimainen**	[pelkurimajnen]

63. Sleep. Dreams

to sleep (vi)	**nukkua**	[nukkua]
sleep, sleeping	**uni**	[uni]
dream	**uni**	[uni]
to dream (in sleep)	**nähdä unta**	[ɲæhdæ unta]
sleepy (adj)	**uninen**	[uninen]
bed	**sänky**	[sæŋky]
mattress	**patja**	[patʲja]
blanket (eiderdown)	**vuodepeite**	[ʋuodepejte]
pillow	**tyyny**	[ty:ny]
sheet	**lakana**	[lakana]
insomnia	**unettomuus**	[unettomu:s]
sleepless (adj)	**uneton**	[uneton]
sleeping pill	**unilääke**	[unilæ:ke]
to take a sleeping pill	**ottaa unilääke**	[otta: unilæ:ke]
to feel sleepy	**haluta nukkua**	[haluta nukkua]
to yawn (vi)	**haukotella**	[haukotella]

to go to bed	**mennä nukkumaan**	[meŋæ nukkumɑ:n]
to make up the bed	**sijata**	[sijɑtɑ]
to fall asleep	**nukahtaa**	[nukɑhtɑ:]
nightmare	**painajainen**	[pɑjnɑjæjnen]
snoring	**kuorsaus**	[kuorsɑus]
to snore (vi)	**kuorsata**	[kuorsɑtɑ]
alarm clock	**herätyskello**	[herætys kello]
to wake (vt)	**herättää**	[herættæ:]
to wake up	**herätä**	[herætæ]
to get up (vi)	**nousta**	[noustɑ]
to wash oneself	**peseytyä**	[peseytyæ]

64. Humour. Laughter. Gladness

humour (wit, fun)	**huumori**	[hu:mori]
sense of humour	**tunne**	[tuŋe]
to have fun	**pitää hauskaa**	[pitæ: hɑuskɑ:]
cheerful (adj)	**iloinen**	[ilojnen]
merriment, fun	**ilo**	[ilo]
smile	**hymy**	[hymy]
to smile (vi)	**hymyillä**	[hymyjʎæ]
to start laughing	**alkaa nauraa**	[ɑlkɑ: nɑurɑ:]
to laugh (vi)	**nauraa**	[nɑurɑ:]
laugh, laughter	**nauru**	[nɑuru]
anecdote	**vitsi**	[ʋit͡si]
funny (amusing)	**hauska**	[hɑuskɑ]
funny (comical)	**lystikäs**	[lystikæs]
to joke (vi)	**laskea leikkiä**	[lɑskeɑ lejkkiæ]
joke (verbal)	**leikinlasku**	[lejkinlɑsku]
joy (emotion)	**ilo**	[ilo]
to rejoice (vi)	**iloita**	[ilojtɑ]
glad, cheerful (adj)	**iloinen**	[ilojnen]

65. Discussion, conversation. Part 1

communication	**viestintä**	[ʋiestintæ]
to communicate	**kommunikoida**	[kommunikojdɑ]
conversation	**puhelu**	[puhelu]
dialogue	**vuoropuhelu**	[ʋuoropuhelu]
discussion (discourse)	**keskustelu**	[keskustelu]
debate	**väittely**	[ʋæjttely]
to debate (vi)	**riidellä**	[ri:ideʎæ]
interlocutor	**keskustelija**	[keskustelijɑ]
topic (theme)	**teema**	[te:mɑ]
point of view	**näkökanta**	[ɲækøkɑntɑ]

opinion (viewpoint)	**mieli**	[mieli]
speech (talk)	**puhe**	[puhe]
discussion (of report, etc.)	**käsittely**	[kæsittely]
to discuss (vt)	**käsitellä**	[kæsiteʎæ]
talk (conversation)	**keskustelu**	[keskustelu]
to talk (vi)	**keskustella**	[keskustellɑ]
meeting	**tapaaminen**	[tɑpɑ:minen]
to meet (vi, vt)	**tavata**	[tɑʋɑtɑ]
proverb	**sananlasku**	[sɑnɑn lɑsku]
saying	**sananparsi**	[sɑnɑn pɑrsi]
riddle (poser)	**arvoitus**	[ɑrʋojtus]
to ask a riddle	**asettaa arvoitus**	[ɑsettɑ: ɑrʋojtus]
password	**tunnussana**	[tuŋussɑnɑ]
secret	**salaisuus**	[sɑlɑjsu:s]
oath (vow)	**vala**	[ʋɑlɑ]
to swear (an oath)	**vannoa**	[ʋɑŋoɑ]
promise	**lupaus**	[lupɑus]
to promise (vt)	**luvata**	[luʋɑtɑ]
advice (counsel)	**neuvo**	[neuʋo]
to advise (vt)	**neuvoa**	[neuʋoɑ]
to listen (to parents)	**totella**	[totellɑ]
news	**uutinen**	[u:tinen]
sensation (news)	**sensaatio**	[sensɑ:tio]
information (facts)	**tiedot**	[tædot]
conclusion (decision)	**johtopäätös**	[øhtopæ:tøs]
voice	**ääni**	[æ:ni]
compliment	**kohteliaisuus**	[kohteliɑjsu:s]
kind (nice)	**ystävällinen**	[ystæʋællinen]
word	**sana**	[sɑnɑ]
phrase	**lause**	[lɑuse]
answer	**vastaus**	[ʋɑstɑus]
truth	**tosi**	[tosi]
lie	**vale**	[ʋɑle]
thought	**ajatus**	[ɑjɑtus]
idea (inspiration)	**idea**	[ideɑ]
fantasy	**mielikuvitus**	[mielikuʋitus]

66. Discussion, conversation. Part 2

respected (adj)	**kunnioitettava**	[kuŋiojtettɑʋɑ]
to respect (vt)	**kunnioittaa**	[kuŋiojttɑ:]
respect	**kunnioitus**	[kuŋiojtus]
Dear ...	**Arvoisa...**	[ɑrʋojsɑ]
to introduce (present)	**tutustuttaa**	[tutustuttɑ:]
intention	**aikomus**	[ɑjkomus]

to intend (have in mind)	**aikoa**	[ɑjkoɑ]
wish	**toivomus**	[tojʋomus]
to wish (~ good luck)	**toivottaa**	[tojʋottɑ:]
surprise (astonishment)	**ihmettely**	[ihmettely]
to surprise (amaze)	**ihmetyttää**	[ihmetyttæ:]
to be surprised	**ihmetellä**	[ihmeteʎæ]
to give (vt)	**antaa**	[ɑntɑ:]
to take (get hold of)	**ottaa**	[ottɑ:]
to give back	**palauttaa**	[pɑlɑuttɑ:]
to return (give back)	**palauttaa**	[pɑlɑuttɑ:]
to apologize (vi)	**pyytää anteeksi**	[py:tæ: ɑnte:ksi]
apology	**anteeksipyyntö**	[ɑnte:ksi py:ntø]
to forgive (vt)	**antaa anteeksi**	[ɑntɑ: ɑnte:ksi]
to talk (speak)	**puhua**	[puhuɑ]
to listen (vi)	**kuunnella**	[ku:ŋellɑ]
to hear out	**kuunnella loppuun**	[ku:ŋellɑ loppu:n]
to understand (vt)	**ymmärtää**	[ymmærtæ:]
to show (display)	**näyttää**	[ɲæyttæ:]
to look at ...	**katsoa**	[kɑʦoɑ]
to call (with one's voice)	**kutsua**	[kuʦuɑ]
to disturb (vt)	**häiritä**	[ɦæjritæ]
to pass (to hand sth)	**antaa**	[ɑntɑ:]
demand (request)	**pyyntö**	[py:ntø]
to request (ask)	**pyytää**	[py:tæ:]
demand (firm request)	**vaatimus**	[ʋɑ:timus]
to demand (request firmly)	**vaatia**	[ʋɑ:tiɑ]
to tease (nickname)	**härnätä**	[ɦærɲætæ]
to mock (deride)	**pilkata**	[pilkɑtɑ]
mockery, derision	**pilkka**	[pilkkɑ]
nickname	**liikanimi**	[li:ikɑnimi]
allusion	**vihjaus**	[ʋih^hjɑus]
to allude (vi)	**vihjata**	[ʋih^hjɑtɑ]
to imply (vt)	**tarkoittaa**	[tɑrkojttɑ:]
description	**kuvaus**	[kuʋɑus]
to describe (vt)	**kuvata**	[kuʋɑtɑ]
praise (compliments)	**kehu**	[kehu]
to praise (vt)	**kehua**	[kehuɑ]
disappointment	**pettymys**	[pettymys]
to disappoint (vt)	**aiheuttaa petyttää**	[ɑjheuttɑ: petyttæ:]
to be disappointed	**pettyä**	[pettyæ]
supposition	**oletus**	[oletus]
to suppose (assume)	**olettaa**	[olettɑ:]
warning (caution)	**varoitus**	[ʋɑrojtus]
to warn (vt)	**varoittaa**	[ʋɑrojttɑ:]

67. Discussion, conversation. Part 3

to talk into (convince)	**suostuttaa**	[suostutta:]
to calm down (vt)	**rauhoittaa**	[rauhojtta:]
silence (~ is golden)	**vaitiolo**	[ʋajtiolo]
to keep silent	**olla vaiti**	[olla ʋajti]
to whisper (vi, vt)	**kuiskata**	[kujskata]
whisper	**kuiske**	[kujske]
frankly, sincerely (adv)	**avomielisesti**	[aʋomielisesti]
in my opinion …	**minusta**	[minusta]
detail (of the story)	**yksityiskohta**	[yksityjs kohta]
detailed (adj)	**yksityiskohtainen**	[yksityjs kohtajnen]
in detail (adv)	**yksityiskohtaisesti**	[yksityjs kohtajsesti]
hint, clue	**vihje**	[ʋihʰe]
to give a hint	**vihjata**	[ʋihʰjata]
look (glance)	**katse**	[katse]
to have a look	**katsahtaa**	[katsahta:]
fixed (look)	**liikkumaton katse**	[li:ikkumaton katse]
to blink (vi)	**räpyttää**	[ræpyttæ:]
to wink (vi)	**iskeä silmää**	[iskeæ silmæ:]
to nod (in assent)	**nyökätä**	[nyøkætæ]
sigh	**huokaus**	[huokaus]
to sigh (vi)	**huokaista**	[huokajsta]
to shudder (vi)	**vavahdella**	[ʋaʋahdella]
gesture	**ele**	[ele]
to touch (one's arm, etc.)	**koskea**	[koskea]
to seize (by the arm)	**tarttua**	[tarttua]
to tap (on the shoulder)	**taputtaa**	[taputta:]
Look out!	**Varo!**	[ʋaro]
Really?	**Ihanko totta?**	[ihaŋko totta]
Are you sure?	**Oletko varma?**	[oletko ʋarma]
Good luck!	**Toivotan onnea!**	[tojʋotan oŋea]
I see!	**Selvä!**	[selʋæ]
It's a pity!	**Onpa ikävä!**	[onpa ikæʋæ]

68. Agreement. Refusal

consent (mutual ~)	**suostumus**	[suostumus]
to agree (say yes)	**suostua**	[suostua]
approval	**hyväksyminen**	[hyʋæksyminen]
to approve (vt)	**hyväksyä**	[hyʋæksyæ]
refusal	**kielto**	[kielto]
to refuse (vi, vt)	**kieltäytyä**	[kæltæytyæ]
Great!	**Loistava!**	[lojstaʋa]
All right!	**Hyvä!**	[hyʋæ]

Okay! (I agree)	**Hyvä on!**	[hyʊæ on]
forbidden (adj)	**kielletty**	[kielletty]
it's forbidden	**on kielletty**	[on kielletty]
it's impossible	**mahdottoman**	[mɑhdottomɑn]
incorrect (adj)	**virheellinen**	[ʊirhe:llinen]
to reject (~ a demand)	**evätä**	[eʊætæ]
to support (cause, idea)	**kannattaa**	[kɑŋɑttɑ:]
to accept (~ an apology)	**hyväksyä**	[hyʊæksyæ]
to confirm (vt)	**vahvistaa**	[ʊɑhʊistɑ:]
confirmation	**vahvistus**	[ʊɑhʊistus]
permission	**lupa**	[lupɑ]
to permit (vt)	**antaa lupa**	[ɑntɑ: lupɑ]
decision	**ratkaisu**	[rɑtkɑjsu]
to say nothing	**olla vaiti**	[ollɑ ʊɑjti]
condition (term)	**ehto**	[ehto]
excuse (pretext)	**tekosyy**	[tekosy:]
praise (compliments)	**kehu**	[kehu]
to praise (vt)	**kehua**	[kehuɑ]

69. Success. Good luck. Failure

success	**menestys**	[menestys]
successfully (adv)	**menestyksekkäästi**	[menestyksekkæ:sti]
successful (adj)	**menestyksellinen**	[menestyksellinen]
good luck	**menestys**	[menestys]
Good luck!	**Onnea!**	[oŋeɑ]
lucky (e.g. ~ day)	**onnistunut**	[oŋistunut]
lucky (fortunate)	**onnellinen**	[oŋellinen]
failure	**romahdus**	[romɑhdus]
misfortune	**epäonni**	[epæoŋi]
bad luck	**huono onni**	[huono oŋi]
unsuccessful (adj)	**epäonnistunut**	[epæoŋistunut]
catastrophe	**onnettomuus**	[oŋettomu:s]
pride	**ylpeys**	[ylpeys]
proud (adj)	**ylpeä**	[ylpeæ]
to be proud	**ylpeillä**	[ylpejʎæ]
winner	**voittaja**	[ʊojttɑjɑ]
to win (vi)	**voittaa**	[ʊojttɑ:]
to lose (not win)	**hävitä**	[ɦæʊitæ]
try	**yritys**	[yritys]
to try (vi)	**yrittää**	[yrittæ:]
chance (opportunity)	**mahdollisuus**	[mɑhdollisu:s]

70. Quarrels. Negative emotions

shout (scream)	**huuto**	[hu:to]
to shout (vi)	**huutaa**	[hu:tɑ:]

to start to cry out	**alkaa huutaa**	[alka: hu:ta:]
quarrel	**riita**	[ri:ita]
to quarrel (vi)	**riidellä**	[ri:ideʎæ]
fight (scandal)	**skandaali**	[skanda:li]
to have a fight	**riidellä**	[ri:ideʎæ]
conflict	**konflikti**	[konflikti]
misunderstanding	**väärinkäsitys**	[ʋæ:rin kæsitys]
insult	**loukkaus**	[loukkaus]
to insult (vt)	**loukata**	[loukata]
insulted (adj)	**loukkaantunut**	[loukka:ntunut]
offence (to take ~)	**loukkaus**	[loukkaus]
to offend (vt)	**loukata**	[loukata]
to take offence	**pahastua**	[pahastua]
indignation	**suuttumus**	[su:ttumus]
to be indignant	**olla suutuksissa**	[olla su:tuksissa]
complaint	**valitus**	[ʋalitus]
to complain (vi, vt)	**valittaa**	[ʋalitta:]
apology	**anteeksipyyntö**	[ante:ksi py:ntø]
to apologize (vi)	**pyytää anteeksi**	[py:tæ: ante:ksi]
to beg pardon	**puolustella**	[puolustella]
criticism	**arvostelu**	[arʋostelu]
to criticize (vt)	**arvostella**	[arʋostella]
accusation	**syyte**	[sy:te]
to accuse (vt)	**syyttää**	[sy:ttæ:]
revenge	**kosto**	[kosto]
to avenge (vt)	**kostaa**	[kosta:]
to pay back	**antaa takaisin**	[anta: takajsin]
disdain	**halveksinta**	[halʋeksinta]
to despise (vt)	**halveksia**	[halʋeksia]
hatred, hate	**viha**	[ʋiha]
to hate (vt)	**vihata**	[ʋihata]
nervous (adj)	**hermostunut**	[hermostunut]
to be nervous	**hermostua**	[hermostua]
angry (mad)	**vihainen**	[ʋihajnen]
to make angry	**suututtaa**	[su:tutta:]
humiliation	**alentaminen**	[alentaminen]
to humiliate (vt)	**alentaa**	[alenta:]
to humiliate oneself	**alentua**	[alentua]
shock	**sokki**	[sokki]
to shock (vt)	**sokeerata**	[soke:rata]
trouble (annoyance)	**ikävyys**	[ikæʋy:s]
unpleasant (adj)	**epämiellyttävä**	[epæmiellyttæʋæ]
fear (dread)	**pelko**	[pelko]
terrible (storm, heat)	**hirveä**	[hirʋeæ]
scary (e.g. ~ story)	**kauhea**	[kauheæ]

horror	**kauhu**	[kauhu]
awful (crime, news)	**karmea**	[karmea]
to cry (weep)	**itkeä**	[itkeæ]
to start crying	**ruveta itkemään**	[ruʋeta itkemæ:n]
tear	**kyynel**	[ky:nel]
fault	**syy**	[sy:]
guilt (feeling)	**syyllisyys**	[sy:llisy:s]
dishonour	**häpeä**	[ɦæpeæ]
protest	**vastalause**	[ʋastalause]
stress	**stressi**	[stressi]
to disturb (vt)	**häiritä**	[ɦæjritæ]
to be furious	**vihastua**	[ʋihastua]
angry (adj)	**vihainen**	[ʋihajnen]
to end (e.g. relationship)	**lopettaa**	[lopetta:]
to swear (at sb)	**kiroilla**	[kirojlla]
to be scared	**pelästyä**	[peʎæstyæ]
to hit (strike with hand)	**iskeä**	[iskeæ]
to fight (vi)	**tapella**	[tapella]
to settle (a conflict)	**sovitella**	[soʋitella]
discontented (adj)	**tyytymätön**	[ty:tymætøn]
furious (adj)	**tuima**	[tujma]
It's not good!	**Se ei ole hyvä!**	[se ej ole hyʋæ]
It's bad!	**Se on huono!**	[se on huono]

Medicine

71. Diseases

illness	**sairaus**	[sɑjrɑus]
to be ill	**sairastaa**	[sɑjrɑstɑ:]
health	**terveys**	[terʋeys]
runny nose (coryza)	**nuha**	[nuhɑ]
tonsillitis	**angiina**	[ɑŋi:inɑ]
cold (illness)	**vilustus**	[ʋilustus]
to catch a cold	**vilustua**	[ʋilustuɑ]
bronchitis	**keuhkokatarri**	[keuhko kɑtɑrri]
pneumonia	**keuhkotulehdus**	[keuhko tulehdus]
flu, influenza	**influenssa**	[influenssɑ]
short-sighted (adj)	**likinäköinen**	[likiɲækøjnen]
long-sighted (adj)	**pitkänäköinen**	[pitkæɲækøjnen]
squint	**kierosilmäisyys**	[kiero silmæjsy:s]
squint-eyed (adj)	**kiero**	[kiero]
cataract	**harmaakaihi**	[hɑrmɑ:kɑjhi]
glaucoma	**silmänpainetauti**	[silmæn pɑjne tɑuti]
stroke	**insultti**	[insultti]
heart attack	**infarkti**	[infɑrkti]
myocardial infarction	**sydäninfarkti**	[sydæn infɑrkti]
paralysis	**halvaus**	[hɑlʋɑus]
to paralyse (vt)	**halvauttaa**	[hɑlʋɑuttɑ:]
allergy	**allergia**	[ɑllergi:ɑ]
asthma	**astma**	[ɑstmɑ]
diabetes	**sokeritauti**	[sokeritɑuti]
toothache	**hammassärky**	[hɑmmɑs særky]
caries	**hammasmätä**	[hɑmmɑs mætæ]
diarrhoea	**ripuli**	[ripuli]
constipation	**ummetus**	[ummetus]
stomach upset	**vatsavaiva**	[ʋɑtsɑʋɑjʋɑ]
food poisoning	**myrkytys**	[myrkytys]
to have a food poisoning	**saada myrkytys**	[sɑ:dɑ myrkytys]
arthritis	**niveltulehdus**	[niʋeltulehdus]
rickets	**riisitauti**	[ri:isitɑti]
rheumatism	**reuma**	[reumɑ]
atherosclerosis	**aeroskleroosi**	[ɑterosklero:si]
gastritis	**mahakatarri**	[mɑhɑkɑtɑrri]
appendicitis	**umpilisäketulehdus**	[umpilisæke tulehdus]

cholecystitis	**sappirakon tulehdus**	[sappirakon tulehdus]
ulcer	**haava**	[ha:ʋa]
measles	**tuhkarokko**	[tuhkarokko]
German measles	**vihurirokko**	[ʋihurirokko]
jaundice	**keltatauti**	[keltatauti]
hepatitis	**hepatiitti**	[hepati:itti]
schizophrenia	**jakomielisyys**	[jakomielisy:s]
rabies (hydrophobia)	**raivotauti**	[rajʋotauti]
neurosis	**neuroosi**	[neuro:si]
concussion	**aivotärähdys**	[ajʋotæræhdys]
cancer	**syöpä**	[syøpæ]
sclerosis	**skleroosi**	[sklero:si]
multiple sclerosis	**hajaskleroosi**	[hajasklero:si]
alcoholism	**alkoholismi**	[alkoholismi]
alcoholic (n)	**alkoholisti**	[alkoholisti]
syphilis	**kuppa**	[kuppa]
AIDS	**AIDS**	[ajds]
tumour	**kasvain**	[kasʋajn]
malignant (adj)	**pahanlaatuinen**	[pahan la:jtunen]
benign (adj)	**hyvänlaatuinen**	[hyʋænla:tunen]
fever	**kuume**	[ku:me]
malaria	**malaria**	[malaria]
gangrene	**kuolio**	[kuolio]
seasickness	**merisairaus**	[merisajraus]
epilepsy	**epilepsia**	[epilepsia]
epidemic	**epidemia**	[epidemia]
typhus	**lavantauti**	[laʋantauti]
tuberculosis	**tuberkuloosi**	[tuberkulo:si]
cholera	**kolera**	[kolera]
plague (bubonic ~)	**rutto**	[rutto]

72. Symptoms. Treatments. Part 1

symptom	**oire**	[ojre]
temperature	**kuume**	[ku:me]
fever	**korkea kuume**	[korkea ku:me]
pulse	**syke**	[syke]
giddiness	**pyörrytys**	[pyørrytys]
hot (adj)	**kuuma**	[ku:ma]
shivering	**vilunväristys**	[ʋilun ʋæristys]
pale (e.g. ~ face)	**kalpea**	[kalpea]
cough	**yskä**	[yskæ]
to cough (vi)	**yskiä**	[yskiæ]
to sneeze (vi)	**aivastella**	[ajʋastella]
faint	**pyörtyminen**	[pyørtyminen]

to faint (vi)	**pyörtyä**	[pyørtyæ]
bruise (hématome)	**mustelma**	[mustelma]
bump (lump)	**kuhmu**	[kuhmu]
to bruise oneself	**törmätä**	[tørmætæ]
bruise	**vamma**	[ʋamma]
to get bruised	**loukkaantua**	[loukka:ntua]
to limp (vi)	**ontua**	[ontua]
dislocation	**niukahdus**	[niukahdus]
to dislocate (vt)	**niukahtaa**	[niukahta:]
fracture	**murtuma**	[murtuma]
to have a fracture	**saada murtuma**	[sa:da murtuma]
cut (e.g. paper ~)	**leikkaushaava**	[lejkkaus ha:ʋa]
to cut oneself	**saada haava leikkaamalla**	[sa:da ha:ʋa lejkka:malla]
bleeding	**verenvuoto**	[ʋerenʋuoto]
burn (injury)	**palohaava**	[paloha:ʋa]
to burn oneself	**polttaa itse**	[poltta: itse]
to prick (vt)	**pistää**	[pistæ:]
to prick oneself	**pistää itseä**	[pistæ: itseæ]
to injure (vt)	**vahingoittaa**	[ʋahiŋojtta:]
injury	**vaurio**	[ʋaurio]
wound	**haava**	[ha:ʋa]
trauma	**vamma**	[ʋamma]
to be delirious	**hourailla**	[hourajlla]
to stutter (vi)	**änkyttää**	[æŋkyttæ:]
sunstroke	**auringonpistos**	[auriŋon pistos]

73. Symptoms. Treatments. Part 2

pain	**kipu**	[kipu]
splinter (in foot, etc.)	**tikku**	[tikku]
sweat (perspiration)	**hiki**	[hiki]
to sweat (perspire)	**hikoilla**	[hikojlla]
vomiting	**oksennus**	[okseŋus]
convulsions	**kouristukset**	[kouristukset]
pregnant (adj)	**raskaana oleva**	[raska:na oleʋa]
to be born	**syntyä**	[syntyæ]
delivery, labour	**synnytys**	[syŋytys]
to labour (vi)	**synnyttää**	[syŋyttæ:]
abortion	**raskaudenkeskeytys**	[raskauden keskeytys]
respiration	**hengitys**	[heŋitys]
inhalation	**sisäänhengitys**	[sisæ:n heŋitys]
exhalation	**uloshengitys**	[uloshеŋitys]
to breathe out	**hengittää ulos**	[heŋittæ: ulos]
to breathe in	**vetää henkeä**	[ʋetæ: heŋkeæ]
disabled person	**invalidi**	[inʋalidi]
cripple	**raajarikko**	[ra:jarikko]

drug addict	**narkomaani**	[narkoma:ni]
deaf (adj)	**kuuro**	[ku:ro]
dumb (adj)	**mykkä**	[mykkæ]
deaf-and-dumb (adj)	**kuuromykkä**	[ku:ro mykkæ]
mad, insane (adj)	**mielenvikainen**	[mielen υikajnen]
madman	**hullu**	[hullu]
madwoman	**hullu**	[hullu]
to go insane	**tulla hulluksi**	[tulla hulluksi]
gene	**geeni**	[ge:ni]
immunity	**immuniteetti**	[immunite:tti]
hereditary (adj)	**perintö-**	[perintø]
congenital (adj)	**synnynnäinen**	[syŋyŋæjnen]
virus	**virus**	[υirus]
microbe	**mikrobi**	[mikrobi]
bacterium	**bakteeri**	[bakte:ri]
infection	**tartunta**	[tartunta]

74. Symptoms. Treatments. Part 3

hospital	**sairaala**	[sajra:la]
patient	**potilas**	[potilas]
diagnosis	**diagnoosi**	[diagno:si]
cure	**lääkintä**	[læ:kintæ]
medical treatment	**hoito**	[hojto]
to get treatment	**saada hoitoa**	[sa:da hojtoa]
to treat (vt)	**hoitaa**	[hojta:]
to nurse (look after)	**hoitaa**	[hojta:]
care	**hoito**	[hojto]
operation, surgery	**leikkaus**	[lejkkaus]
to bandage (head, limb)	**sitoa**	[sitoa]
bandaging	**sidonta**	[sidonta]
vaccination	**rokotus**	[rokotus]
to vaccinate (vt)	**rokottaa**	[rokotta:]
injection, shot	**pisto**	[pisto]
to give an injection	**tehdä pisto**	[tehdæ pisto]
attack	**kohtaus**	[kohtaus]
amputation	**amputaatio**	[amputa:tio]
to amputate (vt)	**amputoida**	[amputojda]
coma	**kooma**	[ko:ma]
to be in a coma	**olla koomassa**	[olla ko:massa]
intensive care	**hoitokoti**	[hojtokoti]
to recover (~ from flu)	**parantua**	[parantua]
state (patient's ~)	**terveydentila**	[terυeyden tila]
consciousness	**tajunta**	[tajunta]
memory (faculty)	**muisti**	[mujsti]
to extract (tooth)	**poistaa**	[pojsta:]

filling	**täyte**	[tæyte]
to fill (a tooth)	**paikata**	[pajkata]
hypnosis	**hypnoosi**	[hypno:si]
to hypnotize (vt)	**hypnotisoida**	[hypnotisojda]

75. Doctors

doctor	**lääkäri**	[læ:kæri]
nurse	**sairaanhoitaja**	[sajra:n hojtaja]
private physician	**omalääkäri**	[oma læ:kæri]
dentist	**hammaslääkäri**	[hammas læ:kæri]
ophthalmologist	**silmälääkäri**	[silmæ læ:kæri]
general practitioner	**sisätautilääkäri**	[sisætauti læ:kæri]
surgeon	**kirurgi**	[kirurgi]
psychiatrist	**psykiatri**	[psykiatri]
paediatrician	**lastenlääkäri**	[lasten læ:kæri]
psychologist	**psykologi**	[psykologi]
gynaecologist	**naistentautilääkäri**	[najstentauti læ:kæri]
cardiologist	**kardiologi**	[kardiologi]

76. Medicine. Drugs. Accessories

medicine, drug	**lääke**	[læ:ke]
remedy	**lääke**	[læ:ke]
prescription	**resepti**	[resepti]
tablet, pill	**tabletti**	[tabletti]
ointment	**voide**	[ʋojde]
ampoule	**ampulli**	[ampulli]
mixture	**mikstuura**	[mikstu:ra]
syrup	**siirappi**	[si:irappi]
pill	**pilleri**	[pilleri]
powder	**jauhe**	[jauhe]
bandage	**side**	[side]
cotton wool	**vanu**	[ʋanu]
iodine	**jodi**	[ødi]
plaster	**laastari**	[la:stari]
eyedropper	**pipetti**	[pipetti]
thermometer	**kuumemittari**	[ku:me mittari]
syringe	**ruisku**	[rujsku]
wheelchair	**pyörätuoli**	[pyøræ tuoli]
crutches	**kainalosauvat**	[kajnalo sauʋat]
painkiller	**puudutusaine**	[pu:dutus ajne]
laxative	**ulostuslääke**	[ulostuslæ:ke]
spirit (ethanol)	**sprii**	[spri:i]

medicinal herbs	**yrtti**	[yrtti]
herbal (~ tea)	**yrtti-**	[yrtti]

77. Smoking. Tobacco products

tobacco	**tupakka**	[tupɑkkɑ]
cigarette	**savuke**	[sɑʋuke]
cigar	**sikari**	[sikɑri]
pipe	**piippu**	[pi:ippu]
packet (of cigarettes)	**pakka**	[pɑkkɑ]
matches	**tulitikut**	[tulitikut]
matchbox	**tulitikkurasia**	[tulitikkurɑsiɑ]
lighter	**sytytin**	[sytytin]
ashtray	**tuhkakuppi**	[tuhkɑkuppi]
cigarette case	**savukekotelo**	[sɑʋukekotelo]
cigarette holder	**imuke**	[imuke]
filter	**suodatin**	[suodɑtin]
to smoke (vi, vt)	**tupakoida**	[tupɑkojdɑ]
to light a cigarette	**sytyttää**	[sytyttæ:]
smoking	**tupakanpoltto**	[tupɑkɑnpoltto]
smoker	**tupakanpolttaja**	[tupɑkɑnpolttɑjɑ]
cigarette end	**tumppi**	[tumppi]
smoke, fumes	**savu**	[sɑʋu]
ash	**tuhka**	[tuhkɑ]

HUMAN HABITAT

City

78. City. Life in the city

city, town	**kaupunki**	[kaupuŋki]
capital	**pääkaupunki**	[pæ:kaupuŋki]
village	**kylä**	[kyʎæ]
city map	**kaupungin asemakaava**	[kaupuŋin asema ka:ʋa]
city centre	**kaupungin keskusta**	[kaupuŋin keskusta]
suburb	**esikaupunki**	[esikaupuŋki]
suburban (adj)	**esikaupunki-**	[esikaupuŋki]
outskirts	**laita**	[lajta]
environs (suburbs)	**ympäristö**	[ympæristø]
quarter	**kortteli**	[kortteli]
residential quarter	**asuinkortteli**	[asujŋkortteli]
traffic	**liikenne**	[li:keŋe]
traffic lights	**liikennevalot**	[li:keŋeʋalot]
public transport	**julkiset kulkuvälineet**	[julkiset kulkuʋæline:t]
crossroads	**risteys**	[risteys]
zebra crossing	**suojatie**	[suojatæ]
pedestrian subway	**alikäytävä**	[alikæytæʋæ]
to cross (vt)	**mennä yli**	[meŋæ yli]
pedestrian	**jalankulkija**	[jalaŋkulkija]
pavement	**jalkakäytävä**	[jalkakæytæʋæ]
bridge	**silta**	[silta]
embankment	**rantakatu**	[rantakatu]
fountain	**suihkulähde**	[sujhku ʎæhde]
allée	**lehtikuja**	[lehti kuja]
park	**puisto**	[pujsto]
boulevard	**bulevardi**	[buleʋardi]
square	**aukio**	[aukio]
avenue (wide street)	**valtakatu**	[ʋalta katu]
street	**katu**	[katu]
lane	**kuja**	[kuja]
dead end	**umpikuja**	[umpikuja]
house	**talo**	[talo]
building	**rakennus**	[rakeŋus]
skyscraper	**pilvenpiirtäjä**	[pilʋen pi:irtæjæ]
facade	**julkisivu**	[julkisiʋu]
roof	**katto**	[katto]

window	**ikkuna**	[ikkuna]
arch	**kaari**	[ka:ri]
column	**pylväs**	[pyluæs]
corner	**kulma**	[kulma]
shop window	**näyteikkuna**	[ɲæyte ikkuna]
shop sign	**kyltti**	[kyltti]
poster	**juliste**	[juliste]
advertising poster	**mainosjuliste**	[majnos juliste]
hoarding	**mainoskilpi**	[majnos kilpi]
rubbish	**jätteet**	[jætte:t]
rubbish bin	**roskis**	[roskis]
to litter (vi)	**roskata**	[roskata]
rubbish dump	**kaatopaikka**	[ka:topajkka]
telephone box	**puhelinkoppi**	[puheliŋkoppi]
street light	**lyhtypylväs**	[lyhtypyluæs]
bench (park ~)	**penkki**	[peŋkki]
policeman	**poliisi**	[poli:isi]
police	**poliisi**	[poli:isi]
beggar	**kerjäläinen**	[kerʰjæʎæjnen]
homeless	**koditon**	[koditon]

79. Urban institutions

shop	**kauppa**	[kauppa]
chemist, pharmacy	**apteekki**	[apte:kki]
optician	**optiikka**	[opti:ikka]
shopping centre	**kauppakeskus**	[kauppa keskus]
supermarket	**supermarketti**	[supermarketti]
bakery	**leipäkauppa**	[lejpækauppa]
baker	**leipuri**	[lejpuri]
cake shop	**konditoria**	[konditoria]
grocery shop	**sekatavarakauppa**	[sekatauara kauppa]
butcher shop	**lihakauppa**	[lihakauppa]
greengrocer	**vihanneskauppa**	[uihaŋes kauppa]
market	**kauppatori**	[kauppatori]
coffee bar	**kahvila**	[kahuila]
restaurant	**ravintola**	[rauintola]
pub	**pubi**	[pubi]
pizzeria	**pizzeria**	[pitseria]
hairdresser	**parturinliike**	[parturin li:ike]
post office	**posti**	[posti]
dry cleaners	**kemiallinen pesu**	[kemiallinen pesu]
photo studio	**valokuvausliike**	[ualo kuuaus li:ike]
shoe shop	**kenkäkauppa**	[keŋkækauppa]
bookshop	**kirjakauppa**	[kirʰja kauppa]

sports shop	**urheilukauppa**	[urhejlu kauppa]
clothing repair	**vaatteiden korjaus**	[ʋa:ttejden korʰjaus]
formal wear hire	**vaatteiden vuokra**	[ʋa:ttejden ʋuokra]
DVD rental shop	**elokuvien vuokra**	[elo kuʋien ʋuokra]
circus	**sirkus**	[sirkus]
zoo	**eläintarha**	[eʎæjntarha]
cinema	**elokuvateatteri**	[elokuʋa teatteri]
museum	**museo**	[museo]
library	**kirjasto**	[kirʰjasto]
theatre	**teatteri**	[teatteri]
opera	**ooppera**	[o:ppera]
nightclub	**yökerho**	[yøkerho]
casino	**kasino**	[kasino]
mosque	**moskeija**	[moskeja]
synagogue	**synagoga**	[synagoga]
cathedral	**tuomiokirkko**	[tuomiokirkko]
temple	**temppeli**	[temppeli]
church	**kirkko**	[kirkko]
institute	**instituutti**	[institu:tti]
university	**yliopisto**	[yliopisto]
school	**koulu**	[koulu]
prefecture	**prefektuuri**	[prefektu:ri]
town hall	**kaupunginhallitus**	[kaupuŋin hallitus]
hotel	**hotelli**	[hotelli]
bank	**pankki**	[paŋkki]
embassy	**suurlähetystö**	[su:r ʎæhetystø]
travel agency	**matkatoimisto**	[matka tojmisto]
information office	**neuvontatoimisto**	[neuʋon tatojmisto]
money exchange	**vaihtopiste**	[ʋajhtopiste]
underground, tube	**metro**	[metro]
hospital	**sairaala**	[sajra:la]
petrol station	**bensiiniasema**	[bensi:ini asema]
car park	**parkkipaikka**	[parkki pajkka]

80. Signs

shop sign	**kyltti**	[kyltti]
notice (written text)	**kirjoitus**	[kirʰøjtus]
poster	**juliste**	[juliste]
direction sign	**osoitin**	[osojtin]
arrow (sign)	**nuoli**	[nuoli]
caution	**varoitus**	[ʋarojtus]
warning sign	**varoitus**	[ʋarojtus]
to warn (vt)	**varoittaa**	[ʋarojtta:]
closing day	**vapaapäivä**	[ʋapa:pæjʋæ]

timetable (schedule)	**aikataulu**	[ajkataulu]
opening hours	**aukioloaika**	[aukioloajka]
WELCOME!	**TERVETULOA!**	[terʋetuloa]
ENTRANCE	**SISÄÄN**	[sisæ:n]
WAY OUT	**ULOS**	[ulos]
PUSH	**TYÖNNÄ**	[tyøŋæ]
PULL	**VEDÄ**	[ʋedæ]
OPEN	**AUKI**	[auki]
CLOSED	**KIINNI**	[ki:iŋi]
WOMEN	**NAISET**	[najset]
MEN	**MIEHET**	[miehet]
DISCOUNTS	**ALE**	[ale]
SALE	**ALENNUSMYYNTI**	[aleŋusmy:nti]
NEW!	**UUTUUS!**	[u:tu:s]
FREE	**ILMAISEKSI**	[ilmajseksi]
ATTENTION!	**HUOMIO!**	[huomio]
NO VACANCIES	**EI OLE TILAA**	[ej ole tilæ:]
RESERVED	**VARATTU**	[ʋarattu]
ADMINISTRATION	**HALLINTO**	[hallinto]
STAFF ONLY	**VAIN HENKILÖKUNNALLE**	[ʋajn heŋkilø kuŋalle]
BEWARE OF THE DOG!	**VARO VIHAISTA KOIRAA**	[ʋaro ʋihajsta kojræ:]
NO SMOKING	**TUPAKOINTI KIELLETTY**	[tupakojnti kielletty]
DO NOT TOUCH!	**EI SAA KOSKEA!**	[ej sa: koskea]
DANGEROUS	**ON VAARALLISTA**	[on ʋa:rallista]
DANGER	**HENGENVAARA**	[heŋenʋa:ra]
HIGH TENSION	**SUURJÄNNITE**	[su:rjæŋite]
NO SWIMMING!	**UIMINEN KIELLETTY**	[ujminen kielletty]
OUT OF ORDER	**EI TOIMI**	[ej tojmi]
FLAMMABLE	**SYTTYVÄ**	[syttyʋæ]
FORBIDDEN	**KIELLETTY**	[kielletty]
NO TRESPASSING!	**LÄPIKULKU KIELLETTY**	[ʎæpikulku kielletty]
WET PAINT	**ON MAALATTU**	[on ma:lattu]

81. Urban transport

bus, coach	**bussi**	[bussi]
tram	**raitiovaunu**	[rajtioʋaunu]
trolleybus	**johdinauto**	[øhdin auto]
route (of bus)	**reitti**	[rejtti]
number (e.g. bus ~)	**numero**	[numero]
to go by ...	**mennä...**	[meŋæ]
to get on (~ the bus)	**nousta**	[nousta]
to get off ...	**astua ulos**	[astua ulos]
stop (e.g. bus ~)	**pysäkki**	[pysækki]

next stop	**seuraava pysäkki**	[seura:ʋa pysækki]
terminus	**viimeinen pysäkki**	[ʋi:imejnen pysækki]
timetable	**aikataulu**	[ɑjkɑtɑulu]
to wait (vt)	**odottaa**	[odottɑ:]
ticket	**lippu**	[lippu]
fare	**lipun hinta**	[lipun hintɑ]
cashier	**kassanhoitaja**	[kɑssɑnhojtɑjɑ]
ticket inspection	**tarkastus**	[tɑrkɑstus]
inspector	**tarkastaja**	[tɑrkɑstɑjɑ]
to be late (for ...)	**myöhästyä**	[myøɦæstyæ]
to miss (~ the train, etc.)	**myöhästyä**	[myøɦæstyæ]
to be in a hurry	**kiirehtiä**	[ki:irehtiæ]
taxi, cab	**taksi**	[tɑksi]
taxi driver	**taksinkuljettaja**	[tɑksin kuʎjettɑjɑ]
by taxi	**taksilla**	[tɑksillɑ]
taxi rank	**taksiasema**	[tɑksiɑsemɑ]
to call a taxi	**tilata taksi**	[tilɑtɑ tɑksi]
to take a taxi	**ottaa taksi**	[ottɑ: tɑksi]
traffic	**katuliikenne**	[kɑtuli:keŋe]
traffic jam	**ruuhka**	[ru:hkɑ]
rush hour	**ruuhka-aika**	[ru:hkɑ ɑjkɑ]
to park (vi)	**pysäköidä**	[pysækøjdæ]
to park (vt)	**pysäköidä**	[pysækøjdæ]
car park	**parkkipaikka**	[pɑrkki pɑjkkɑ]
underground, tube	**metro**	[metro]
station	**asema**	[ɑsemɑ]
to take the tube	**mennä metrolla**	[meŋæ metrollɑ]
train	**juna**	[junɑ]
train station	**rautatieasema**	[rɑutɑtieɑsemɑ]

82. Sightseeing

monument	**patsas**	[pɑʦɑs]
fortress	**linna**	[liŋɑ]
palace	**palatsi**	[pɑlɑʦi]
castle	**linna**	[liŋɑ]
tower	**torni**	[torni]
mausoleum	**mausoleumi**	[mɑusoleumi]
architecture	**arkkitehtuuri**	[ɑrrkitehtu:ri]
medieval (adj)	**keskiaikainen**	[keskiɑjkɑjnen]
ancient (adj)	**vanha**	[ʋɑnhɑ]
national (adj)	**kansallinen**	[kɑnsɑllinen]
well-known (adj)	**tunnettu**	[tuŋettu]
tourist	**matkailija**	[mɑtkɑjlijɑ]
guide (person)	**opas**	[opɑs]
excursion	**retki**	[retki]

to show (vt)	**näyttää**	[ɲæyttæ:]
to tell (vt)	**kertoa**	[kertoɑ]
to find (vt)	**löytää**	[løytæ:]
to get lost	**hävitä**	[ɦæʋitæ]
map (e.g. underground ~)	**reittikartta**	[rejtti kɑrttɑ]
map (e.g. city ~)	**asemakaava**	[ɑsemɑ kɑ:ʋɑ]
souvenir, gift	**muistoesine**	[mujstoesine]
gift shop	**matkamuistokauppa**	[mɑtkɑ mujsto kɑuppɑ]
to take pictures	**valokuvata**	[ʋɑlokuʋɑtɑ]
to be photographed	**valokuvauttaa itsensä**	[ʋɑlo kuʋɑuttɑ: itsensæ]

83. Shopping

to buy (purchase)	**ostaa**	[ostɑ:]
purchase	**ostos**	[ostos]
to go shopping	**käydä ostoksilla**	[kæydæ ostoksillɑ]
shopping	**ostoksilla käynti**	[ostoksillɑ kæynti]
to be open (ab. shop)	**toimia**	[tojmiɑ]
to be closed	**olla kiinni**	[ollɑ ki:iŋi]
footwear	**jalkineet**	[jɑlkine:t]
clothes, clothing	**vaatteet**	[ʋɑ:tte:t]
cosmetics	**kosmetiikka**	[kosmeti:ikkɑ]
food products	**ruokatavarat**	[ruokɑ tɑʋɑrɑt]
gift, present	**lahja**	[lɑhʰjɑ]
shop assistant (masc.)	**myyjä**	[my:jæ]
shop assistant (fem.)	**myyjätär**	[my:jætær]
cash desk	**kassa**	[kɑssɑ]
mirror	**peili**	[pejli]
counter (in shop)	**tiski**	[tiski]
fitting room	**sovitushuone**	[soʋitus huone]
to try on	**sovittaa**	[soʋittɑ:]
to fit (ab. dress, etc.)	**sopia**	[sopiɑ]
to fancy (vt)	**miellyttää**	[miellyttæ:]
price	**hinta**	[hintɑ]
price tag	**hintalappu**	[hintɑ lɑppu]
to cost (vt)	**maksaa**	[mɑksɑ:]
How much?	**Kuinka paljon?**	[kuiŋkɑ pɑlʰon]
discount	**alennus**	[ɑleŋus]
inexpensive (adj)	**halpa**	[hɑlpɑ]
cheap (adj)	**halpa**	[hɑlpɑ]
expensive (adj)	**kallis**	[kɑllis]
It's expensive	**Se on kallista**	[se on kɑllistɑ]
hire (n)	**vuokra**	[ʋuokrɑ]
to hire (~ a dinner jacket)	**vuokrata**	[ʋuokrɑtɑ]

credit	**luotto**	[luotto]
on credit (adv)	**luotolla**	[luotolla]

84. Money

money	**rahat**	[rahat]
exchange	**vaihto**	[ʋajhto]
exchange rate	**kurssi**	[kurssi]
cashpoint	**pankkiautomaatti**	[paŋkki automa:tti]
coin	**kolikko**	[kolikko]
dollar	**dollari**	[dollari]
euro	**euro**	[euro]
lira	**liira**	[li:ira]
Deutschmark	**markka**	[markka]
franc	**frangi**	[fraŋi]
pound sterling	**punta**	[punta]
yen	**jeni**	[jeni]
debt	**velka**	[ʋelka]
debtor	**velallinen**	[ʋelallinen]
to lend (money)	**lainata jollekulle**	[lajnata ølekulle]
to borrow (vi, vt)	**lainata joltakulta**	[lajnata øltakulta]
bank	**pankki**	[paŋkki]
account	**tili**	[tili]
to deposit into the account	**tallettaa rahaa tilille**	[talletta: raha: tilille]
to withdraw (vt)	**nostaa rahaa tililtä**	[nosta: raha: tililta]
credit card	**luottokortti**	[luotto kortti]
cash	**käteinen**	[kætejnen]
cheque	**kuitti**	[kujtti]
to write a cheque	**kirjoittaa shekki**	[kir^h ojtta: ʃekki]
chequebook	**sekkivihko**	[se:kkiʋihko]
wallet	**lompakko**	[lompakko]
purse	**kukkaro**	[kukkaro]
billfold	**kukkaro**	[kukkaro]
safe	**kassakaappi**	[kassaka:ppi]
heir	**perillinen**	[perillinen]
inheritance	**perintö**	[perintø]
fortune (wealth)	**omaisuus**	[omajsu:s]
lease, let	**vuokraus**	[ʋuokraus]
rent money	**asuntovuokra**	[asuntoʋuokra]
to rent (sth from sb)	**vuokrata**	[ʋuokrata]
price	**hinta**	[hinta]
cost	**hinta**	[hinta]
sum	**summa**	[summa]
to spend (vt)	**kuluttaa**	[kulutta:]
expenses	**kulut**	[kulut]

to economize (vi, vt) **säästää** [sæ:stæ:]
economical **säästäväinen** [sæ:stæʋæjnen]

to pay (vi, vt) **maksaa** [mɑksɑ:]
payment **maksu** [mɑksu]
change (give the ~) **vaihtoraha** [ʋɑjhtorɑhɑ]

tax **vero** [ʋero]
fine **sakko** [sɑkko]
to fine (vt) **sakottaa** [sɑkottɑ:]

85. Post. Postal service

post office **posti** [posti]
post (letters, etc.) **posti** [posti]
postman **postikantaja** [postiŋkɑntɑjæ]
opening hours **virka-aika** [ʋirkɑ ɑjkɑ]

letter **kirje** [kirʰje]
registered letter **kirjattu kirje** [kirʰjɑttu kirʰje]
postcard **postikortti** [posti kortti]
telegram **sähke** [sæhke]
parcel **paketti** [pɑketti]
money transfer **rahalähetys** [rɑhɑ ʎæhetys]

to receive (vt) **saada** [sɑ:dɑ]
to send (vt) **lähettää** [ʎæhettæ:]
sending **kirjeen lähetys** [kirʰje:n ʎæhetys]

address **osoite** [osojte]
postcode **postinumero** [postinumero]
sender **lähettäjä** [ʎæhettæjæ]
receiver, addressee **saaja** [sɑ:jɑ]

name **nimi** [nimi]
family name **sukunimi** [sukunimi]

rate (of postage) **tariffi** [tɑriffi]
standard (adj) **tavallinen** [tɑʋɑllinen]
economical (adj) **edullinen** [edullinen]

weight **paino** [pɑjno]
to weigh up (vt) **punnita** [puŋitɑ]
envelope **kirjekuori** [kirʰjekuori]
postage stamp **postimerkki** [postimerkki]
to stamp an envelope **liimata postimerkki** [li:imɑtɑ postimerkki]

Dwelling. House. Home

86. House. Dwelling

house	**koti**	[koti]
at home (adv)	**kotona**	[kotona]
courtyard	**piha**	[piha]
fence	**aita**	[ajta]
brick (n)	**tiili**	[ti:ili]
brick (as adj)	**tiili-**	[ti:ili]
stone (n)	**kivi**	[kiʋi]
stone (as adj)	**kivinen**	[kiʋinen]
concrete (n)	**betoni**	[betoni]
concrete (as adj)	**betoninen**	[betoninen]
new (adj)	**uusi**	[u:si]
old (adj)	**vanha**	[ʋanha]
decrepit (house)	**ränsistynyt**	[rænsistynyt]
modern (adj)	**nykyaikainen**	[nyky ajkajnen]
multistorey (adj)	**monikerroksinen**	[moni kerroksinen]
high (adj)	**korkea**	[korkea]
floor, storey	**kerros**	[kerros]
single-storey (adj)	**yksikerroksinen**	[yksikerroksinen]
ground floor	**alakerros**	[alakerros]
top floor	**yläkerta**	[yʎækerta]
roof	**katto**	[katto]
chimney (stack)	**savupiippu**	[saʋupi:ippu]
roof tiles	**kattotiili**	[kattoti:ili]
tiled (adj)	**kattotiili-**	[kattoti:ili]
loft (attic)	**ullakko**	[ullakko]
window	**ikkuna**	[ikkuna]
glass	**lasi**	[lasi]
window ledge	**ikkunalauta**	[ikkuna lauta]
shutters	**ikkunaluukut**	[ikkuna lu:kut]
wall	**seinä**	[sejɲæ]
balcony	**parveke**	[parʋeke]
downpipe	**vesikouru**	[ʋesikouru]
upstairs (to be ~)	**ylhäällä**	[ylhæ:ʎæ]
to go upstairs	**nousta**	[nousta]
to come down	**laskeutua**	[laskeutua]
to move (to new premises)	**muuttaa**	[mu:tta:]

87. House. Entrance. Lift

entrance	**rappu**	[rappu]
stairs (stairway)	**portaat**	[porta:t]
steps	**askelmat**	[askelmat]
banisters	**kaide**	[kajde]
lobby (hotel ~)	**halli**	[halli]
postbox	**postilaatikko**	[postila:tikko]
rubbish container	**roskis**	[roskis]
refuse chute	**roskakuilu**	[roskakujlu]
lift	**hissi**	[hissi]
goods lift	**tavarahissi**	[tauara hissi]
lift cage	**hissi**	[hissi]
to take the lift	**mennä hissillä**	[meŋæ hissiʎæ]
flat	**asunto**	[asunto]
residents, inhabitants	**asukkaat**	[asukka:t]
neighbour (masc.)	**naapuri**	[na:puri]
neighbour (fem.)	**naapuri**	[na:puri]
neighbours	**naapurit**	[na:purit]

88. House. Electricity

electricity	**sähkö**	[sæhkø]
light bulb	**lamppu**	[lamppu]
switch	**kytkin**	[kytkin]
fuse	**sulake**	[sulake]
cable, wire (electric ~)	**johdin**	[øhdin]
wiring	**johde**	[øhde]
electricity meter	**mittari**	[mittari]
readings	**lukema**	[lukema]

89. House. Doors. Locks

door	**ovi**	[oui]
vehicle gate	**portti**	[portti]
handle, doorknob	**kahva**	[kahua]
to unlock (unbolt)	**avata lukko**	[auata lukko]
to open (vt)	**avata**	[auata]
to close (vt)	**sulkea**	[sulkea]
key	**avain**	[auajn]
bunch (of keys)	**nippu**	[nippu]
to creak (door hinge)	**narista**	[narista]
creak	**narina**	[narina]
hinge (of door)	**sarana**	[sarana]
doormat	**matto**	[matto]
door lock	**lukko**	[lukko]

keyhole	**avaimenreikä**	[aʋajmenrejkæ]
bolt (sliding bar)	**salpa**	[salpa]
door latch	**salpa**	[salpa]
padlock	**munalukko**	[muna lukko]
to ring (~ the door bell)	**soittaa**	[sojtta:]
ringing (sound)	**soitto**	[sojtto]
doorbell	**ovikello**	[oʋikello]
button	**nappi**	[nappi]
knock (at the door)	**koputus**	[koputus]
to knock (vi)	**koputtaa**	[koputta:]
code	**koodi**	[ko:di]
code lock	**koodilukko**	[ko:dilukko]
door phone	**ovipuhelin**	[oʋipuhelin]
number (on the door)	**numero**	[numero]
doorplate	**taulu**	[taulu]
peephole	**ovisilmä**	[oʋisilmæ]

90. Country house

village	**kylä**	[kyʎæ]
vegetable garden	**kasvitarha**	[kasʋitarha]
fence	**aita**	[ajta]
paling	**aita**	[ajta]
wicket gate	**portti**	[portti]
granary	**aitta**	[ajtta]
cellar	**kellari**	[kellari]
shed (in garden)	**vaja**	[ʋaja]
well (water)	**kaivo**	[kajʋo]
stove (wood-fired ~)	**uuni**	[u:ni]
to heat the stove	**lämmittää**	[ʎæmmittæ:]
firewood	**polttopuut**	[polttopu:t]
log (firewood)	**halko**	[halko]
veranda	**vilpola**	[ʋilpola]
terrace (patio)	**terassi**	[terassi]
front steps	**kuisti**	[kuisti]
swing (hanging seat)	**keinu**	[kejnu]

91. Villa. Mansion

country house	**maatalo**	[ma:talo]
villa (by sea)	**huvila**	[huʋila]
wing (of building)	**siipi**	[si:ipi]
garden	**puutarha**	[pu:tarha]
park	**puisto**	[pujsto]
tropical glasshouse	**ansari**	[ansari]
to look after (garden, etc.)	**hoitaa**	[hojta:]

swimming pool	**uima-allas**	[ujma allas]
gym	**urheiluhalli**	[urhejluhalli]
tennis court	**tenniskenttä**	[teŋis kenttæ]
home cinema room	**elokuvateatteri**	[elokuʋa teatteri]
garage	**autotalli**	[autotalli]
private property	**yksityisomaisuus**	[yksityjs omajsu:s]
private land	**yksityisomistukset**	[yksityjs omistukset]
warning (caution)	**varoitus**	[ʋarojtus]
warning sign	**varoituskirjoitus**	[ʋarojtus kirʰøjtus]
security	**vartio**	[ʋartio]
security guard	**vartija**	[ʋartija]
burglar alarm	**hälytyslaite**	[ɦælytyslajte]

92. Castle. Palace

castle	**linna**	[liŋa]
palace	**palatsi**	[palatsi]
fortress	**linna**	[liŋa]
wall (round castle)	**seinä**	[sejɲæ]
tower	**torni**	[torni]
main tower, donjon	**päätorni**	[pæ:torni]
portcullis	**nostoportti**	[nosto portti]
subterranean passage	**maanalainen käytävä**	[ma:nalajnen kæytæʋæ]
moat	**kaivanto**	[kajʋanto]
chain	**ketju**	[ketju]
arrow loop	**ampuma-aukko**	[ampuma aukko]
magnificent (adj)	**upea**	[upea]
majestic (adj)	**valtava**	[ʋaltaʋa]
impregnable (adj)	**valloittamaton**	[ʋallojttamaton]
knightly (adj)	**ritari-**	[ritari]
medieval (adj)	**keskiaikainen**	[keskiajkajnen]

93. Flat

flat	**asunto**	[asunto]
room	**huone**	[huone]
bedroom	**makuuhuone**	[maku: huone]
dining room	**ruokailuhuone**	[ruokajlu huone]
living room	**vierashuone**	[ʋieras huone]
study	**työhuone**	[tyøhuone]
entry room	**eteinen**	[etejnen]
bathroom	**kylpyhuone**	[kylpyhuone]
water closet	**vessa**	[ʋessa]
ceiling	**katto**	[katto]
floor	**lattia**	[lattia]
corner	**nurkka**	[nurkka]

94. Flat. Cleaning

to clean (vi, vt)	**siivota**	[si:iʋota]
to put away (to stow)	**korjata pois**	[korʰjata pojs]
dust	**pöly**	[pøly]
dusty (adj)	**pölyinen**	[pølyjnen]
to dust (vt)	**pyyhkiä pölyt pois**	[py:hkiæ pølyt pojs]
vacuum cleaner	**pölynimuri**	[pølynimuri]
to vacuum (vt)	**imuroida**	[imurojda]
to sweep (vi, vt)	**lakaista**	[lakajsta]
sweepings	**roskat**	[roskat]
order	**kunto**	[kunto]
disorder, mess	**epäjärjestys**	[epæjærʰjestys]
mop	**lattiaharja**	[lattiaharʰæ]
duster	**rätti**	[rætti]
broom	**luuta**	[lu:ta]
dustpan	**rikkalapio**	[rikkalapio]

95. Furniture. Interior

furniture	**huonekalut**	[huonekalut]
table	**pöytä**	[pøytæ]
chair	**tuoli**	[tuoli]
bed	**sänky**	[sæŋky]
sofa, settee	**sohva**	[sohʋa]
armchair	**nojatuoli**	[nojatuoli]
bookcase	**kaappi**	[ka:ppi]
shelf	**hylly**	[hylly]
set of shelves	**hyllykkö**	[hyllykkø]
wardrobe	**vaatekaappi**	[ʋa:te ka:ppi]
coat rack	**ripustin**	[ripustin]
coat stand	**naulakko**	[naulakko]
chest of drawers	**lipasto**	[lipasto]
coffee table	**sohvapöytä**	[sohʋapøjtæ]
mirror	**peili**	[pejli]
carpet	**matto**	[matto]
small carpet	**pieni matto**	[pjeni matto]
fireplace	**takka**	[takka]
candle	**kynttilä**	[kynttiʎæ]
candlestick	**kynttilänjalka**	[kynttiʎænjalka]
drapes	**kaihtimet**	[kajhtimet]
wallpaper	**tapetit**	[tapetit]
blinds (jalousie)	**rullaverhot**	[rulle ʋerhot]
table lamp	**pöytälamppu**	[pøytæ lamppu]
wall lamp	**seinävalaisin**	[sejna ʋalajsin]

standard lamp	**lattialamppu**	[lattia lamppu]
chandelier	**kattokruunu**	[kattokru:nu]
leg (of chair, table)	**jalka**	[jalka]
armrest	**käsinoja**	[kæsinoja]
back	**selkänoja**	[selkænoja]
drawer	**laatikko**	[la:tikko]

96. Bedding

bedclothes	**vuodevaatteet**	[ʋuodeʋa:tte:t]
pillow	**tyyny**	[ty:ny]
pillowslip	**tyynyliina**	[ty:ny li:ina]
blanket (eiderdown)	**vuodepeite**	[ʋuodepejte]
sheet	**lakana**	[lakana]
bedspread	**peite**	[pejte]

97. Kitchen

kitchen	**keittiö**	[kejttiø]
gas	**kaasu**	[ka:su]
gas cooker	**kaasuliesi**	[ka:su liesi]
electric cooker	**sähköhella**	[sæhkø hella]
oven	**paistinuuni**	[pajstinu:ni]
microwave oven	**mikroaaltouuni**	[mikro a:lto u:ni]
refrigerator	**jääkaappi**	[jæ:ka:ppi]
freezer	**pakastin**	[pakastin]
dishwasher	**astianpesukone**	[astianpesukone]
mincer	**lihamylly**	[lihamylly]
juicer	**mehunpuristin**	[mehun puristin]
toaster	**leivänpaahdin**	[lejʋæn pa:hdin]
mixer	**sekoitin**	[sekojtin]
coffee maker	**kahvinkeitin**	[kahʋiŋkejtin]
coffee pot	**kahvipannu**	[kahʋipaŋu]
coffee grinder	**kahvimylly**	[kahʋimylly]
kettle	**teepannu**	[te:paŋu]
teapot	**teekannu**	[te:kaŋu]
lid	**kansi**	[kansi]
tea strainer	**teesiivilä**	[te:si:iʋiʎæ]
spoon	**lusikka**	[lusikka]
teaspoon	**teelusikka**	[te: lusikka]
tablespoon	**ruokalusikka**	[ruoka lusikka]
fork	**haarukka**	[ha:rukka]
knife	**veitsi**	[ʋejʦi]
tableware (dishes)	**astiat**	[astiat]
plate (dinner ~)	**lautanen**	[lautanen]

saucer	**teevati**	[te:ʋati]
shot glass	**pikari**	[pikari]
glass (~ of water)	**lasi**	[lasi]
cup	**kuppi**	[kuppi]
sugar bowl	**sokeriastia**	[sokeriastia]
salt shaker	**suola-astia**	[suola astia]
pepper shaker	**pippuriastia**	[pippuriastia]
butter dish	**voiastia**	[ʋojastia]
stew pot	**kasari**	[kasari]
frying pan	**pannu**	[paŋu]
ladle	**liemikauha**	[liemikauha]
colander	**lävikkö**	[ʎæʋikkø]
tray	**tarjotin**	[tarʰøtin]
bottle	**pullo**	[pullo]
jar (glass)	**lasitölkki**	[lasitølkki]
tin, can	**peltitölkki**	[peltitølkki]
bottle opener	**pullonavaaja**	[pullonaʋa:jæ]
tin opener	**purkinavaaja**	[purkinaʋa:jæ]
corkscrew	**korkkiruuvi**	[korkkiru:ʋi]
filter	**suodatin**	[suodatin]
to filter (vt)	**suodattaa**	[suodatta:]
rubbish, refuse	**jätteet**	[jætte:t]
rubbish bin	**roskasanko**	[roskasaŋko]

98. Bathroom

bathroom	**kylpyhuone**	[kylpyhuone]
water	**vesi**	[ʋesi]
tap	**hana**	[hana]
hot water	**kuuma vesi**	[ku:ma ʋesi]
cold water	**kylmä vesi**	[kylmæ ʋesi]
toothpaste	**hammastahna**	[hammas tahna]
to clean one's teeth	**harjata hampaita**	[harʰjata hampajta]
to shave (vi)	**ajaa parta**	[aja: parta:]
shaving foam	**partavaahdoke**	[partaʋa:hdoke]
razor	**partaveitsi**	[partaʋejtsi]
to wash (clean)	**pestä**	[pestæ]
to have a bath	**peseytyä**	[peseytyæ]
shower	**suihku**	[sujhku]
to have a shower	**käydä suihkussa**	[kæydæ suihkussa]
bath (tub)	**amme**	[amme]
toilet	**vessanpönttö**	[ʋessanpønttø]
sink (washbasin)	**pesuallas**	[pesuallas]
soap	**saippua**	[sajppua]
soap dish	**saippuakotelo**	[sajppua kotelo]

sponge	**pesusieni**	[pesusieni]
shampoo	**sampoo**	[sampo:]
towel	**pyyhe**	[py:he]
bathrobe	**froteinen aamutakki**	[frotejnen ɑ:mutakki]
laundry (process)	**pyykin pesu**	[py:kin pesu]
washing machine	**pesukone**	[pesu kone]
to do the laundry	**pestä pyykkiä**	[pestæ py:kkiæ]
washing powder	**pesujauhe**	[pesujauhe]

99. Household appliances

TV, telly	**televisio**	[teleʋisio]
tape recorder	**nauhuri**	[nauhuri]
video	**videonauhuri**	[ʋideonauhuri]
radio	**vastaanotin**	[ʋasta:notin]
player (CD, MP3, etc.)	**korvalappustereot**	[korʋalappustereot]
video projector	**videoheitin**	[ʋideohejtin]
home cinema	**kotiteatteri**	[kotiteatteri]
DVD player	**DVD-soitin**	[deʋede sojtin]
amplifier	**vahvistin**	[ʋahʋistin]
video game console	**pelikonsoli**	[pelikonsoli]
video camera	**videokamera**	[ʋideokamera]
camera (photo)	**kamera**	[kamera]
digital camera	**digitaalikamera**	[digita:li kamera]
vacuum cleaner	**pölynimuri**	[pølynimuri]
iron (e.g. steam ~)	**silitysrauta**	[silitys rauta]
ironing board	**silityslauta**	[silitys lauta]
telephone	**puhelin**	[puhelin]
mobile phone	**matkapuhelin**	[matka puhelin]
typewriter	**kirjoituskone**	[kirʰøjtus kone]
sewing machine	**ompelukone**	[ompelu kone]
microphone	**mikrofoni**	[mikrofoni]
headphones	**kuulokkeet**	[ku:lokke:t]
remote control (TV)	**kaukosäädin**	[kaukosæ:din]
CD, compact disc	**CD-levy**	[sede leʋy]
cassette	**kasetti**	[kasetti]
vinyl record	**levy**	[leʋy]

100. Repairs. Renovation

renovations	**remontti**	[remontti]
to renovate (vt)	**remontoida**	[remontoida]
to repair (vt)	**korjata**	[korʰjata]
to put in order	**panna järjestykseen**	[paŋa jærʰjestykse:n]
to redo (do again)	**tehdä uudelleen**	[tehdæ u:delle:n]

paint	**maali**	[mɑ:li]
to paint (~ a wall)	**maalata**	[mɑ:lɑtɑ]
house painter	**maalari**	[mɑ:lɑri]
brush	**pensseli**	[pensseli]
whitewash	**valkaisu**	[ʋɑlkɑjsu]
to whitewash (vt)	**valkaista**	[ʋɑlkɑjstɑ]
wallpaper	**tapetit**	[tɑpetit]
to wallpaper (vt)	**tapetoida**	[tɑpetojdɑ]
varnish	**lakka**	[lɑkkɑ]
to varnish (vt)	**lakata**	[lɑkɑtɑ]

101. Plumbing

water	**vesi**	[ʋesi]
hot water	**kuuma vesi**	[ku:mɑ ʋesi]
cold water	**kylmä vesi**	[kylmæ ʋesi]
tap	**hana**	[hɑnɑ]
drop (of water)	**pisara**	[pisɑrɑ]
to drip (vi)	**tippua**	[tippuɑ]
to leak (ab. pipe)	**vuotaa**	[ʋuotɑ:]
leak (pipe ~)	**vuoto**	[ʋuoto]
puddle	**lätäkkö**	[ʎætækkø]
pipe	**putki**	[putki]
valve	**venttiili**	[ʋentti:ili]
to be clogged up	**tukkeutua**	[tukkeutuɑ]
tools	**instrumentti**	[instrumentti]
adjustable spanner	**mutteriavain**	[mutteriɑʋɑjn]
to unscrew, untwist (vt)	**kiertää irti**	[kiertæ: irti]
to screw (tighten)	**kiertää**	[kærtæ:]
to unclog (vt)	**puhdistaa**	[puhdistɑ:]
plumber	**putkimies**	[putkimies]
basement	**kellari**	[kellɑri]
sewerage (system)	**viemäri**	[ʋiemæri]

102. Fire. Conflagration

fire (to catch ~)	**tuli**	[tuli]
flame	**liekki**	[liekki]
spark	**kipinä**	[kipiɲæ]
smoke (from fire)	**savu**	[sɑʋu]
torch (flaming stick)	**soihtu**	[sojhtu]
campfire	**nuotio**	[nuotio]
petrol	**bensiini**	[bensi:ini]
paraffin	**paloöljy**	[pɑloøl[h]y]
flammable (adj)	**poltto-**	[poltto]

explosive (adj)	**räjähdysvaarallinen**	[ræjæhdys ʋɑ:rɑllinen]
NO SMOKING	**EI SAA POLTTAA!**	[ej sɑ: polttɑ:]
safety	**turvallisuus**	[turʋɑllisu:s]
danger	**vaara**	[ʋɑ:rɑ]
dangerous (adj)	**vaarallinen**	[ʋɑ:rɑlinen]
to catch fire	**syttyä tuleen**	[syttyæ tule:n]
explosion	**räjähdys**	[ræjæhdys]
to set fire	**sytyttää**	[sytyttæ:]
incendiary (arsonist)	**palon sytyttäjä**	[pɑlon sytyttæjæ]
arson	**tuhopoltto**	[tuhopoltto]
to blaze (vi)	**leimuta**	[lejmutɑ]
to burn (be on fire)	**palaa**	[pɑlɑ:]
to burn down	**palaa loppuun**	[pɑlɑ: loppu:n]
firefighter	**palomies**	[pɑlomies]
fire engine	**paloauto**	[pɑloɑuto]
fire brigade	**palokunta**	[pɑlokuntɑ]
fire engine ladder	**tikkaat**	[tikkɑ:t]
fire hose	**letku**	[letku]
fire extinguisher	**tulensammutin**	[tulen sɑmmutin]
helmet	**kypärä**	[kypæræ]
siren	**sireeni**	[sire:ni]
to call out	**huutaa**	[hu:tɑ:]
to call for help	**kutsua avuksi**	[kutsuɑ ɑʋuksi]
rescuer	**pelastaja**	[pelɑstɑjɑ]
to rescue (vt)	**pelastaa**	[pelɑstɑ:]
to arrive (vi)	**saapua**	[sɑ:puɑ]
to extinguish (vt)	**sammuttaa**	[sɑmmuttɑ:]
water	**vesi**	[ʋesi]
sand	**hiekka**	[hiekkɑ]
ruins (destruction)	**rauniot**	[rɑuniot]
to collapse (building, etc.)	**romahtaa**	[romɑhtɑ:]
to fall down (vi)	**luhistua**	[luhistuɑ]
to cave in (ceiling, floor)	**luhistua**	[luhistuɑ]
fragment (piece of wall, etc.)	**pirstale**	[pirstɑle]
ash	**tuhka**	[tuhkɑ]
to suffocate (die)	**tukehtua**	[tukehtuɑ]
to be killed (perish)	**tuhoutua**	[tuhoutuɑ]

HUMAN ACTIVITIES

Job. Business. Part 1

103. Office. Working in the office

office (of firm)	**toimisto**	[tojmisto]
office (of director, etc.)	**työhuone**	[tyøhuone]
secretary	**sihteeri**	[sihte:ri]
director	**johtaja**	[øhtaja]
manager	**manageri**	[manageri]
accountant	**kirjanpitäjä**	[kirʰjanpitæjæ]
employee	**työntekijä**	[tyøntekiæ]
furniture	**huonekalut**	[huonekalut]
desk	**pöytä**	[pøytæ]
desk chair	**nojatuoli**	[nojatuoli]
chest of drawers	**pieni kaappi**	[pieni ka:ppi]
coat stand	**naulakko**	[naulakko]
computer	**tietokone**	[tietokone]
printer	**tulostin**	[tulostin]
fax machine	**faksi**	[faksi]
photocopier	**kopiokone**	[kopiokone]
paper	**paperi**	[paperi]
office supplies	**toimistotarvikkeet**	[tojmisto tarʋikke:t]
mouse mat	**hiirimatto**	[hi:irimatto]
sheet of paper	**arkki**	[arkki]
folder, binder	**kansio**	[kansio]
catalogue	**luettelo**	[luettelo]
directory (of addresses)	**hakemisto**	[hakemisto]
documentation	**asiakirjat**	[asiakirʰjat]
brochure	**brosyyri**	[brosy:ri]
leaflet	**lehtinen**	[lehtinen]
sample	**malli**	[malli]
training meeting	**harjoittelu**	[harʰøjttelu]
meeting (of managers)	**neuvottelu**	[neuʋottelu]
lunch time	**ruokatunti**	[ruokatunti]
to make a copy	**ottaa kopio**	[otta: kopio]
to make copies	**monistaa**	[monista:]
to receive a fax	**saada faksi**	[sa:da faksi]
to send a fax	**lähettää faksilla**	[ʎæhettæ: faksilla]
to ring (telephone)	**soittaa**	[sojtta:]
to answer (vt)	**vastata**	[ʋastata]

to put through	**yhdistää**	[yhdistæ:]
to arrange, to set up	**sopia tapaamisesta**	[sopia tapa:misesta]
to demonstrate (vt)	**esittää**	[esittæ:]
to be absent	**olla poissa**	[olla pojssa]
absence	**poissaolo**	[pojssaolo]

104. Business processes. Part 1

occupation	**toimi**	[tojmi]
firm	**liike**	[li:ike]
company	**yhtiö**	[yhtiø]
corporation	**korporaatio**	[korpora:tio]
enterprise	**yritys**	[yritys]
agency	**toimisto**	[tojmisto]
agreement (contract)	**sopimus**	[sopimus]
contract	**sopimus**	[sopimus]
deal	**kauppa**	[kauppa]
order (to place an ~)	**tilaus**	[tilaus]
term (of contract)	**ehto**	[ehto]
wholesale (adv)	**tukussa**	[tukussa]
wholesale (adj)	**tukku-**	[tukku]
wholesale (n)	**tukkumyynti**	[tukkumy:nti]
retail (adj)	**vähittäis-**	[ʋæhittæjs]
retail (n)	**vähittäismyynti**	[ʋæhittæjs my:nti]
competitor	**kilpailija**	[kilpajlija]
competition	**kilpailu**	[kilpajlu]
to compete (vi)	**kilpailla**	[kilpajlla]
partner (associate)	**partneri**	[partneri]
partnership	**kumppanuus**	[kumppanu:s]
crisis	**kriisi**	[kri:isi]
bankruptcy	**vararikko**	[ʋararikko]
to go bankrupt	**tehdä vararikko**	[tehdæ ʋararikko]
difficulty	**vaikeus**	[ʋajkeus]
problem	**ongelma**	[oŋelma]
catastrophe	**onnettomuus**	[oŋettomu:s]
economy	**taloustiede**	[taloustiede]
economic (~ growth)	**taloudellinen**	[taloudellinen]
economic recession	**taloudellinen lasku**	[taloudellinen lasku]
goal (aim)	**päämäärä**	[pæ:mæ:ræ]
task	**tarkoitus**	[tarkojtus]
to trade (vi)	**käydä kauppaa**	[kæydæ kauppa:]
network (distribution ~)	**verkko**	[ʋerkko]
inventory (stock)	**varasto**	[ʋarasto]
assortment	**valikoima**	[ʋali kojma]
leader	**johtaja**	[øhtaja]
large (~ company)	**suuri**	[su:ri]

monopoly	**monopoli**	[monopoli]
theory	**teoria**	[teoria]
practice	**käytäntö**	[kæyntæntø]
experience (in my ~)	**kokemus**	[kokemus]
trend (tendency)	**tendenssi**	[tendenssi]
development	**kehitys**	[kehitys]

105. Business processes. Part 2

profitability	**etu**	[etu]
profitable (adj)	**edullinen**	[edullinen]
delegation (group)	**valtuuskunta**	[ʋaltu:skunta]
salary	**palkka**	[palkka]
to correct (an error)	**korjata**	[korʰjata]
business trip	**työmatka**	[tyømatka]
commission	**lautakunta**	[lautakunta]
to control (vt)	**tarkastaa**	[tarkasta:]
conference	**konferenssi**	[konferenssi]
licence	**lisenssi**	[lisenssi]
reliable (~ partner)	**luotettava**	[luotettaʋa]
initiative (undertaking)	**aloite**	[alojte]
norm (standard)	**normi**	[normi]
circumstance	**seikka**	[sejkka]
duty (of employee)	**velvollisuus**	[ʋelʋollisu:s]
enterprise	**järjestö**	[jærʰjestø]
organization (process)	**järjestely**	[jærʰjestely]
organized (adj)	**järjestynyt**	[jærʰjestynyt]
cancellation	**peruutus**	[peru:tus]
to cancel (call off)	**peruuttaa**	[peru:tta:]
report (official ~)	**selostus**	[selostus]
patent	**patentti**	[patentti]
to patent (obtain patent)	**patentoida**	[patentojda]
to plan (vt)	**suunnitella**	[su:ŋitella]
bonus (money)	**palkinto**	[palkinto]
professional (adj)	**ammatti-**	[amatti]
procedure	**menettely**	[menettely]
to examine (contract, etc.)	**käsitellä**	[kæsiteʎæ]
calculation	**laskelma**	[laskelma]
reputation	**maine**	[majne]
risk	**riski**	[riski]
to manage, to run	**johtaa**	[øhta:]
information	**tiedot**	[tædot]
property	**omaisuus**	[omajsu:s]
union	**liitto**	[li:itto]
life insurance	**hengen vakuutus**	[heŋen ʋaku:tus]
to insure (vt)	**vakuuttaa**	[ʋaku:tta:]

insurance	**vakuutus**	[ʋaku:tus]
auction	**huutokauppa**	[hu:tokauppa]
to notify (inform)	**tiedottaa**	[tiedotta:]
management (process)	**hallinto**	[hallinto]
service (~ industry)	**palvelus**	[palʋelus]
forum	**foorumi**	[fo:rumi]
to function (vi)	**toimia**	[tojmia]
stage (phase)	**vaihe**	[ʋajhe]
legal (~ services)	**oikeustieteellinen**	[ojkeus tiete:llinen]
lawyer (legal expert)	**lakimies**	[lakimies]

106. Production. Works

plant	**tehdas**	[tehdas]
factory	**tehdas**	[tehdas]
workshop	**osasto**	[osasto]
production site	**tuotanto**	[tuotanto]
industry	**teollisuus**	[teollisu:s]
industrial (adj)	**teollinen**	[teollinen]
heavy industry	**raskas teollisuus**	[raskas teollisu:s]
light industry	**kevyt teollisuus**	[keʋyt teollisu:s]
products	**tuotanto**	[tuotanto]
to produce (vt)	**tuottaa**	[tuotta:]
raw materials	**raaka-aine**	[ra:ka ajne]
foreman	**työnjohtaja**	[tø:niohtaæ]
workers team	**prikaati**	[prika:ti]
worker	**työläinen**	[tyøʎæjnen]
working day	**työpäivä**	[tyøpæjʋæ]
pause	**väliaika**	[ʋæliajka]
meeting	**kokous**	[kokous]
to discuss (vt)	**käsitellä**	[kæsiteʎæ]
plan	**suunnitelma**	[su:ŋitelma]
to fulfil the plan	**täyttää suunnitelma**	[te:ttæ: su:ŋitelma]
rate of output	**normi**	[normi]
quality	**laatu**	[la:tu]
checking (control)	**tarkastus**	[tarkastus]
quality control	**laadunvalvonta**	[la:dun ʋalʋonta]
safety of work	**työturva**	[tyøturʋa]
discipline	**kuri**	[kuri]
infraction	**rikkomus**	[rikkomus]
to violate (rules)	**rikkoa**	[rikkoa]
strike	**lakko**	[lakko]
striker	**lakkolainen**	[lakkolajnen]
to be on strike	**lakkoilla**	[lakkojla]
trade union	**ammattiliitto**	[ammatti li:itto]
to invent (machine, etc.)	**keksiä**	[keksiæ]
invention	**keksintö**	[keksintø]

research	**tutkimus**	[tutkimus]
to improve (make better)	**parantaa**	[paranta:]
technology	**teknologia**	[teknologia]
technical drawing	**piirros**	[pi:irros]
load, cargo	**lasti**	[lasti]
loader (person)	**lastaaja**	[lasta:ja]
to load (vehicle, etc.)	**kuormata**	[kuormata]
loading (process)	**kuormaaminen**	[kuorma:minen]
to unload (vi, vt)	**purkaa lasti**	[purka: lasti]
unloading	**purkaminen**	[purkaminen]
transport	**kulkuneuvot**	[kulkuneuʋot]
transport company	**kuljetusyhtiö**	[kul^{h}jetus yhtiø]
to transport (vt)	**kuljettaa**	[kul^{h}jetta:]
wagon	**tavaravaunu**	[taʋaraʋaunu]
cistern	**säiliö**	[sæjliø]
lorry	**kuorma-auto**	[kuorma auto]
machine tool	**kone**	[kone]
mechanism	**koneisto**	[konejsto]
industrial waste	**jätteet**	[jætte:t]
packing (process)	**pakkaus**	[pakkaus]
to pack (vt)	**pakata**	[pakata]

107. Contract. Agreement

contract	**sopimus**	[sopimus]
agreement	**sopimus**	[sopimus]
addendum	**liite**	[li:ite]
to sign a contract	**tehdä sopimus**	[tehdæ sopimus]
signature	**allekirjoitus**	[allekir^{h}øjtus]
to sign (vt)	**allekirjoittaa**	[allekir^{h}ojtta:]
stamp (seal)	**leima**	[lejma]
subject of contract	**sopimuksen aihe**	[sopimuksen ajhe]
clause	**kohta**	[kohta]
parties (in contract)	**puolet**	[puolet]
legal address	**juridinen osoite**	[juridinen osojte]
to break the contract	**rikkoa sopimus**	[rikkoa sopimus]
commitment	**sitoumus**	[sitoumus]
responsibility	**vastuu**	[ʋastu:]
force majeure	**yli voimainen este**	[yli ʋojmajnen este]
dispute	**kiista**	[ki:ista]
penalties	**sakkosanktiot**	[sakko saŋktiot]

108. Import & Export

import	**tuonti**	[tuonti]
importer	**tuoja**	[tuoja]
to import (vt)	**tuoda maahan**	[tuoda ma:han]
import (e.g. ~ goods)	**tuonti-**	[tuonti]
exporter	**viejä**	[ʋiejæ]
to export (vi, vt)	**viedä**	[ʋiedæ]
goods	**tavara**	[taʋara]
consignment, lot	**erä**	[eræ]
weight	**paino**	[pajno]
volume	**tilavuus**	[tilaʋu:s]
cubic metre	**kuutiometri**	[ku:tio metri]
manufacturer	**tuottaja**	[tuottaja]
transport company	**liikenneyhtiö**	[li:keŋe yhtiø]
container	**kontti**	[kontti]
border	**raja**	[raja]
customs	**tulli**	[tulli]
customs duty	**tullimaksu**	[tulli maksu]
customs officer	**tullimies**	[tullimies]
smuggling	**salakuljetus**	[salakul^{h}jetus]
contraband (goods)	**salakuljetustavara**	[sala kul^{h}jetus taʋara]

109. Finances

share, stock	**osake**	[osake]
bond (certificate)	**obligaatio**	[obliga:tio]
bill of exchange	**vekseli**	[ʋekseli]
stock exchange	**pörssi**	[pørssi]
stock price	**osakkeiden kurssi**	[osakkejden kurssi]
to become cheaper	**halventua**	[halʋentua]
to rise in price	**kallistua**	[kallistua]
share	**osuus**	[osu:s]
controlling interest	**osake-enemmistö**	[osake enemmistø]
investment	**sijoitukset**	[si:ojtukset]
to invest (vt)	**investoida**	[inʋestojda]
percent	**prosentti**	[prosentti]
interest (on investment)	**korko**	[korko]
profit	**voitto**	[ʋojtto]
profitable (adj)	**edullinen**	[edullinen]
tax	**vero**	[ʋero]
currency (foreign ~)	**valuutta**	[ʋalu:tta]
national (adj)	**kansallinen**	[kansallinen]

exchange (currency ~)	**vaihto**	[ʋajhto]
accountant	**kirjanpitäjä**	[kirʰjanpitæjæ]
accounting	**kirjanpito**	[kirʰjan pito]
bankruptcy	**konkurssi**	[koŋkursi]
collapse, ruin	**vararikko**	[ʋararikko]
ruin	**perikato**	[perikato]
to be ruined	**joutua perikatoon**	[øutua perikato:n]
inflation	**inflaatio**	[infla:tio]
devaluation	**devalvointi**	[deʋalʋojnti]
capital	**pääoma**	[pæ:oma]
income	**tulo**	[tulo]
turnover	**kierto**	[kierto]
resources	**varat**	[ʋarat]
monetary resources	**rahavarat**	[rahaʋarat]
to reduce (expenses)	**supistaa**	[supista:]

110. Marketing

marketing	**markkinointi**	[markkinointi]
market	**markkinat**	[markkinat]
market segment	**markkinoiden segmentti**	[markkinojden segmentti]
product	**tuote**	[tuote]
goods	**tavara**	[taʋara]
trademark	**merkki**	[merkki]
logotype	**yrityksen merkki**	[yrityksen merkki]
logo	**logotyyppi**	[logoty:ppi]
demand	**kysyntä**	[kysyntæ]
supply	**tarjous**	[tarʰøus]
need	**tarve**	[tarʋe]
consumer	**kuluttaja**	[kuluttaja]
analysis	**analyysi**	[analy:si]
to analyse (vt)	**analysoida**	[analysojda]
positioning	**asemointi**	[asemojnti]
to position (vt)	**asemoida**	[asemojda]
price	**hinta**	[hinta]
pricing policy	**hintapolitiikka**	[hinta politi:ikka]
pricing	**hinnanmuodostus**	[hiŋan muodostus]

111. Advertising

advertising	**mainos**	[majnos]
to advertise (vt)	**mainostaa**	[majnosta:]
budget	**budjetti**	[budʰjetti]
ad, advertisement	**mainos**	[majnos]
TV advertising	**televisiomainos**	[teleʋisio majnos]

radio advertising	**radiomainos**	[radio majnos]
outdoor advertising	**katumainos**	[katumajnos]
mass medias	**joukkotiedotusvälineet**	[øukko tiedotus ʋæline:t]
periodical (n)	**aikakausjulkaisu**	[ajkakaus julkajsu]
image (public appearance)	**imago**	[imago]
slogan	**iskulause**	[iskulause]
motto (maxim)	**tunnuslause**	[tuŋuslause]
campaign	**kampanja**	[kampanʰja]
advertising campaign	**mainoskampanja**	[majnos kampanʰja]
target group	**kohderyhmä**	[kohderyhmæ]
business card	**nimikortti**	[nimikortti]
leaflet	**lehtinen**	[lehtinen]
brochure	**brosyyri**	[brosy:ri]
pamphlet	**kirjanen**	[kirʰjænen]
newsletter	**vaalilippu**	[ʋa:lilippu]
shop sign	**kyltti**	[kyltti]
poster	**juliste**	[juliste]
hoarding	**mainoskilpi**	[majnos kilpi]

112. Banking

bank	**pankki**	[paŋkki]
branch (of bank, etc.)	**osasto**	[osasto]
consultant	**neuvoja**	[neuʋoja]
manager (director)	**johtaja**	[øhtaja]
bank account	**tili**	[tili]
account number	**tilinumero**	[tili numero]
current account	**käyttötili**	[kæyttø tili]
deposit account	**säästötili**	[sæ:stø tili]
to open an account	**avata tili**	[aʋata tili]
to close the account	**kuolettaa tili**	[kuoletta: tili]
to deposit into the account	**panna tilille**	[paŋa tilille]
to withdraw (vt)	**nostaa rahat tililtä**	[nosta: rahat tililta]
deposit	**talletus**	[talletus]
to make a deposit	**tallettaa**	[talletta:]
wire transfer	**siirto**	[si:irto]
to wire (money)	**siirtää**	[si:irtæ:]
sum	**summa**	[summa]
How much?	**paljonko**	[palʰøŋko]
signature	**allekirjoitus**	[allekirʰøjtus]
to sign (vt)	**allekirjoittaa**	[allekirʰojtta:]
credit card	**luottokortti**	[luotto kortti]
code	**koodi**	[ko:di]

credit card number	**luottokortin numero**	[luotto kortin numero]
cashpoint	**pankkiautomaatti**	[paŋkki automa:tti]
cheque	**kuitti**	[kujtti]
to write a cheque	**kirjoittaa shekki**	[kirʰojtta: ʃekki]
chequebook	**sekkivihko**	[se:kkiʋihko]
loan (bank ~)	**luotto**	[luotto]
to apply for a loan	**hakea luottoa**	[hakea luottoa]
to get a loan	**saada luotto**	[sa:da luotto]
to give a loan	**antaa luottoa**	[anta: luottoa]
guarantee	**takuu**	[taku:]

113. Telephone. Phone conversation

telephone	**puhelin**	[puhelin]
mobile phone	**matkapuhelin**	[matka puhelin]
answering machine	**puhelinvastaaja**	[puhelin ʋasta:ja]
to ring (telephone)	**soittaa**	[sojtta:]
call, ring	**soitto**	[sojtto]
to dial a number	**valita numero**	[ʋalita numero]
Hello!	**Hei!**	[hej]
to ask (vt)	**kysyä**	[kysyæ]
to answer (vi, vt)	**vastata**	[ʋastata]
to hear (vt)	**kuulla**	[ku:lla]
well (adv)	**hyvin**	[hyʋin]
not well (adv)	**huonosti**	[huonosti]
noises (interference)	**häiriöt**	[ɦæjriøt]
receiver	**kuuloke**	[ku:loke]
to pick up (~ the phone)	**nostaa luuri**	[nosta: lu:ri]
to hang up (~ the phone)	**laskea luuri**	[laskea lu:ri]
engaged (adj)	**varattu**	[ʋarattu]
to ring (ab. phone)	**soittaa**	[sojtta:]
telephone book	**puhelinluettelo**	[puhelin luettelo]
local (adj)	**paikallinen**	[pajkallinen]
trunk (e.g. ~ call)	**kauko-**	[kauko]
international (adj)	**kansainvälinen**	[kansajnʋælinen]

114. Mobile telephone

mobile phone	**matkapuhelin**	[matka puhelin]
display	**näyttö**	[ɲæyttø]
button	**nappula**	[nappula]
SIM card	**SIM-kortti**	[sim kortti]
battery	**paristo**	[paristo]
to be flat (battery)	**olla tyhjä**	[olla ty:ɦʲa]

charger	**laturi**	[ɑturi]
menu	**valikko**	[ʋɑlikko]
settings	**asetukset**	[ɑsetukset]
tune (melody)	**melodia**	[melodiɑ]
to select (vt)	**valita**	[ʋɑlitɑ]
calculator	**laskin**	[lɑskin]
answering machine	**puhelinvastaaja**	[puhelin ʋɑstɑ:jɑ]
alarm clock	**herätyskello**	[herætys kello]
contacts	**puhelinluettelo**	[puhelin luettelo]
SMS (text message)	**SMS-viesti**	[esemes ʋiesti]
subscriber	**tilaaja**	[tilɑ:jɑ]

115. Stationery

ballpoint pen	**täytekynä**	[tæytekyɲæ]
fountain pen	**sulkakynä**	[sulkɑkyɲæ]
pencil	**lyijykynä**	[ly:kyɲæ]
highlighter	**korostuskynä**	[korostuskyɲæ]
felt-tip pen	**huopakynä**	[huopɑkyɲæ]
notepad	**lehtiö**	[lehtiø]
diary	**päivyri**	[pæjʋyri]
ruler	**viivoitin**	[ʋi:iʋojtin]
calculator	**laskin**	[lɑskin]
rubber	**kumi**	[kumi]
drawing pin	**nasta**	[nɑstɑ]
paper clip	**paperiliitin**	[pɑperi li:itin]
glue	**liima**	[li:imɑ]
stapler	**nitoja**	[nitojɑ]
hole punch	**rei'itin**	[rejıtin]
pencil sharpener	**teroitin**	[terojtin]

116. Various kinds of documents

account (report)	**selostus**	[selostus]
agreement	**sopimus**	[sopimus]
application form	**tilaus**	[tilɑus]
authentic (adj)	**alkuperäinen**	[ɑlkuperæjnen]
badge (identity tag)	**rintamerkki**	[rintɑmerkki]
business card	**nimikortti**	[nimikortti]
certificate (~ of quality)	**sertifikaatti**	[sertifikɑ:tti]
cheque (e.g. draw a ~)	**sekki**	[sekki]
bill (in restaurant)	**lasku**	[lɑsku]
constitution	**perustuslaki**	[perustuslɑki]
contract	**sopimus**	[sopimus]
copy	**kopio**	[kopio]

copy (of contract, etc.)	**kappale**	[kappale]
customs declaration	**selvityskirja**	[selυityskirʰa]
document	**asiakirja**	[asiakirʰæ]
driving licence	**ajokortti**	[aøkortti]
addendum	**liite**	[li:ite]
form	**lomake**	[lomake]
identity card, ID	**todistus**	[todistus]
inquiry (request)	**kysely**	[kysely]
invitation card	**kutsulippu**	[kutsulippu]
invoice	**lasku**	[lasku]
law	**laki**	[laki]
letter (mail)	**kirje**	[kirʰje]
letterhead	**lomake**	[lomake]
list (of names, etc.)	**luettelo**	[luettelo]
manuscript	**käsikirjoitus**	[kæsikirʰøjtus]
newsletter	**vaalilippu**	[υa:lilippu]
note (short message)	**kirjelappu**	[kirʰjelappu]
pass (for worker, visitor)	**kulkulupa**	[kulkulupa]
passport	**passi**	[passi]
permit	**lupa**	[lupa]
curriculum vitae, CV	**ansioluettelo**	[ansioluettelo]
debt note, IOU	**kuitti**	[kujtti]
receipt (for purchase)	**kuitti**	[kujtti]
till receipt	**sekki**	[sekki]
report	**raportti**	[raportti]
to show (ID, etc.)	**esittää**	[esittæ:]
to sign (vt)	**allekirjoittaa**	[allekirʰojtta:]
signature	**allekirjoitus**	[allekirʰøjtus]
stamp (seal)	**leima**	[lejma]
text	**teksti**	[teksti]
ticket (for entry)	**lippu**	[lippu]
to cross out	**yliviivata**	[yliυi:iυata]
to fill in (~ a form)	**täyttää**	[tæyttæ:]
waybill	**rahtikirja**	[rahtikirʰja]
will (testament)	**testamentti**	[testamentti]

117. Kinds of business

accounting services	**kirjanpitopalvelut**	[kirʰjan pito palυelut]
advertising	**mainos**	[majnos]
advertising agency	**mainostoimisto**	[majnos tojmisto]
air-conditioners	**ilmastointilaitteet**	[ilmastojnti lajtte:t]
airline	**lentoyhtiö**	[lentoyhtiø]
alcoholic drinks	**alkoholijuomat**	[alkoholi juomat]
antiques	**antiikki**	[anti:ikki]
art gallery	**galleria**	[galleria]
audit services	**tilintarkastuspalvelut**	[tilin tarkastus palυelut]

banks **pankkitoiminta** [paŋkki tojminta]
beauty salon **kauneushoitola** [kauneus hojtola]
bookshop **kirjakauppa** [kir^{h}ja kauppa]
brewery **olutpanimo** [olutpanimo]
business centre **liiketoimisto** [li:ike tojmisto]
business school **liikekoulu** [li:ike koulu]

casino **kasino** [kasino]
chemist, pharmacy **apteekki** [apte:kki]
cinema **elokuvateatteri** [elokuʋa teatteri]
construction **rakennusala** [rakeŋus ala]
consulting **neuvola** [neuʋola]

dentistry **hammashoito** [hammas hojto]
design **muotoilu** [muotojlu]
dry cleaners **kemiallinen pesu** [kemiallinen pesu]

employment agency **henkilöstön valintatoimisto** [heŋkiløstøn ʋalinta tojmisto]

financial services **rahoituspalvelut** [rahojtus palʋelut]
food products **ruokatavarat** [ruoka taʋarat]
furniture (for house) **huonekalut** [huonekalut]
garment **vaatteet** [ʋa:tte:t]
hotel **hotelli** [hotelli]

ice-cream **jäätelö** [jæ:telø]
industry **teollisuus** [teollisu:s]
insurance **vakuutus** [ʋaku:tus]
Internet **netti** [netti]
investment **sijoitukset** [si:ojtukset]
jeweller **kultaseppä** [kultaseppæ]
jewellery **koruesineet** [koruesine:t]

laundry (room, shop) **pesula** [pesula]
legal adviser **oikeudelliset palvelut** [ojkeudelliset palʋelut]
light industry **kevyt teollisuus** [keʋyt teollisu:s]

magazine **aikakauslehti** [ajkakaus lehti]
mail-order selling **postiluettelokauppa** [posti luettelo kauppa]
medicine **lääketiede** [læ:ketiede]
museum **museo** [museo]

news agency **tietotoimisto** [tieto tojmisto]
newspaper **lehti** [lehti]
nightclub **yökerho** [yøkerho]

oil (petroleum) **öljy** [øl^{h}y]
parcels service **lähetintoimisto** [ʎæhetin tojmisto]
pharmaceuticals **farmasia** [farmasia]
printing (industry) **kirjapainoala** [kir^{h}ja pajno ala]
pub **baari** [ba:ri]
publishing house **kustantamo** [kustantamo]

radio **radio** [radio]
real estate **kiinteistö** [ki:intejstø]
restaurant **ravintola** [raʋintola]

security agency	**vartioimisliike**	[ʋartiojmis li:ike]
shop	**kauppa**	[kauppa]
sport	**urheilu**	[urhejlu]
stock exchange	**pörssi**	[pørssi]
supermarket	**supermarketi**	[supermarketi]
swimming pool	**uimahalli**	[ujmahalli]
tailors	**ateljee**	[atelʰje:]
television	**televisio**	[teleʋisio]
theatre	**teatteri**	[teatteri]
trade	**kauppa**	[kauppa]
transport companies	**kuljetukset**	[kulʰjetukset]
travel	**matkailu**	[matkajlu]
undertakers	**hautaustoimisto**	[hautaus tojmisto]
veterinary surgeon	**eläinlääkäri**	[eʎæjn læ:kari]
warehouse	**varasto**	[ʋarasto]
waste collection	**roskan vienti**	[roskan ʋienti]

Job. Business. Part 2

118. Show. Exhibition

exhibition, show	**näyttely**	[ɲæyttely]
trade show	**kauppanäyttely**	[kauppa ɲæyttely]
participation	**osanotto**	[osanotto]
to participate (vi)	**osallistua**	[osallistua]
participant (exhibitor)	**osanottaja**	[osanottaja]
director	**johtaja**	[øhtaja]
organizer's office	**johtokunta**	[øhtokunta]
organizer	**järjestäjä**	[jærʰjestæjæ]
to organize (vt)	**järjestää**	[jærʰjestæ:]
participation form	**hakemus osallistumiseen**	[hakemus osallistumise:n]
to fill in (vt)	**täyttää**	[tæyttæ:]
details	**yksityiskohdat**	[yksityjskohdat]
information	**tiedotus**	[tiedotus]
price	**hinta**	[hinta]
including	**sisältäen**	[sisæltæen]
to include (vt)	**sisältää**	[sisæltæ:]
to pay (vi, vt)	**maksaa**	[maksa:]
registration fee	**rekisterimaksu**	[rekisteri maksu]
entrance	**pääsy**	[pæ:sy]
pavilion, hall	**paviljonki**	[pauilʰøŋki]
to register (vt)	**rekisteröidä**	[rekisterøjdæ]
badge (identity tag)	**rintamerkki**	[rintamerkki]
stand	**näyttelyteline**	[ɲæyttely teline]
to reserve, to book	**reservoida**	[reseruojda]
display case	**näyteikkuna**	[ɲæyte ikkuna]
spotlight	**valaisin**	[ualajsin]
design	**muotoilu**	[muotojlu]
to place (put, set)	**sijoittaa**	[si:ojtta:]
distributor	**tukkumyyjä**	[tukkumy:jæ]
supplier	**toimittaja**	[tojmittaja]
country	**maa**	[ma:]
foreign (adj)	**ulkomainen**	[ulkomajnen]
product	**tuote**	[tuote]
association	**yhdistys**	[yhdistys]
conference hall	**kokoussali**	[kokoussali]
congress	**kongressi**	[koŋressi]

contest (competition)	**kilpailu**	[kilpajlu]
visitor	**kävijä**	[kæʋijæ]
to visit (attend)	**käydä**	[kæydæ]
customer	**tilaaja**	[tila:ja]

119. Mass Media

newspaper	**lehti**	[lehti]
magazine	**aikakauslehti**	[ajkakaus lehti]
press (printed media)	**lehdistö**	[lehdistø]
radio	**radio**	[radio]
radio station	**radioasema**	[radio asema]
television	**televisio**	[teleʋisio]
presenter, host	**juontaja**	[juontaja]
newsreader	**kuuluttaja**	[ku:luttaja]
commentator	**kommentoija**	[kommentoja]
journalist	**lehtimies**	[lehtimies]
correspondent (reporter)	**kirjeenvaihtaja**	[kirʰje:n ʋajhtaja]
press photographer	**lehtivalokuvaaja**	[lehti ʋalo kuʋa:ja]
reporter	**reportteri**	[reportteri]
editor	**toimittaja**	[tojmittaja]
editor-in-chief	**päätoimittaja**	[pæ: tojmittaja]
to subscribe (to …)	**tilata**	[tilata]
subscription	**tilaus**	[tilaus]
subscriber	**tilaaja**	[tila:ja]
to read (vi, vt)	**lukea**	[lukea]
reader	**lukija**	[lukija]
circulation (of newspaper)	**levikki**	[leʋikke]
monthly (adj)	**kuukautinen**	[ku:kautinen]
weekly (adj)	**jokaviikkoinen**	[økaʋi:ikkojnen]
issue (edition)	**numero**	[numero]
new (~ issue)	**tuore**	[tuore]
headline	**otsikko**	[otsikko]
short article	**lehtikirjoitus**	[lehtikirʰøjtus]
column (regular article)	**otsikko**	[otsikko]
article	**artikkeli**	[artikkeli]
page	**sivu**	[siʋu]
reportage, report	**reportaasi**	[reporta:si]
event	**tapahtuma**	[tapahtuma]
sensation (news)	**sensaatio**	[sensa:tio]
scandal	**skandaali**	[skanda:li]
scandalous (adj)	**skandaalimainen**	[skanda:limajnen]
great (~ scandal)	**kova**	[koʋa]
programme	**ohjelma**	[ohʰelma]
interview	**haastattelu**	[ha:stattelu]
live broadcast	**suora lähetys**	[suora ʎæhetys]
channel	**kanava**	[kanaʋa]

120. Agriculture

agriculture	**maatalous**	[mɑ:tɑlous]
peasant (masc.)	**talonpoika**	[tɑlon pojkɑ]
peasant (fem.)	**talonpoikaisnainen**	[tɑlon pojkɑjs nɑjnen]
farmer	**farmari**	[fɑrmɑri]
tractor	**traktori**	[trɑktori]
combine, harvester	**leikkuupuimuri**	[lejkku: pujmuri]
plough	**aura**	[ɑurɑ]
to plough (vi, vt)	**kyntää**	[kyntæ:]
ploughland	**kynnös**	[kyŋøs]
furrow (in field)	**vako**	[ʋɑko]
to sow (vi, vt)	**kylvää**	[kylʋæ:]
seeder	**kylvökone**	[kylʋøkone]
sowing (process)	**kylvö**	[kylʋø]
scythe	**viikate**	[ʋi:ikɑte]
to mow, to scythe	**niittää**	[ni:ittæ:]
shovel (tool)	**lapio**	[lɑpio]
to dig (cultivate)	**kaivaa**	[kɑjʋɑ:]
hoe	**kuokka**	[kuokkɑ]
to hoe, to weed	**kitkeä**	[kitkeɑ]
weed (plant)	**rikkaruoho**	[rikkɑ ruoho]
watering can	**kastelukannu**	[kɑstelukɑŋu]
to water (plants)	**kastella**	[kɑstellɑ]
watering (act)	**kastelu**	[kɑstelu]
pitchfork	**hanko**	[hɑŋko]
rake	**harava**	[hɑrɑʋɑ]
fertilizer	**lannoite**	[lɑŋojte]
to fertilize (vt)	**lannoittaa**	[lɑŋojttɑ:]
manure (fertilizer)	**lanta**	[lɑntɑ]
field	**pelto**	[pelto]
meadow	**niitty**	[ni:itty]
vegetable garden	**kasvitarha**	[kɑsʋitɑrhɑ]
orchard (e.g. apple ~)	**puutarha**	[pu:tɑrhɑ]
to pasture (vt)	**paimentaa**	[pɑjmentɑ:]
herdsman	**paimen**	[pɑjmen]
pastureland	**laidun**	[lɑjdun]
cattle breeding	**karjanhoito**	[kɑr^{h}jɑn hojto]
sheep farming	**lampaanhoito**	[lɑmpɑ:n hojto]
plantation	**viljelys**	[ʋil^{h}elys]
row (garden bed ~s)	**kasvipenkki**	[kɑsʋipeŋkki]
greenhouse (hotbed)	**lämpölava**	[ʎæmpølɑʋɑ]

drought (lack of rain)	**kuivuus**	[kujʋu:s]
dry (~ summer)	**kuiva**	[kujʋɑ]
cereal plants	**vilja**	[ʋilʰjɑ]
to harvest, to gather	**korjata**	[korʰjɑtɑ]
miller (person)	**mylläri**	[myʎæri]
mill (e.g. gristmill)	**mylly**	[mylly]
to grind (grain)	**jauhaa viljaa**	[jɑuhɑ: ʋilʰæ:]
flour	**jauhot**	[jɑuhot]
straw	**oljet**	[olʰjet]

121. Building. Building process

building site	**rakennustyömaa**	[rɑkeŋus tyø mɑ:]
to build (vt)	**rakentaa**	[rɑkentɑ:]
building worker	**rakentaja**	[rɑkentɑjɑ]
project	**hanke**	[hɑŋke]
architect	**arkkitehti**	[ɑrkkitehti]
worker	**työläinen**	[tyøʎæjnen]
foundations (of building)	**perustus**	[perustus]
roof	**katto**	[kɑtto]
foundation pile	**paalu**	[pɑ:lu]
wall	**seinä**	[sejɲæ]
reinforcing bars	**kalusteet**	[kɑluste:t]
scaffolding	**rakennustelineet**	[rɑkeŋus teline:t]
concrete	**betoni**	[betoni]
granite	**graniitti**	[grɑni:itti]
stone	**kivi**	[kiʋi]
brick	**tiili**	[ti:ili]
sand	**hiekka**	[hiekkɑ]
cement	**sementti**	[sementti]
plaster (for walls)	**rappaus**	[rɑppɑus]
to plaster (vt)	**rapata**	[rɑpɑtɑ]
paint	**maali**	[mɑ:li]
to paint (~ a wall)	**maalata**	[mɑ:lɑtɑ]
barrel	**tynnyri**	[tyŋyri]
crane	**nosturi**	[nosturi]
to lift (vt)	**nostaa**	[nostɑ:]
to lower (vt)	**laskea**	[lɑskeɑ]
bulldozer	**raivaustraktori**	[rɑjʋɑus trɑktori]
excavator	**kaivuri**	[kɑjʋuri]
scoop, bucket	**kauha**	[kɑuhɑ]
to dig (excavate)	**kaivaa**	[kɑjʋɑ:]
hard hat	**kypärä**	[kypæræ]

122. Science. Research. Scientists

science	**tiede**	[tiede]
scientific (adj)	**tieteellinen**	[tiete:llinen]
scientist	**tiedemies**	[tiedemies]
theory	**teoria**	[teoria]
axiom	**aksiomi**	[aksiomi]
analysis	**analyysi**	[analy:si]
to analyse (vt)	**analysoida**	[analysojda]
argument (strong ~)	**argumentti**	[argumentti]
substance (matter)	**aine**	[ajne]
hypothesis	**hypoteesi**	[hypote:si]
dilemma	**dilemma**	[dilemma]
dissertation	**väitöskirja**	[ʋæjtøskirʰja]
dogma	**dogmi**	[dogmi]
doctrine	**oppi**	[oppi]
research	**tutkimus**	[tutkimus]
to do research	**tutkia**	[tutkia]
testing	**tarkastus**	[tarkastus]
laboratory	**laboratorio**	[laboratorio]
method	**metodi**	[metodi]
molecule	**molekyyli**	[moleky:li]
monitoring	**valvonta**	[ʋaʎʋonta]
discovery (act, event)	**löytö**	[løytø]
postulate	**oletus**	[oletus]
principle	**periaate**	[peria:te]
forecast	**ennustus**	[eŋustus]
to forecast (vt)	**ennustaa**	[eŋusta:]
synthesis	**synteesi**	[synte:si]
trend (tendency)	**tendenssi**	[tendenssi]
theorem	**olettamus**	[olettamus]
teachings	**oppi**	[oppi]
fact	**tosiasia**	[tosiasia]
expedition	**retkikunta**	[retkikunta]
experiment	**koe**	[koe]
academician	**akateemikko**	[akate:mikko]
bachelor (e.g. ~ of Arts)	**kandidaatti**	[kandida:tti]
doctor (PhD)	**tohtori**	[tohtori]
Associate Professor	**dosentti**	[dosentti]
Master (e.g. ~ of Arts)	**maisteri**	[majsteri]
professor	**professori**	[professori]

Professions and occupations

123. Job search. Dismissal

job	**työ**	[tyø]
personnel	**henkilökunta**	[heŋkiløkunta]
career	**virkaura**	[ʋirkaura]
prospect	**tulevaisuuden näkymät**	[tuleʋajsu:den nakymat]
skills (mastery)	**mestaruus**	[mestaru:s]
selection (for job)	**valinta**	[ʋalinta]
employment agency	**työnvälitys toimisto**	[tøjnʋælitys tojmisto]
curriculum vitae, CV	**ansioluettelo**	[ansioluettelo]
interview (for job)	**työhaastattelussa**	[tyoha:stattelussa]
vacancy	**vakanssi**	[ʋakanssi]
salary, pay	**palkka**	[palkka]
fixed salary	**kiinteä palkka**	[ki:inteæ palkka]
pay, compensation	**maksu**	[maksu]
position (job)	**virka**	[ʋirka]
duty (of employee)	**velvollisuus**	[ʋelʋollisu:s]
range of duties	**velvollisuudet**	[ʋelʋollisu:det]
busy (I'm ~)	**varattu**	[ʋarattu]
to fire (dismiss)	**antaa potkut**	[anta: potkut]
dismissal	**irtisanominen**	[irtisanominen]
unemployment	**työttömyys**	[tyøttømy:s]
unemployed (n)	**työtön**	[tyøtøn]
retirement	**eläke**	[eʎæke]
to retire (from job)	**jäädä eläkkeelle**	[jæ:dæ eʎække:lle]

124. Business people

director	**johtaja**	[øhtaja]
manager (director)	**johtaja**	[øhtaja]
boss	**esimies**	[esimies]
superior	**päällikkö**	[pæ:likkø]
superiors	**päällystö**	[pæ:llystø]
president	**presidentti**	[presidentti]
chairman	**puheenjohtaja**	[puhe:n øhtaja]
deputy (substitute)	**sijainen**	[sijajnen]
assistant	**apulainen**	[apulajnen]
secretary	**sihteeri**	[sihte:ri]

personal assistant	**henkilökohtainen avustaja**	[heŋkylø kohtajnen auustaæ]
businessman	**liikemies**	[li:ikemies]
entrepreneur	**yrittäjä**	[yrittæjæ]
founder	**perustaja**	[perustaja]
to found (vt)	**perustaa**	[perusta:]
founding member	**kumppani**	[kumppani]
partner	**partneri**	[partneri]
shareholder	**osakkeenomistaja**	[osakke:n omistaæ]
millionaire	**miljonääri**	[milʰønæ:ri]
billionaire	**miljardööri**	[milʰærdø:ri]
owner, proprietor	**omistaja**	[omistaja]
landowner	**maanomistaja**	[ma:nomistaja]
client	**asiakas**	[asiakas]
regular client	**vakituinen asiakas**	[υakitujnen asiakas]
buyer (customer)	**ostaja**	[ostaja]
visitor	**kävijä**	[kæυijæ]
professional (n)	**ammattilainen**	[ammattilajnen]
expert	**asiantuntija**	[asiantuntija]
specialist	**ammattimies**	[ammattimies]
banker	**pankkiiri**	[paŋkki:iri]
broker	**välittäjä**	[υælittæjæ]
cashier	**kassanhoitaja**	[kassanhojtaja]
accountant	**kirjanpitäjä**	[kirʰjanpitæjæ]
security guard	**vartija**	[υartija]
investor	**sijoittaja**	[siøjttaja]
debtor	**velallinen**	[υelallinen]
creditor	**luotonantaja**	[luotonantaja]
borrower	**lainanottaja**	[lajnanottajæ]
importer	**maahantuoja**	[ma:hantuoja]
exporter	**viejä**	[υiejæ]
manufacturer	**tuottaja**	[tuottaja]
distributor	**tukkumyyjä**	[tukkumy:jæ]
middleman	**välittäjä**	[υælittæjæ]
consultant	**neuvoja**	[neuυoja]
representative	**edustaja**	[edustaja]
agent	**asiamies**	[asiamies]
insurance agent	**vakuutusasiamies**	[υaku:tus asiamies]

125. Service professions

cook	**kokki**	[kokki]
chef	**keittiömestari**	[kejttiø mestari]
baker	**leipuri**	[lejpuri]
barman	**baarimestari**	[ba:rimestari]

waiter	**tarjoilija**	[tarʰøjlija]
waitress	**tarjoilijatar**	[tarʰøjlijatar]
lawyer, barrister	**asianajaja**	[asianajaja]
lawyer (legal expert)	**lakimies**	[lakimies]
notary	**notaari**	[nota:ri]
electrician	**sähkömies**	[sæhkømies]
plumber	**putkimies**	[putkimies]
carpenter	**kirvesmies**	[kirʋesmies]
masseur	**hieroja**	[hieroja]
masseuse	**naishieroja**	[najs hieroja]
doctor	**lääkäri**	[læ:kæri]
taxi driver	**taksinkuljettaja**	[taksin kuʎjettaja]
driver	**kuljettaja**	[kuʎættaja]
delivery man	**lähetti**	[ʎæhetti]
chambermaid	**sisäkkö**	[sisækkø]
security guard	**vartija**	[ʋartija]
stewardess	**lentoemäntä**	[lentoemæntæ]
teacher (in primary school)	**opettaja**	[opettaja]
librarian	**kirjastonhoitaja**	[kirʰjaston hojtaja]
translator	**kääntäjä**	[kæ:ntæjæ]
interpreter	**tulkki**	[tulkki]
guide	**opas**	[opas]
hairdresser	**parturi**	[parturi]
postman	**postinkantaja**	[postin kantaja]
shop assistant (masc.)	**myyjä**	[my:jæ]
gardener	**puutarhuri**	[pu:tarhuri]
servant (in household)	**palvelija**	[palʋelija]
maid	**palvelijatar**	[palʋelijatar]
cleaner (cleaning lady)	**siivooja**	[si:iʋo:ja]

126. Military professions and ranks

private	**rivimies**	[riʋimies]
sergeant	**kersantti**	[kersantti]
lieutenant	**luutnantti**	[lu:tnantti]
captain	**kapteeni**	[kapte:ni]
major	**majuri**	[majuri]
colonel	**eversti**	[eʋersti]
general	**kenraali**	[kenra:li]
marshal	**marsalkka**	[marsalkka]
admiral	**amiraali**	[amira:li]
military man	**sotilashenkilö**	[sotilas heŋkilø]
soldier	**sotilas**	[sotilas]
officer	**upseeri**	[upse:ri]

commander	**komentaja**	[komentaja]
border guard	**rajavartija**	[raja uartija]
radio operator	**radisti**	[radisti]
scout (searcher)	**tiedustelija**	[tiedustelija]
pioneer (sapper)	**pioneeri**	[pione:ri]
marksman	**ampuja**	[ampuja]
navigator	**perämies**	[peræmies]

127. Officials. Priests

king	**kuningas**	[kuniŋas]
queen	**kuningatar**	[kuniŋatar]
prince	**prinssi**	[prinssi]
princess	**prinsessa**	[prinsessa]
tsar, czar	**tsaari**	[ʦa:ri]
czarina	**tsaaritar**	[ʦa:ritar]
president	**presidentti**	[presidentti]
Minister	**ministeri**	[ministeri]
prime minister	**pääministeri**	[pæ: ministeri]
senator	**senaattori**	[sena:ttori]
diplomat	**diplomaatti**	[diploma:tti]
consul	**konsuli**	[konsuli]
ambassador	**suurlähettiläs**	[su:rʎæhettiʎæs]
advisor (military ~)	**neuvos**	[neuuos]
official (civil servant)	**virkamies**	[uirkamies]
prefect	**prefekti**	[prefekti]
mayor	**kaupunginjohtaja**	[kaupuŋin øhtaja]
judge	**tuomari**	[tuomari]
prosecutor	**syyttäjä**	[sy:ttæjæ]
missionary	**lähetystyöntekijä**	[ʎæhentystyøntekija]
monk	**munkki**	[muŋkki]
abbot	**apotti**	[apotti]
rabbi	**rabbi**	[rrabbi]
vizier	**visiiri**	[uisi:iri]
shah	**šaahi**	[ʃa:hi]
sheikh	**šeikki**	[ʃejkki]

128. Agricultural professions

beekeeper	**mehiläishoitaja**	[mehiʎæjs hojtaja]
herdsman	**paimen**	[pajmen]
agronomist	**agronomi**	[agronomi]
cattle breeder	**karjanhoitaja**	[karʰjan hojtaja]
veterinary surgeon	**eläinlääkäri**	[eʎæjn læ:kari]

farmer	**farmari**	[farmari]
winemaker	**viininvalmistaja**	[ʋi:inin ʋalmistaja]
zoologist	**eläintieteilijä**	[eʎæjn tietejlijæ]
cowboy	**cowboy**	[kauboj]

129. Art professions

actor	**näyttelijä**	[ɲæyttelijæ]
actress	**näyttelijätär**	[ɲæytteʎætær]
singer (masc.)	**laulaja**	[laulaja]
singer (fem.)	**naislaulaja**	[najslaulaja]
dancer (masc.)	**tanssija**	[tanssija]
dancer (fem.)	**tanssijatar**	[tanssijatar]
performing artist (masc.)	**näyttelijä**	[ɲæyttelijæ]
performing artist (fem.)	**näyttelijätär**	[ɲæytteʎætær]
musician	**muusikko**	[mu:sikko]
pianist	**pianisti**	[pianisti]
guitar player	**kitaransoittaja**	[kitaran sojttaja]
conductor (of musicians)	**kapellimestari**	[kapelli mestari]
composer	**säveltäjä**	[sæʋeltæjæ]
impresario	**järjestäjä**	[jærʰjestæjæ]
film director	**ohjaaja**	[ohʰja:ja]
producer	**tuottaja**	[tuottaja]
scriptwriter	**skenaristi**	[skenaristi]
critic	**arvostelija**	[arʋostelija]
writer	**kirjailija**	[kirʰjajlija]
poet	**runoilija**	[runojlija]
sculptor	**kuvanveistäjä**	[kuʋanʋejstæjæ]
artist (painter)	**taiteilija**	[tajtejlija]
juggler	**jonglööri**	[øŋlø:ri]
clown	**klovni**	[kloʋni]
acrobat	**akrobaatti**	[akroba:tti]
magician	**taikuri**	[tajkuri]

130. Various professions

doctor	**lääkäri**	[læ:kæri]
nurse	**sairaanhoitaja**	[sajra:n hojtaja]
psychiatrist	**psykiatri**	[psykiatri]
stomatologist	**hammaslääkäri**	[hammas læ:kæri]
surgeon	**kirurgi**	[kirurgi]
astronaut	**astronautti**	[astronautti]
astronomer	**tähtitieteilijä**	[tæhti tietejlijæ]

pilot	**lentäjä**	[lentæjæ]
driver (of taxi, etc.)	**kuljettaja**	[kuʎættaja]
train driver	**junankuljettaja**	[yneŋkuʎættaja]
mechanic	**mekaanikko**	[meka:nikko]
miner	**kaivosmies**	[kajʋosmies]
worker	**työläinen**	[tyøʎæjnen]
metalworker	**viilaaja**	[ʋi:ila:ja]
joiner (carpenter)	**puuseppä**	[pu:seppæ]
turner	**sorvari**	[sorʋari]
building worker	**rakentaja**	[rakentaja]
welder	**hitsari**	[hitsari]
professor (title)	**professori**	[professori]
architect	**arkkitehti**	[arkkitehti]
historian	**historioitsija**	[historiojtsija]
scientist	**tiedemies**	[tiedemies]
physicist	**fyysikko**	[fy:sikko]
chemist (scientist)	**kemisti**	[kemisti]
archaeologist	**arkeologi**	[arkeologi]
geologist	**geologi**	[geologi]
researcher	**tutkija**	[tutkija]
babysitter	**lastenhoitaja**	[lasten hojtaja]
teacher, educator	**pedagogi**	[pedagogi]
editor	**toimittaja**	[tojmittaja]
editor-in-chief	**päätoimittaja**	[pæ: tojmittaja]
correspondent	**kirjeenvaihtaja**	[kirʰje:n ʋajhtaja]
typist (fem.)	**konekirjoittaja**	[kone kirʰøjttaja]
designer	**muotoilija**	[muotojlija]
computer expert	**tietokoneasiantuntija**	[tietokone asiantuntija]
programmer	**ohjelmoija**	[ohʰjelmoja]
engineer (designer)	**insinööri**	[insinø:ri]
sailor	**merimies**	[merimies]
seaman	**matruusi**	[matru:si]
rescuer	**pelastaja**	[pelastaja]
firefighter	**palomies**	[palomies]
policeman	**poliisi**	[poli:isi]
watchman	**vahti**	[ʋahti]
detective	**etsivä**	[etsiʋæ]
customs officer	**tullimies**	[tullimies]
bodyguard	**henkivartija**	[heŋkiʋartija]
prison officer	**vanginvartija**	[ʋaŋinʋartija]
inspector	**tarkastaja**	[tarkastaja]
sportsman	**urheilija**	[urhejlija]
trainer, coach	**valmentaja**	[ʋalmentaja]
butcher	**lihanleikkaaja**	[lihanlejka:æ]
cobbler	**suutari**	[su:tari]
merchant	**liikemies**	[li:ikemies]

loader (person)	**lastaaja**	[lasta:ja]
fashion designer	**muotisuunnittelija**	[muoti su:ŋittelija]
model (fem.)	**malli**	[malli]

131. Occupations. Social status

schoolboy	**koululainen**	[koululajnen]
student (college ~)	**ylioppilas**	[ylioppilas]
philosopher	**filosofi**	[filosofi]
economist	**taloustieteilijä**	[talous tietejlijæ]
inventor	**keksijä**	[keksiæ]
unemployed (n)	**työtön**	[tyøtøn]
pensioner	**eläkeläinen**	[eʎækeʎæjnen]
spy, secret agent	**vakoilija**	[ʋakojlija]
prisoner	**vanki**	[ʋaŋki]
striker	**lakkolainen**	[lakkolajnen]
bureaucrat	**virkamies**	[ʋirkamies]
traveller	**matkailija**	[matkajlija]
homosexual	**homoseksuaali**	[homoseksua:li]
hacker	**hakkeri**	[hakkeri]
bandit	**rosvo**	[rosʋo]
hit man, killer	**salamurhaaja**	[sala murha:ja]
drug addict	**narkomaani**	[narkoma:ni]
drug dealer	**huumekauppias**	[hu:me kauppias]
prostitute (fem.)	**prostituoitu**	[prostituojtu]
pimp	**sutenööri**	[sutenø:ri]
sorcerer	**noita**	[nojta]
sorceress	**noita**	[nojta]
pirate	**merirosvo**	[merirosʋo]
slave	**orja**	[or^{h}ja]
samurai	**samurai**	[samuraj]
savage (primitive)	**villi-ihminen**	[ʋilli ihminen]

Sports

132. Kinds of sports. Sportspersons

sportsman	**urheilija**	[urhejlijɑ]
kind of sport	**urheilulaji**	[urhejlulɑjı]
basketball	**koripallo**	[koripɑllo]
basketball player	**koripalloilija**	[koripɑllojlijɑ]
baseball	**pesäpallo**	[pesæpɑllo]
baseball player	**pesäpallon pelaaja**	[pesæpɑllon pelɑ:æ]
football	**jalkapallo**	[jɑlkɑ pɑllo]
football player	**jalkapalloilija**	[jɑlkɑ pɑllojlijɑ]
goalkeeper	**maalivahti**	[mɑ:liʋɑhti]
ice hockey	**jääkiekko**	[jæ:kækko]
ice hockey player	**jääkiekkoilija**	[jæ:kiekkojlijɑ]
volleyball	**lentopallo**	[lento pɑllo]
volleyball player	**lentopalloilija**	[lento pɑllojlijɑ]
boxing	**nyrkkeily**	[nyrkkejly]
boxer	**nyrkkeilijä**	[nyrkkejlijæ]
wrestling	**taistelu**	[tɑjstelu]
wrestler	**taistelija**	[tɑjstelijɑ]
karate	**karate**	[kɑrɑte]
karate fighter	**karateka**	[kɑrɑtekɑ]
judo	**judo**	[judo]
judo athlete	**judoka**	[judokɑ]
tennis	**tennis**	[teŋis]
tennis player	**tenniksen pelaaja**	[teŋiksen pelɑ:jɑ]
swimming	**uinti**	[ujnti]
swimmer	**uimari**	[ujmɑri]
fencing	**miekkailu**	[miekkɑjlu]
fencer	**miekkailija**	[miekkɑjlijɑ]
chess	**šakki**	[ʃɑkki]
chess player	**šakinpelaaja**	[ʃɑkinpelɑ:jɑ]
alpinism	**vuorikiipeily**	[ʋuoriki:ipejly]
alpinist	**vuorikiipeilijä**	[ʋuoriki:ipejlijæ]
running	**juoksu**	[juoksu]

runner	**juoksija**	[juoksija]
athletics	**yleisurheilu**	[ylejsurhejlu]
athlete	**yleisurheilija**	[ylejsurhejlija]
horse riding	**ratsastusurheilu**	[ratsastus urhejlu]
horse rider	**ratsastaja**	[ratsastaja]
figure skating	**taitoluistelu**	[tajto lujstelu]
figure skater (masc.)	**taitoluistelija**	[tajto lujstelija]
figure skater (fem.)	**taitoluistelija**	[tajto lujstelija]
weightlifting	**painonnosto**	[pajnoŋosto]
weightlifter	**painonnostaja**	[pajnon nostaja]
car racing	**kilpa-autoilu**	[kilpa autojlu]
racing driver	**kilpa-ajaja**	[kilpa ajaja]
cycling	**pyöräily**	[pyøræjly]
cyclist	**pyöräilijä**	[pyøræjlijæ]
long jump	**pituushyppy**	[pitu:s hyppy]
pole vaulting	**seiväshyppy**	[sejʊæs hyppy]
jumper	**hyppääjä**	[hyppæ:jæ]

133. Kinds of sports. Miscellaneous

American football	**Amerikkalainen jalkapallo**	[amerikkalajnen jalkapallo]
badminton	**sulkapallo**	[sulkapallo]
biathlon	**ampumahiihto**	[ampumahi:ihto]
billiards	**biljardi**	[bilʰjardi]
bobsleigh	**rattikelkka**	[ratti kelkka]
bodybuilding	**kehonrakennus**	[kehonrakeŋus]
water polo	**vesipallo**	[ʊesi pallo]
handball	**käsipallo**	[kæsi pallo]
golf	**golf**	[goʎf]
rowing	**soutu**	[soutu]
diving	**sukellus**	[sukellus]
cross-country skiing	**murtomaahiihto**	[murtoma:hi:iɦto]
ping-pong	**pöytätennis**	[pøytæ teŋis]
sailing	**purjehdus**	[purʰjehdus]
rally	**ralli**	[ralli]
rugby	**rugby**	[ragbi]
snowboarding	**lumilautailu**	[lumi lautajlu]
archery	**jousiammunta**	[øusiam munta]

134. Gym

barbell	**painonnostotanko**	[pajnoŋosto taŋko]
dumbbells	**käsipainot**	[kæsipajnot]

training machine	**kuntolaite**	[kuntolajte]
bicycle trainer	**kuntopyörä**	[kuntopyøræ]
treadmill	**juoksurata**	[juoksurata]
horizontal bar	**tanko**	[taŋko]
parallel bars	**nojapuut**	[noja pu:t]
vaulting horse	**ratsu**	[ratsu]
mat (in gym)	**matto**	[matto]
aerobics	**aerobick**	[aerobik]
yoga	**jooga**	[ø:ga]

135. Ice hockey

ice hockey	**jääkiekko**	[jæ:kækko]
ice hockey player	**jääkiekkoilija**	[jæ:kiekkojlija]
to play ice hockey	**pelata jääkiekkoa**	[pelata jæ:kjekkoa]
ice	**jää**	[jæ:]
puck	**kiekko**	[kækko]
ice hockey stick	**maila**	[majla]
ice skates	**luistimet**	[lujstimet]
board	**laita**	[lajta]
shot	**laukaus**	[laukaus]
goaltender	**maalivahti**	[ma:liυahti]
goal (score)	**maali**	[ma:li]
to score a goal	**tehdä maali**	[tehdæ ma:li]
period	**erä**	[eræ]
substitutes bench	**varamiespenkki**	[υaramies peŋkki]

136. Football

football	**jalkapallo**	[jalka pallo]
football player	**jalkapalloilija**	[jalka pallojlija]
to play football	**pelata jalkapalloa**	[pelata ælkapaloa]
major league	**korkein liiga**	[korkejn li:iga]
football club	**jalkapallokerho**	[jalka pallo kerho]
coach	**valmentaja**	[υalmentaja]
owner, proprietor	**omistaja**	[omistaja]
team	**joukkue**	[øukkue]
team captain	**joukkueen kapteeni**	[øukkue:n kapte:ni]
player	**pelaaja**	[pela:ja]
substitute	**varamies**	[υaramies]
forward	**hyökkääjä**	[hyøkkæ:jæ]
centre forward	**keskushyökkääjä**	[keskus hyøkkæ:jæ]
striker, scorer	**maalintekijä**	[ma:lintekijæ]

defender, back	**puolustaja**	[puolustaja]
halfback	**tukimies**	[tukimies]
match	**matsi**	[matsi]
to meet (vi, vt)	**tavata**	[tauata]
final	**finaali**	[fina:li]
semi-final	**välierä**	[uæli eræ]
championship	**mestaruuskilpailut**	[mestaru:s kilpajlut]
period, half	**puoliaika**	[puoliajka]
first period	**ensimmäinen puoliaika**	[ensimmæjnen puoliajka]
half-time	**tauko**	[tauko]
goal	**maali**	[ma:li]
goalkeeper	**maalivahti**	[ma:liuahti]
goalpost	**poikkihirsi**	[pojkki hirsi]
crossbar	**poikkipuu**	[pojkki pu:]
net	**verkko**	[uerkko]
to concede a goal	**ohita pallo maaliin**	[ohita pallo ma:li:in]
ball	**pallo**	[pallo]
pass	**syöttö**	[syøttø]
kick	**isku**	[isku]
to kick (~ the ball)	**iskeä**	[iskeæ]
free kick	**rangaistuspotku**	[raŋajstus potku]
corner kick	**kulmuri**	[kulmuri]
attack	**hyökkäys**	[hyøkkæys]
counterattack	**vastahyökkäys**	[uasta hyøkkæys]
combination	**yhdistelmä**	[yhdistelmæ]
referee	**erotuomari**	[erotuomari]
to whistle (vi)	**viheltää**	[uiheltæ:]
whistle (sound)	**pilli**	[pilli]
foul, misconduct	**rikkomus**	[rikkomus]
to commit a foul	**rikkoa**	[rikkoa]
to send off	**poistaa kentältä**	[pojsta: kentæltæ]
yellow card	**keltainen kortti**	[keltajnen kortti]
red card	**punainen kortti**	[punajnen kortti]
disqualification	**esteellisuus**	[este:llisu:s]
to disqualify (vt)	**diskvalifioida**	[diskualifiojda]
penalty kick	**rangaistuspotku**	[raŋajstus potku]
wall	**seinä**	[sejɲæ]
to score (vi, vt)	**potkaista**	[potkajsta]
goal (score)	**maali**	[ma:li]
to score a goal	**tehdä maali**	[tehdæ ma:li]
substitution	**vaihto**	[uajhto]
to replace (vt)	**vaihtaa**	[uajhta:]
rules	**säännöt**	[sæ:ŋøt]
tactics	**taktiikka**	[takti:ikka]

stadium	**urheilukenttä**	[urhejlukenttæ]
stand (at stadium)	**katsomo**	[kɑtsomo]
fan, supporter	**fani**	[fɑni]
to shout (vi)	**huutaa**	[hu:tɑ:]
scoreboard	**tulostaulu**	[tulostɑulu]
score	**maaliluku**	[mɑ:liluku]
defeat	**häviö**	[ɦæʋiø]
to lose (not win)	**hävitä**	[ɦæʋitæ]
draw	**tasapeli**	[tɑsɑpeli]
to draw (vi)	**pelata tasan**	[pelɑtɑ tɑsɑn]
victory	**voitto**	[ʋojtto]
to win (vi, vt)	**voittaa**	[ʋojttɑ:]
champion	**mestari**	[mestɑri]
best (adj)	**paras**	[pɑrɑs]
to congratulate (vt)	**onnitella**	[oŋitellɑ]
commentator	**kommentoija**	[kommentojɑ]
to commentate (vt)	**kommentoida**	[kommentojdɑ]
broadcast	**televisiointi**	[teleʋisiojnti]

137. Alpine skiing

skis	**sukset**	[sukset]
to ski (vi)	**hiihdellä**	[hi:ihdeʎæ]
mountain-ski resort	**hiihtokeskus**	[hi:ihto keskus]
ski lift	**hiihtohissi**	[hi:ihto hissi]
ski poles	**suksisauvat**	[suksisɑuʋɑt]
slope	**rinne**	[riŋe]
slalom	**pujottelu**	[puøttelu]

138. Tennis. Golf

golf	**golff**	[goʎf]
golf club	**golfkerho**	[goʎf kerho]
golfer	**golfin pelaaja**	[goʎfin pelɑ:jɑ]
hole	**kuoppa**	[kuoppɑ]
club	**maila**	[mɑjlɑ]
golf trolley	**golfkärryt**	[goʎf kɑrryt]
tennis	**tennis**	[teŋis]
tennis court	**tenniskenttä**	[teŋis kenttæ]
serve	**syöttö**	[syøttø]
to serve (vt)	**syöttää**	[syøttæ:]
racket	**maila**	[mɑjlɑ]
net	**verkko**	[ʋerkko]
ball	**pallo**	[pɑllo]

139. Chess

chess	**šakki**	[ʃakki]
chessmen	**šakkinappulat**	[ʃakki nappulat]
chess player	**šakinpelaaja**	[ʃakinpela:ja]
chessboard	**šakkilauta**	[ʃakki lauta]
chessman	**nappula**	[nappula]
White (white pieces)	**valkeat**	[ʋalkeat]
Black (black pieces)	**mustat**	[mustat]
pawn	**sotilas**	[sotilas]
bishop	**norsu**	[norsu]
knight	**ratsu**	[ratsu]
rook (castle)	**torni**	[torni]
queen	**kuningatar**	[kuniŋatar]
king	**kuningas**	[kuniŋas]
move	**siirto**	[si:irto]
to move (vi, vt)	**siirtää**	[si:irtæ:]
to sacrifice (vt)	**uhrata**	[uhrata]
castling	**linnoitus**	[liŋojtus]
check	**šakki**	[ʃakki]
checkmate	**matti**	[matti]
chess tournament	**šakkiturnaus**	[ʃakki turnaus]
Grand Master	**suurmestari**	[su:rmestari]
combination	**yhdistelmä**	[yhdistelmæ]
game (in chess)	**peli**	[peli]
draughts	**tammi**	[tammi]

140. Boxing

boxing	**nyrkkeily**	[nyrkkejly]
fight (bout)	**ottelu**	[ottelu]
boxing match	**nyrkkeilyottelu**	[nyrkkejly ottelu]
round (in boxing)	**erä**	[eræ]
ring	**kehä**	[keɦæ]
gong	**gongi**	[goŋi]
punch	**isku**	[isku]
knock-down	**knock down**	[nokdaun]
knockout	**tyrmäys**	[tyrmæys]
to knock out	**tyrmätä**	[tyrmætæ]
boxing glove	**nyrkkeilyhansikas**	[nyrkkejlu hansikas]
referee	**tuomari**	[tuomari]
lightweight	**kevyt sarja**	[keʋyt sar^{h}ja]
middleweight	**keskisarja**	[keskisar^{h}ja]
heavyweight	**raskas sarja**	[raskas sar^{h}ja]

141. Sports. Miscellaneous

Olympic Games	**Olympiakisat**	[olympia kisat]
winner	**voittaja**	[ʋojttaja]
to be winning	**voittaa**	[ʋojtta:]
to win (vi)	**voittaa**	[ʋojtta:]
leader	**johtaja**	[øhtaja]
to lead (vi)	**johtaa**	[øhta:]
first place	**ensimmäinen sija**	[ensimmæjnen sija]
second place	**toinen sija**	[tojnen sija]
third place	**kolmas sija**	[kolmas sija]
medal	**mitali**	[mitali]
trophy	**saalis**	[sa:lis]
prize cup (trophy)	**pokaali**	[poka:li]
prize (in game)	**palkinto**	[palkinto]
main prize	**pääpalkinto**	[pæ: palkinto]
record	**ennätys**	[eŋætys]
to set a record	**saavuttaa ennätys**	[sa:ʋutta: eŋætys]
final	**loppuottelu**	[loppuottelu]
final (adj)	**finaali-**	[fina:li]
champion	**mestari**	[mestari]
championship	**mestaruuskilpailut**	[mestaru:s kilpajlut]
stadium	**stadion**	[stadion]
stand (at stadium)	**katsomo**	[kaʦomo]
fan, supporter	**penkkiurheilija**	[peŋkki urhejlija]
opponent, rival	**vastustaja**	[ʋastustaja]
start	**lähtö**	[ʎæhtø]
finish line	**maali**	[ma:li]
defeat	**häviö**	[ɦæʋiø]
to lose (not win)	**hävitä**	[ɦæʋitæ]
referee	**tuomari**	[tuomari]
judges	**tuomaristo**	[tuomaristo]
score	**maaliluku**	[ma:liluku]
draw	**tasapeli**	[tasapeli]
to draw (vi)	**pelata tasan**	[pelata tasan]
point	**piste**	[piste]
result (final score)	**tulos**	[tulos]
half-time	**tauko**	[tauko]
doping	**doping**	[dopiŋ]
to penalise (vt)	**rangaista**	[raŋajsta]
to disqualify (vt)	**diskvalifioida**	[diskʋalifiojda]
apparatus	**teline**	[teline]
javelin	**keihäs**	[kejɦæs]

shot put ball	**kuula**	[ku:la]
ball (snooker, etc.)	**biljardipallo**	[bil^{h}jardi pallo]
aim (target)	**maali**	[ma:li]
target	**maali**	[ma:li]
to shoot (vi)	**ampua**	[ampua]
precise (~ shot)	**tarkka**	[tarkka]
trainer, coach	**valmentaja**	[ʋalmentaja]
to train (sb)	**valmentaa**	[ʋalmenta:]
to train (vi)	**valmentautua**	[ʋalmentautua]
training	**valmennus**	[ʋalmeŋus]
gym	**voimistelusali**	[ʋojmistelu sali]
exercise (physical)	**liike**	[li:ike]
warm-up (of athlete)	**verryttely**	[ʋerryttely]

Education

142. School

school	**koulu**	[koulu]
headmaster	**koulun rehtori**	[koulun rehtori]
pupil (boy)	**oppilas**	[oppilas]
pupil (girl)	**tyttöoppilas**	[tyttø oppilas]
schoolboy	**koululainen**	[koululajnen]
schoolgirl	**koululainen**	[koululajnen]
to teach (sb)	**opettaa**	[opetta:]
to learn (language, etc.)	**opetella**	[opetella]
to learn by heart	**oppia ulkoa**	[oppia ulkoa]
to study (work to learn)	**opiskella**	[opiskella]
to be at school	**käydä koulua**	[kæydæ koulua]
to go to school	**mennä kouluun**	[meŋa koulu:n]
alphabet	**aakkoset**	[a:kkoset]
subject (at school)	**oppiaine**	[oppiajne]
classroom	**luokka**	[luokka]
lesson	**tunti**	[tunti]
playtime, break	**tauko**	[tauko]
school bell	**soitto**	[sojtto]
desk (for pupil)	**pulpetti**	[pulpetti]
blackboard	**taulu**	[taulu]
mark	**arvosana**	[aruosana]
good mark	**hyvä arvosana**	[hyuæ aruosana]
bad mark	**huono arvosana**	[huono aruosana]
to give a mark	**merkitä arvosana**	[merkitæ aruosana]
mistake	**virhe**	[uirhe]
to make mistakes	**tehdä virheet**	[tehdæ uirhe:t]
to correct (an error)	**korjata**	[korʰjata]
crib	**lunttilappu**	[lunttilappu]
homework	**kotitehtävä**	[kotitehtæuæ]
exercise (in education)	**harjoitus**	[harʰøjtus]
to be present	**olla läsnä**	[olla ʎæsɲæ]
to be absent	**olla poissa**	[olla pojssa]
to punish (vt)	**rangaista**	[raŋajsta]
punishment	**rangaistus**	[raŋajstus]
conduct (behaviour)	**käytös**	[kæytøs]

school report	**oppilaan päiväkirja**	[oppila:n pæjʋækirʰja]
pencil	**lyijykynä**	[ly:kyɲæ]
rubber	**kumi**	[kumi]
chalk	**liitu**	[li:itu]
pencil case	**kynäkotelo**	[kyɲækotelo]
schoolbag	**salkku**	[salkku]
pen	**kynä**	[kyɲæ]
exercise book	**vihko**	[ʋihko]
textbook	**oppikirja**	[oppikirʰja]
compasses	**harppi**	[harppi]
to draw (a blueprint, etc.)	**piirtää**	[pi:irtæ:]
technical drawing	**piirros**	[pi:irros]
poem	**runo**	[runo]
by heart (adv)	**ulkoa**	[ulkoa]
to learn by heart	**oppia ulkoa**	[oppia ulkoa]
school holidays	**loma**	[loma]
to be on holiday	**olla lomalla**	[olla lomalla]
test (at school)	**koe**	[koe]
essay (composition)	**ainekirjoitus**	[ajnekirʰøjtus]
dictation	**sanelu**	[sanelu]
exam	**tentti**	[tentti]
to take an exam	**suorittaa tentit**	[suoritta: tentit]
experiment (chemical ~)	**koe**	[koe]

143. College. University

academy	**akatemia**	[akatemia]
university	**yliopisto**	[yliopisto]
faculty (section)	**tiedekunta**	[tiede kunta]
student (masc.)	**opiskelija**	[opiskelija]
student (fem.)	**opiskelija**	[opiskelija]
lecturer (teacher)	**opettaja**	[opettaja]
lecture hall, room	**luentosali**	[luentosali]
graduate	**valmistunut**	[ʋalmistunut]
diploma	**diplomi**	[diplomi]
dissertation	**väitöskirja**	[ʋæjtøskirʰja]
study (report)	**tutkimus**	[tutkimus]
laboratory	**laboratorio**	[laboratorio]
lecture	**luento**	[luento]
course mate	**kurssitoveri**	[kurssitoʋeri]
scholarship	**opintotuki**	[opinto tuki]
academic degree	**oppiarvo**	[oppi arʋo]

144. Sciences. Disciplines

mathematics	**matematiikka**	[matemati:ikka]
algebra	**algebra**	[algebra]
geometry	**geometria**	[geometria]
astronomy	**tähtitiede**	[tæhti tiede]
biology	**biologia**	[biologia]
geography	**maantiede**	[ma:ntiede]
geology	**geologia**	[geologia]
history	**historia**	[historia]
medicine	**lääketiede**	[læ:ketiede]
pedagogy	**pedagogiikka**	[pedagogi:ikka]
law	**oikeustiede**	[ojkeustiede]
physics	**fysiikka**	[fysi:ikka]
chemistry	**kemia**	[kemia]
philosophy	**filosofia**	[filosofia]
psychology	**psykologia**	[psykologia]

145. Writing system. Orthography

grammar	**kielioppi**	[kielioppi]
vocabulary	**sanasto**	[sanasto]
phonetics	**äänneoppi**	[æ:ŋeoppi]
noun	**substantiivi**	[substanti:ivi]
adjective	**adjektiivi**	[adjekti:ivi]
verb	**verbi**	[verbi]
adverb	**adverbi**	[adverbi]
pronoun	**pronomini**	[pronomini]
interjection	**interjektio**	[inter^{h}jektio]
preposition	**prepositio**	[prepositio]
root	**sanan kanta**	[sanan kanta]
ending	**pääte**	[pæ:te]
prefix	**etuliite**	[etuli:ite]
syllable	**tavu**	[tavu]
suffix	**johdin**	[øhdin]
stress mark	**paino**	[pajno]
apostrophe	**heittomerkki**	[hejttomerkki]
full stop	**piste**	[piste]
comma	**pilkku**	[pilkku]
semicolon	**puolipiste**	[puolipiste]
colon	**kaksoispiste**	[kaksojspiste]
ellipsis	**pisteryhmä**	[pisteryhmæ]
question mark	**kysymysmerkki**	[kysymys merkki]
exclamation mark	**huutomerkki**	[hu:tomerkki]

inverted commas	**lainausmerkit**	[lajnaus merkit]
in inverted commas	**lainausmerkeissä**	[lajnaus merkejssæ]
parenthesis	**sulkumerkit**	[sulkumerkit]
in parenthesis	**sulkumerkeissä**	[sulkumerkejssæ]
hyphen	**tavuviiva**	[taʋu ʋi:iʋa]
dash	**ajatusviiva**	[aætusʋi:iʋa]
space (between words)	**väli**	[ʋæli]
letter	**kirjain**	[kir^{h}jajn]
capital letter	**iso kirjain**	[iso kir^{h}jajn]
vowel (n)	**vokaali**	[ʋoka:li]
consonant (n)	**konsonantti**	[konsonantti]
sentence	**lause**	[lause]
subject	**subjekti**	[sub^{h}jekti]
predicate	**predikaatti**	[predika:tti]
line	**rivi**	[riʋi]
on a new line	**uudella rivillä**	[u:dela riʋilla]
paragraph	**kappale**	[kappale]
word	**sana**	[sana]
word group	**sanaliitto**	[sana li:itto]
expression	**ilmaisu**	[ilmajsu]
synonym	**synonyymi**	[synony:mi]
antonym	**antonyymi**	[antony:mi]
rule	**sääntö**	[sæ:ntø]
exception	**poikkeus**	[pojkkeus]
correct (adj)	**oikea**	[ojkea]
conjugation	**verbien taivutus**	[ʋerbien tajʋutus]
declension	**nominien taivutus**	[nominien tajʋutus]
nominal case	**sija**	[sija]
question	**kysymys**	[kysymys]
to underline (vt)	**alleviivata**	[alleʋi:iʋata]
dotted line	**pisteviiva**	[pisteʋi:iʋa]

146. Foreign languages

language	**kieli**	[kieli]
foreign language	**vieras kieli**	[ʋieras kieli]
to study (vt)	**opiskella**	[opiskella]
to learn (language, etc.)	**opetella**	[opetella]
to read (vi, vt)	**lukea**	[lukea]
to speak (vi, vt)	**puhua**	[puhua]
to understand (vt)	**ymmärtää**	[ymmærtæ:]
to write (vt)	**kirjoittaa**	[kir^{h}ojtta:]
fast (adv)	**nopeasti**	[nopeasti]
slowly (adv)	**hitaasti**	[hita:sti]

fluently (adv)	**sujuvasti**	[sujuʋɑsti]
rules	**säännöt**	[sæ:ŋøt]
grammar	**kielioppi**	[kielioppi]
vocabulary	**sanasto**	[sɑnɑsto]
phonetics	**äänneoppi**	[æ:ŋeoppi]
textbook	**oppikirja**	[oppikir^{h}jɑ]
dictionary	**sanakirja**	[sɑnɑkir^{h}jɑ]
teach-yourself book	**itseopiskeluopas**	[itseopiskelu opɑs]
phrasebook	**fraasisanakirja**	[frɑ:si sɑnɑkir^{j}ɑ]
cassette	**kasetti**	[kɑsetti]
videotape	**videokasetti**	[ʋideokɑsetti]
CD, compact disc	**CD-levy**	[sede leʋy]
DVD	**DVD-levy**	[deʋede leʋy]
alphabet	**aakkoset**	[ɑ:kkoset]
to spell (vt)	**tavata**	[tɑʋɑtɑ]
pronunciation	**ääntäminen**	[æ:ntæminen]
accent	**korostus**	[korostus]
with an accent	**vieraasti korostaen**	[ʋierɑ:sti korostɑen]
without an accent	**ilman korostusta**	[ilmɑn korostustɑ]
word	**sana**	[sɑnɑ]
meaning	**merkitys**	[merkitys]
course (e.g. a French ~)	**kurssit**	[kurssit]
to sign up	**ilmoittautua**	[ilmojttɑutuɑ]
teacher	**opettaja**	[opettɑjɑ]
translation (process)	**kääntäminen**	[kæ:ntæminen]
translation (text, etc.)	**käännös**	[kæ:ŋøs]
translator	**kääntäjä**	[kæ:ntæjæ]
interpreter	**tulkki**	[tulkki]
polyglot	**monikielinen**	[moni kielinen]
memory	**muisti**	[mujsti]

147. Fairy tale characters

Santa Claus	**Santa Claus**	[sɑntɑ klɑus]
mermaid	**merenneito**	[mereŋejto]
magician, wizard	**noita**	[nojtɑ]
fairy	**hyvä noita**	[hyʋɑ nojtɑ]
magic (adj)	**taika-**	[tɑjkɑ]
magic wand	**taikasauva**	[tɑjkɑ sɑuʋɑ]
fairy tale	**satu**	[sɑtu]
miracle	**ihme**	[ihme]
dwarf	**tonttu**	[tonttu]
to turn into ...	**muuttua...**	[mu:ttuɑ]
ghost	**kummitus**	[kummitus]

phantom	**haamu**	[ha:mu]
monster	**hirviö**	[hirυiø]
dragon	**lohikäärme**	[lohikæ:rme]
giant	**jättiläinen**	[jættiʎæjnen]

148. Zodiac Signs

Aries	**Oinas**	[ojnas]
Taurus	**Härkä**	[ɦærkæ]
Gemini	**Kaksoset**	[kaksoset]
Cancer	**Rapu**	[rapu]
Leo	**Leijona**	[leiøna]
Virgo	**Neitsyt**	[nejʦyt]
Libra	**Vaaka**	[υa:ka]
Scorpio	**Skorpioni**	[skorpioni]
Sagittarius	**Jousimies**	[øusimies]
Capricorn	**Kauris**	[kauris]
Aquarius	**Vesimies**	[υesimies]
Pisces	**Kalat**	[kalat]
character	**luonne**	[luoŋe]
features of character	**luonteenpiirteet**	[luonte:n pi:irte:t]
behaviour	**käytös**	[kæytøs]
to tell fortunes	**ennustaa**	[eŋusta:]
fortune-teller	**ennustaja**	[eŋustaja]
horoscope	**horoskooppi**	[horosko:ppi]

Arts

149. Theatre

theatre	**teatteri**	[teatteri]
opera	**ooppera**	[o:ppera]
operetta	**operetti**	[operetti]
ballet	**baletti**	[baletti]
playbill	**juliste**	[juliste]
theatrical company	**seurue**	[seurue]
tour	**kiertue**	[kjertue]
to be on tour	**vierailla**	[ʋierajlla]
to rehearse (vi, vt)	**harjoitella**	[harʰøjtella]
rehearsal	**harjoitus**	[harʰøjtus]
repertoire	**ohjelmisto**	[ohjelmisto]
performance	**esitys**	[esitys]
stage show	**näytelmä**	[ɲæytelmæ]
play	**näytelmä**	[ɲæytelmæ]
ticket	**lippu**	[lippu]
Box office	**lippukassa**	[lippukassa]
lobby, foyer	**aula**	[aula]
coat check	**naulakko**	[naulakko]
cloakroom ticket	**vaatelappu**	[ʋa:te lappu]
binoculars	**kiikari**	[ki:ikari]
usher	**tarkastaja**	[tarkastaja]
stalls	**permanto**	[permanto]
balcony	**parveke**	[parʋeke]
dress circle	**ensi parvi**	[ensi parʋi]
box	**aitio**	[ajtio]
row	**rivi**	[riʋi]
seat	**paikka**	[pajkka]
audience	**yleisö**	[ylejsø]
spectator	**katsoja**	[katsoja]
to clap (vi, vt)	**taputtaa käsiä**	[taputta: kæsiæ]
applause	**aplodit**	[aplodit]
ovation	**suosionosoitukset**	[suosionosojtukset]
stage	**näyttämö**	[ɲæyttæmø]
curtain	**esirippu**	[esirippu]
scenery	**lavastus**	[laʋastus]
backstage	**kulissit**	[kulissit]
scene (e.g. the last ~)	**kohtaus**	[kohtaus]
act	**näytös**	[ɲæutøs]
interval	**väliaika**	[ʋæliajka]

150. Cinema

actor	**näyttelijä**	[ɲæyttelijæ]
actress	**näyttelijätär**	[ɲæytteʎætær]
cinema (industry)	**elokuvat**	[elokuʋɑt]
film	**elokuva**	[elokuʋɑ]
episode	**sarja**	[sɑr^{h}jɑ]
detective	**dekkari**	[dekkɑri]
action film	**toimintaelokuva**	[tojmintɑ elokuʋɑ]
adventure film	**seikkailuelokuva**	[sejkkɑjlu elokuʋɑ]
science fiction film	**tieteisfiktioelokuva**	[tjetesfiktio elokuʋɑ]
horror film	**kauhuelokuva**	[kɑuhu elokuʋɑ]
comedy film	**komedia**	[komediɑ]
melodrama	**melodraama**	[melodrɑ:mɑ]
drama	**draama**	[drɑ:mɑ]
fictional film	**kuvitteellinen elokuva**	[kuʋite:linen elokuʋɑ]
documentary	**dokumenttielokuva**	[dokumentti elokuʋɑ]
cartoon	**piirrosfilmi**	[pi:irros filmi]
silent films	**mykkäelokuva**	[mykkæ elokuʋɑ]
role	**osa**	[osɑ]
leading role	**pääosa**	[pæ:osɑ]
to play (vi, vt)	**näytellä**	[ɲæyteʎæ]
film star	**filmitähti**	[filmitæhti]
well-known (adj)	**tunnettu**	[tuŋettu]
famous (adj)	**kuulu**	[ku:lu]
popular (adj)	**suosittu**	[suosittu]
script (screenplay)	**käsikirjoitus**	[kæsikir^{h}øjtus]
scriptwriter	**skenaristi**	[skenɑristi]
film director	**ohjaaja**	[oh^{h}jɑ:jɑ]
producer	**tuottaja**	[tuottɑjɑ]
assistant	**avustaja**	[ɑʋustɑjɑ]
cameraman	**operaattori**	[operɑ:ttori]
stuntman	**temppumies**	[temppumies]
to shoot a film	**elokuvata**	[elokuʋɑtɑ]
audition, screen test	**kokeilut**	[kokejlut]
shooting	**filmaus**	[filmɑus]
film crew	**filmausryhmä**	[filmɑus ryhmæ]
film set	**filmauskenttä**	[filmɑus kenttæ]
camera	**elokuvakamera**	[elokuʋɑ kɑmerɑ]
cinema	**elokuvateatteri**	[elokuʋɑ teɑtteri]
screen (e.g. big ~)	**valkokangas**	[ʋɑlkokɑŋɑs]
to show a film	**esittää elokuvaa**	[esittæ: elokuʋɑ:]
soundtrack	**ääniraita**	[æ:nirɑjtɑ]
special effects	**tehosteet**	[tehoste:t]
subtitles	**tekstitykset**	[tekstitykset]

credits **lopputekstit** [lopputekstit]
translation **käännös** [kæ:ŋøs]

151. Painting

art **taide** [tajde]
fine arts **kaunotaiteet** [kaunotajte:t]
art gallery **galleria** [galleria]
art exhibition **taidenäyttely** [tajdeɲæyttely]

painting **maalaustaide** [ma:laus tajde]
graphic art **piirrostaide** [pi:irros tajde]
abstract art **abstraktinen taide** [abstraktinen tajde]
impressionism **impressionismi** [impressionismi]

picture (painting) **taulu** [taulu]
drawing **piirros** [pi:irros]
poster **juliste** [juliste]

illustration (picture) **kuva** [kuʋa]
miniature **pienoiskuva** [pienojskuʋa]
copy (of painting, etc.) **kopio** [kopio]
reproduction **jäljennös** [jæl^{h}jeŋøs]

mosaic **mosaiikki** [mosai:ikki]
stained glass **ikkunamaalaus** [ikkunama:laus]
fresco **fresko** [fresko]
engraving **kaiverrus** [kajʋerrus]

bust (sculpture) **rintakuva** [rintakuʋa]
sculpture **kuvanveisto** [kuʋanʋejsto]
statue **kuvapatsas** [kuʋapatsas]
plaster of Paris **kipsi** [kipsi]
plaster (as adj) **kipsistä** [kipsistæ]

portrait **muotokuva** [muotokuʋa]
self-portrait **omakuva** [omakuʋa]
landscape **maisemakuva** [majsemakuʋa]
still life **asetelma** [asetelma]
caricature **pilakuva** [pilakuʋa]
sketch **hahmotelma** [hahmotelma]

paint **väri** [ʋæri]
watercolour **akvarelliväri** [akʋarelliʋæri]
oil (paint) **öljyväri** [øl^{h}yʋæri]
pencil **lyijykynä** [ly:kyɲæ]
Indian ink **tussi** [tussi]
charcoal **hiili** [hi:ili]

to draw (vi, vt) **piirtää** [pi:irtæ:]
to paint (vi, vt) **maalata** [ma:lata]

to pose (vi) **poseerata** [pose:rata]
artist's model (masc.) **poseeraaja** [pose:ra:ja]

artist's model (fem.)	**poseeraaja**	[pose:ra:ja]
artist (painter)	**taiteilija**	[tajtejlija]
work of art	**teos**	[teos]
masterpiece	**mestariteos**	[mestariteos]
workshop (of artist)	**verstas**	[ʋerstas]
canvas (cloth)	**kangas**	[kaŋas]
easel	**maalausteline**	[ma:lausteline]
palette	**paletti**	[paletti]
frame (of picture, etc.)	**kehys**	[kehys]
restoration	**entistys**	[entistys]
to restore (vt)	**entistää**	[entistæ:]

152. Literature & Poetry

literature	**kirjallisuus**	[kirʰjallisu:s]
author (writer)	**tekijä**	[tekijæ]
pseudonym	**salanimi**	[sala nimi]
book	**kirja**	[kirʰja]
volume	**nide**	[nide]
table of contents	**sisällysluettelo**	[sisællys luettelo]
page	**sivu**	[siʋu]
main character	**päähenkilö**	[pæ:heŋkilø]
autograph	**nimikirjoitus**	[nimi kirʰøjtus]
short story	**kertomus**	[kertomus]
story (novella)	**novelli**	[noʋelli]
novel	**romaani**	[roma:ni]
work (writing)	**teos**	[teos]
fable	**satu**	[satu]
detective novel	**salapoliisiromaani**	[sala poli:isi roma:ni]
poem (verse)	**runo**	[runo]
poetry	**runous**	[runous]
poem (epic, ballad)	**runoelma**	[runoelma]
poet	**runoilija**	[runojlija]
fiction	**kaunokirjallisuus**	[kauno kirʰjallisu:s]
science fiction	**tieteiskirjallisuus**	[tietejs kirʰjallisu:s]
adventures	**seikkailut**	[sejkkajlut]
educational literature	**oppikirjallisuus**	[oppi kirʰællisu:s]
children's literature	**lastenkirjallisuus**	[lasten kirʰjallisu:s]

153. Circus

circus	**sirkus**	[sirkus]
big top (circus)	**kiertävä sirkus**	[kiertæʋæ sirkus]
programme	**ohjelma**	[ohʰjelma]
performance	**esitys**	[esitys]
act (circus ~)	**numero**	[numero]

circus ring	**areena**	[are:na]
pantomime (act)	**pantomiimi**	[pantomi:imi]
clown	**klovni**	[klouni]
acrobat	**akrobaatti**	[akroba:tti]
acrobatics	**voimistelutaito**	[uojmistelu tajto]
gymnast	**voimistelija**	[uojmistelija]
gymnastics	**voimistelu**	[uojmistelu]
somersault	**hypähdys**	[hypæhdys]
strongman	**atleetti**	[atle:tti]
animal-tamer	**kesyttäjä**	[kesyttæjæ]
equestrian	**ratsastaja**	[ratsastaja]
assistant	**avustaja**	[auustaja]
stunt	**trikki**	[trikki]
magic trick	**temppu**	[temppu]
conjurer, magician	**taikuri**	[tajkuri]
juggler	**jonglööri**	[øŋlø:ri]
to juggle (vi, vt)	**jongleerata**	[øŋle:rata]
animal trainer	**kouluttaja**	[kouluttaja]
animal training	**koulutus**	[koulutus]
to train (animals)	**kouluttaa**	[koulutta:]

154. Music. Pop music

music	**musiikki**	[musi:ikki]
musician	**muusikko**	[mu:sikko]
musical instrument	**soitin**	[sojtin]
to play ...	**soittaa**	[sojtta:]
guitar	**kitara**	[kitara]
violin	**viulu**	[uiulu]
cello	**sello**	[sello]
double bass	**bassoviulu**	[bassouiulu]
harp	**harppu**	[harppu]
piano	**piano**	[piano]
grand piano	**flyygeli**	[fly:geli]
organ	**urut**	[urut]
wind instruments	**puhallussoitimet**	[puhallus sojtimet]
oboe	**oboe**	[oboj]
saxophone	**saksofoni**	[saksofoni]
clarinet	**klarinetti**	[klarinetti]
flute	**huilu**	[hujlu]
trumpet	**torvi**	[torui]
accordion	**pianoharmonikka**	[piano harmonikka]
drum	**rumpu**	[rumpu]
duo	**duo**	[duo]
trio	**trio**	[trio]

quartet	**kvartetti**	[kʊartetti]
choir	**kuoro**	[kuoro]
orchestra	**orkesteri**	[orkesteri]
pop music	**pop musiikki**	[pop musi:ikki]
rock music	**rokki**	[rokki]
rock group	**rokkiyhtye**	[rokki yhtye]
jazz	**jatsi**	[jatsi]
idol	**idoli**	[idoli]
admirer, fan	**ihailija**	[ihajlija]
concert	**konsertti**	[konsertti]
symphony	**sinfonia**	[sinfonia]
composition	**sävellys**	[sæʊellys]
to compose (write)	**säveltää**	[sæʊeltæ:]
singing	**laulaminen**	[lauluminen]
song	**laulu**	[laulu]
tune (melody)	**melodia**	[melodia]
rhythm	**rytmi**	[rytmi]
blues	**blues**	[blyes]
sheet music	**nuotit**	[nuotit]
baton	**tahtipuikko**	[tahti pujkko]
bow	**jousi**	[øusi]
string	**kieli**	[kieli]
case (e.g. guitar ~)	**kotelo**	[kotelo]

Rest. Entertainment. Travel

155. Trip. Travel

tourism	**matkailu**	[matkajlu]
tourist	**matkailija**	[matkajlija]
trip, voyage	**matka**	[matka]
adventure	**seikkailu**	[sejkkajlu]
trip, journey	**matka**	[matka]
holiday	**loma**	[loma]
to be on holiday	**olla lomalla**	[olla lomalla]
rest	**lepo**	[lepo]
train	**juna**	[juna]
by train	**junalla**	[junalla]
aeroplane	**lentokone**	[lentokone]
by aeroplane	**lentokoneella**	[lentokone:lla]
by car	**autolla**	[autolla]
by ship	**laivalla**	[lajυalla]
luggage	**matkatavarat**	[matkataυarat]
suitcase, luggage	**matkalaukku**	[matkalaukku]
luggage trolley	**matkatavarakärryt**	[matkataυarat kærryt]
passport	**passi**	[passi]
visa	**viisumi**	[υi:isumi]
ticket	**lippu**	[lippu]
air ticket	**lentolippu**	[lentolippu]
guidebook	**opas**	[opas]
map	**kartta**	[kartta]
area (rural ~)	**seutu**	[seutu]
place, site	**paikka**	[pajkka]
exotica	**eksoottisuus**	[ekso:ttisu:s]
exotic (adj)	**eksoottinen**	[ekso:ttinen]
amazing (adj)	**ihmeellinen**	[ihme:llinen]
group	**ryhmä**	[ryhmæ]
excursion	**retki**	[retki]
guide (person)	**opas**	[opas]

156. Hotel

hotel	**hotelli**	[hotelli]
motel	**motelli**	[motelli]
three-star (adj)	**kolme tähteä**	[kolme tæhteæ]

five-star	**viisi tähteä**	[ʋi:isi tæhteæ]
to stay (in hotel, etc.)	**majoittua**	[mɑøjttuɑ]
room	**huone**	[huone]
single room	**yhden hengen huone**	[yhden heŋen huone]
double room	**kahden hengen huone**	[kɑhden heŋen huone]
to book a room	**varata huone**	[ʋɑrɑtɑ huone]
half board	**puolihoito**	[puolihojto]
full board	**täysihoito**	[tæysihojto]
with bath	**ammeen kanssa**	[ɑmme:n kɑnssɑ]
with shower	**suihkun kanssa**	[sujhkun kɑnssɑ]
satellite television	**satelliittitelevisio**	[sɑtelli:itti teleʋisio]
air-conditioner	**ilmastointilaite**	[ilmɑstojntilɑjte]
towel	**pyyhe**	[py:he]
key	**avain**	[ɑʋɑjn]
administrator	**vastaanottaja**	[ʋɑstɑ:nottɑjæ]
chambermaid	**kerrossiivooja**	[kerrossi:iʋo:jɑ]
porter, bellboy	**kantaja**	[kɑntɑjɑ]
doorman	**vahtimestari**	[ʋɑhti mestɑri]
restaurant	**ravintola**	[rɑʋintolɑ]
pub, bar	**baari**	[bɑ:ri]
breakfast	**aamiainen**	[ɑ:miɑjnen]
dinner	**illallinen**	[illɑllinen]
buffet	**noutopöytä**	[nouto pøytæ]
lobby	**eteishalli**	[etejshɑlli]
lift	**hissi**	[hissi]
DO NOT DISTURB	**ÄLKÄÄ HÄIRITKÖ**	[ælkæ: ɦæjritkø]
NO SMOKING	**EI SAA POLTTAA!**	[ej sɑ: polttɑ:]

157. Books. Reading

book	**kirja**	[kirʰjɑ]
author	**tekijä**	[tekijæ]
writer	**kirjailija**	[kirʰjɑjlijɑ]
to write (~ a book)	**kirjoittaa**	[kirʰojttɑ:]
reader	**lukija**	[lukijɑ]
to read (vi, vt)	**lukea**	[lukeɑ]
reading (activity)	**lukeminen**	[lukeminen]
silently (to oneself)	**hiljaa**	[hiʎʲɑ:]
aloud (adv)	**ääneen**	[æ:ne:n]
to publish (vt)	**julkaista**	[julkɑjstɑ]
publishing (process)	**julkaisu**	[julkɑjsu]
publisher	**julkaisija**	[julkɑjsijɑ]
publishing house	**kustantamo**	[kustɑntɑmo]
to come out	**ilmestyä**	[ilmestyæ]

release (of a book)	**julkaisu**	[julkajsu]
print run	**painosmäärä**	[pajnosmæ:ræ]
bookshop	**kirjakauppa**	[kir^{h}ja kauppa]
library	**kirjasto**	[kir^{h}jasto]
story (novella)	**novelli**	[noʋelli]
short story	**kertomus**	[kertomus]
novel	**romaani**	[roma:ni]
detective novel	**salapoliisiromaani**	[sala poli:isi roma:ni]
memoirs	**muistelmat**	[mujstelmat]
legend	**tarina**	[tarina]
myth	**myytti**	[my:tti]
poetry, poems	**runot**	[runot]
autobiography	**omaelämäkerta**	[omaeʎæmækerta]
selected works	**valitut teokset**	[ʋalitut teokset]
science fiction	**tieteiskirjallisuus**	[tietejs kir^{h}jallisu:s]
title	**nimi**	[nimi]
introduction	**johdanto**	[øhdanto]
title page	**nimilehti**	[nimilehti]
chapter	**luku**	[luku]
extract	**katkelma**	[katkelma]
episode	**jakso**	[jakso]
plot (storyline)	**juoni**	[juoni]
contents	**sisältö**	[sisæltø]
table of contents	**sisällysluettelo**	[sisællys luettelo]
main character	**pääsankari**	[pæ: saŋkari]
volume	**nide**	[nide]
cover	**kansi**	[kansi]
binding	**sidonta**	[sidonta]
bookmark	**kirjanmerkki**	[kir^{h}janmerkki]
page	**sivu**	[siʋu]
to flick through	**selailla**	[selajlla]
margins	**reunat**	[reunat]
annotation	**merkintä**	[merkintæ]
footnote	**huomautus**	[huomautus]
text	**teksti**	[teksti]
type, fount	**kirjainlaji**	[kir^{h}jajnlajı]
misprint, typo	**painovirhe**	[pajnoʋirhe]
translation	**käännös**	[kæ:ŋøs]
to translate (vt)	**kääntää**	[kæ:ntæ:]
original (n)	**alkuperäiskappale**	[alkuperæjskappale]
famous (adj)	**kuulu**	[ku:lu]
unknown (adj)	**tuntematon**	[tuntematon]
interesting (adj)	**mielenkiintoinen**	[mielen ki:intojnen]
bestseller	**menekkiteos**	[menekkiteos]

dictionary	**sanakirja**	[sanakir^{h}ja]
textbook	**oppikirja**	[oppikir^{h}ja]
encyclopedia	**tietosanakirja**	[tietosanakir^{h}ja]

158. Hunting. Fishing

hunt (of animal)	**metsästys**	[metsæstys]
to hunt (vi, vt)	**metsästää**	[metsæstæ:]
hunter	**metsästäjä**	[metsæstæjæ]
to shoot (vi)	**ampua**	[ampua]
rifle	**pyssy**	[pyssy]
bullet (cartridge)	**patruuna**	[patru:na]
shotgun pellets	**haulit**	[haulit]
trap (e.g. bear ~)	**raudat**	[raudat]
snare (for birds, etc.)	**pyydys**	[py:dys]
to lay a trap	**asettaa raudat**	[asetta: raudat]
poacher	**salametsästäjä**	[salametsæstæjæ]
game (in hunting)	**riista**	[ri:ista]
hound	**metsästyskoira**	[metsæstyskojra]
safari	**safari**	[safari]
mounted animal	**täytetty eläin**	[tæytetty eʎæjn]
fisherman	**kalastaja**	[kalastaja]
fishing	**kalastus**	[kalastus]
to fish (vi)	**kalastaa**	[kalasta:]
fishing rod	**onki**	[oŋki]
fishing line	**siima**	[si:ima]
hook	**koukku**	[koukku]
float	**koho**	[koho]
bait	**syötti**	[syøtti]
to cast a line	**heittää onki**	[hejttæ: oŋki]
to bite (ab. fish)	**käydä onkeen**	[kæydæ oŋke:n]
catch (of fish)	**saalis**	[sa:lis]
ice-hole	**avanto**	[aʋanto]
net	**verkko**	[ʋerkko]
boat	**vene**	[ʋene]
to net (catch with net)	**laskea verkot**	[laskea ʋerkot]
to cast the net	**heittää verkko**	[hejttæ: ʋerkko]
to haul in the net	**vetää verkko**	[ʋetæ: ʋerkko]
whaler (person)	**valaanpyytäjä**	[ʋala:n py:tæjæ]
whaler (vessel)	**valaanpyyntialus**	[ʋala:n py:ntialus]
harpoon	**harppuuna**	[harppu:na]

159. Games. Billiards

billiards	**biljardi**	[bil^{h}jardi]
billiard room, hall	**biljardisali**	[bil^{h}jardi sali]

ball	**biljardipallo**	[bilʰjardi pallo]
to pocket a ball	**työntää pallo pussiin**	[tyøntæ: pallo pussi:in]
cue	**biljardikeppi**	[bilʰjardi keppi]
pocket	**pussi**	[pussi]

160. Games. Playing cards

diamonds	**ruutu**	[ru:tu]
spades	**pata**	[pata]
hearts	**hertta**	[hertta]
clubs	**risti**	[risti]
ace	**ässä**	[æssæ]
king	**kuningas**	[kuniŋas]
queen	**rouva**	[rouʋa]
jack, knave	**sotamies**	[sotamies]
playing card	**kortti**	[kortti]
cards	**kortit**	[kortit]
trump	**valtti**	[ʋaltti]
pack of cards	**pakka**	[pakka]
to deal (vi, vt)	**jakaa**	[jaka:]
to shuffle (cards)	**sekoittaa**	[sekojtta:]
lead, turn (n)	**siirto**	[si:irto]
cardsharp	**korttihuijari**	[korttihuijari]

161. Casino. Roulette

casino	**kasino**	[kasino]
roulette (game)	**ruletti**	[ruletti]
bet, stake	**panos**	[panos]
to place bets	**panna panos**	[paŋa panos]
red	**punainen**	[punajnen]
black	**musta**	[musta]
to bet on red	**panna panos punaisen varaan**	[paŋa panos punajsen ʋara:n]
to bet on black	**panna panos mustan varaan**	[paŋa panos mustan ʋara:n]
croupier (dealer)	**pelipankin hoitaja**	[peli paŋkin hojtaja]
to turn the wheel	**pyörittää**	[pyørittæ:]
rules (of game)	**pelisäännöt**	[pelisæ:ŋøt]
chip	**peliraha**	[peliraha]
to win (vi, vt)	**voittaa**	[ʋojtta:]
winnings	**voitto**	[ʋojtto]
to lose (~ 100 dollars)	**hävitä**	[ɦæʋitæ]
loss	**häviö**	[ɦæʋiø]
player	**pelaaja**	[pela:ja]

blackjack (card game)	**Black Jack**	[blek ʤek]
game of dice	**noppapeli**	[noppɑpeli]
fruit machine	**peliautomaatti**	[peli ɑutomɑ:tti]

162. Rest. Games. Miscellaneous

to take a walk	**kävellä**	[kæʋeʎæ]
walk, stroll	**kävely**	[kæʋely]
road trip	**retki**	[retki]
adventure	**seikkailu**	[sejkkɑjlu]
picnic	**piknikki**	[piknikki]
game (chess, etc.)	**peli**	[peli]
player	**pelaaja**	[pelɑ:jɑ]
game (one ~ of chess)	**erä**	[eræ]
collector (e.g. philatelist)	**keräilijä**	[keræjlijæ]
to collect (vt)	**keräillä**	[keræjʎæ]
collection	**kokoelma**	[kokoelmɑ]
crossword puzzle	**sanaristikko**	[sɑnɑristikko]
racecourse (hippodrome)	**ravirata**	[rɑʋirɑtɑ]
discotheque	**disko**	[disko]
sauna	**sauna**	[sɑunɑ]
lottery	**arpajaiset**	[ɑrpɑjɑjset]
camping trip	**retki**	[retki]
camp	**leiri**	[lejri]
tent (for camping)	**teltta**	[telttɑ]
compass	**kompassi**	[kompɑssi]
camper	**retkeilijä**	[retkejlijæ]
to watch (film, etc.)	**katsoa**	[kɑʦoɑ]
viewer	**television katsoja**	[teleʋision kɑʦojɑ]
TV program	**televisiolähetys**	[teleʋisio ʎæhetys]

163. Photography

camera (photo)	**kamera**	[kɑmerɑ]
photo, picture	**valokuva**	[ʋɑlokuʋɑ]
photographer	**valokuvaaja**	[ʋɑlokuʋɑ:jɑ]
photo studio	**valokuvaamo**	[ʋɑlokuʋɑ:mo]
photo album	**valokuvakansio**	[ʋɑlokuʋɑkɑnsio]
camera lens	**objektiivi**	[objekti:iʋi]
telephoto lens	**teleobjektiivi**	[teleobjekti:iʋi]
filter	**suodatin**	[suodɑtin]
lens	**linssi**	[linssi]
optics (high-quality ~)	**optiikka**	[opti:ikkɑ]
diaphragm (aperture)	**himmennin**	[himmeŋin]

exposure time	**valotus**	[ʋalotus]
viewfinder	**tähtäin**	[tæhtæjn]
digital camera	**digitaalikamera**	[digita:li kamera]
tripod	**jalusta**	[jalusta]
flash	**leimahdus**	[lejmahdus]
to photograph (vt)	**valokuvata**	[ʋalokuʋata]
to take pictures	**kuvata**	[kuʋata]
to be photographed	**käydä valokuvassa**	[kæydæ ʋalokuʋassa]
focus	**terävyys**	[teræʋy:s]
to adjust the focus	**tarkentaa**	[tarkenta:]
sharp, in focus (adj)	**terävä**	[teræʋæ]
sharpness	**terävyys**	[teræʋy:s]
contrast	**kontrasti**	[kontrasti]
contrasty (adj)	**kontrasti-**	[kontrasti]
picture (photo)	**kuva**	[kuʋa]
negative (n)	**negatiivi**	[negati:iʋi]
film (a roll of ~)	**filmi**	[filmi]
frame (still)	**otos**	[otos]
to print (photos)	**painaa**	[pajna:]

164. Beach. Swimming

beach	**uimaranta**	[ujmaranta]
sand	**hiekka**	[hiekka]
deserted (beach)	**aavikko-**	[a:ʋikko]
suntan	**rusketus**	[rusketus]
to get a tan	**ottaa aurinkoa**	[otta: auriŋkoa]
tanned (adj)	**ruskettunut**	[ruskettunut]
sunscreen	**aurinkovoide**	[auriŋko ʋojde]
bikini	**bikinit**	[bikinit]
swimsuit, bikini	**uimapuku**	[ujmapuku]
swim trunks	**uimahousut**	[ujmahousut]
swimming pool	**uimahalli**	[ujmahalli]
to swim (vi)	**uida**	[ujda]
shower	**suihku**	[sujhku]
to change (one's clothes)	**vaihtaa vaatteet**	[ʋajhta: ʋa:tte:t]
towel	**pyyhe**	[py:he]
boat	**vene**	[ʋene]
motorboat	**moottorivene**	[mo:ttoriʋene]
water ski	**vesihiihto**	[ʋesi hi:ihto]
pedalo	**vesipolkupyörä**	[ʋesi polkupyøræ]
surfing	**lainelautailu**	[lajnelautajlu]
surfer	**lainelautailija**	[lajnelautajlija]
scuba set	**happilaite**	[happilajte]

flippers (swimfins)	**räpylät**	[ræpyʎæt]
mask	**naamari**	[nɑ:mɑri]
diver	**sukeltaja**	[sukeltɑjɑ]
to dive (vi)	**sukeltaa**	[sukeltɑ:]
underwater (adv)	**veden alla**	[ʋeden ɑllɑ]
beach umbrella	**sateenvarjo**	[sɑte:nʋɑrø]
beach chair	**telttatuoli**	[telttɑtuoli]
sunglasses	**aurinkolasit**	[ɑuriŋkolɑsit]
air mattress	**uimapatja**	[ujmɑpɑtjɑ]
to play (amuse oneself)	**leikkiä**	[lejkkiæ]
to go for a swim	**kylpeä**	[kylpeæ]
beach ball	**pallo**	[pɑllo]
to inflate (vt)	**puhaltaa täyteen**	[puhɑltɑ: tæyte:n]
inflatable, air (adj)	**ilma-**	[ilmɑ]
wave	**aalto**	[ɑ:lto]
buoy	**poiju**	[poiju]
to drown (ab. person)	**hukkua**	[hukkuɑ]
to save, to rescue	**pelastaa**	[pelɑstɑ:]
lifejacket	**pelastusliivi**	[pelɑstusli:iʋi]
to observe, to watch	**valvoa**	[ʋɑlʋoɑ]
lifeguard	**pelastaja**	[pelɑstɑjɑ]

TECHNICAL EQUIPMENT. TRANSPORT

Technical equipment

165. Computer

computer	**tietokone**	[tietokone]
notebook, laptop	**kannettava tietokone**	[kaŋettaʋa tietokone]
to switch on	**avata**	[aʋata]
to turn off	**sammuttaa**	[sammutta:]
keyboard	**näppäimistö**	[ɲæppæjmistø]
key	**näppäin**	[ɲæppæjn]
mouse	**hiiri**	[hi:iri]
mouse mat	**hiirimatto**	[hi:irimatto]
button	**näppäin**	[ɲæppæjn]
cursor	**kursori**	[kursori]
monitor	**monitori**	[monitori]
screen	**näyttö**	[ɲæyttø]
hard disk	**kiintolevy**	[ki:intoleʋy]
hard disk volume	**levytila**	[leʋytila]
memory	**muisti**	[mujsti]
random access memory	**työmuisti**	[tyømujsti]
file	**tiedosto**	[tædosto]
folder	**kansio**	[kansio]
to open (vt)	**avata**	[aʋata]
to close (vt)	**sulkea**	[sulkea]
to save (vt)	**tallentaa**	[tallenta:]
to delete (vt)	**poistaa**	[pojsta:]
to copy (vt)	**kopioida**	[kopiojda]
to sort (vt)	**lajitella**	[lajıtella]
to transfer (copy)	**kopioida**	[kopiojda]
programme	**ohjelma**	[oh^{h}jelma]
software	**ohjelmisto**	[ohjelmisto]
programmer	**ohjelmoija**	[oh^{h}jelmoja]
to program (vt)	**ohjelmoida**	[oh^{h}jelmojda]
hacker	**murtaja**	[murtaja]
password	**tunnussana**	[tuŋussana]
virus	**virus**	[ʋirus]
to find, to detect	**löytää**	[løytæ:]
byte	**tavu**	[taʋu]

megabyte	**megatavu**	[megataʋu]
data	**tiedot**	[tædot]
database	**tietokanta**	[tieto kanta]
cable (wire)	**kaapeli**	[ka:peli]
to disconnect (vt)	**kytkeä irti**	[kytkeæ irti]
to connect (sth to sth)	**yhdistää**	[yhdistæ:]

166. Internet. E-mail

Internet	**netti**	[netti]
browser	**selain**	[selajn]
search engine	**hakupalvelu**	[hakupalʋelu]
provider	**internet-palveluntarjoaja**	[internet palʋelun tarʰøaja]
web master	**webmaster**	[ʋebmaster]
website	**nettisivusto**	[nettisiʋusto]
web page	**nettisivu**	[nettisiʋu]
address	**osoite**	[osojte]
address book	**osoitekirja**	[osojte kirʰja]
postbox	**postilaatikko**	[postila:tikko]
post	**posti**	[posti]
message	**viesti**	[ʋiesti]
sender	**lähettäjä**	[ʎæhettæjæ]
to send (vt)	**lähettää**	[ʎæhettæ:]
sending (of mail)	**kirjeen lähetys**	[kirʰje:n ʎæhetys]
receiver	**saaja**	[sa:ja]
to receive (vt)	**saada**	[sa:da]
correspondence	**kirjeenvaihto**	[kirʰje:n ʋajhto]
to correspond (vi)	**olla kirjeenvaihdossa**	[olla kirʰje:n ʋajhdossa]
file	**tiedosto**	[tædosto]
to download (vt)	**jäljentää**	[jæljentæ:]
to create (vt)	**luoda**	[luoda]
to delete (vt)	**poistaa**	[pojsta:]
deleted (adj)	**poistettu**	[pojstettu]
connection (ADSL, etc.)	**yhteys**	[yhteys]
speed	**nopeus**	[nopeus]
modem	**modeemi**	[mode:mi]
access	**saavutus**	[sa:ʋutus]
port (e.g. input ~)	**portti**	[portti]
connection (make a ~)	**liittymä**	[li:ittymæ]
to connect (vi)	**liittyä**	[li:ittyæ]
to select (vt)	**valita**	[ʋalita]
to search (for ...)	**etsiä**	[etsiæ]

167. Electricity

electricity	**sähkö**	[sæhkø]
electrical (adj)	**sähkö-**	[sæhkø]
electric power station	**voimala**	[ʋojmɑlɑ]
energy	**energia**	[energiɑ]
electric power	**sähköenergia**	[sæhkøenergiɑ]
light bulb	**lamppu**	[lɑmppu]
torch	**taskulamppu**	[tɑskulɑmppu]
street light	**lyhty**	[lyhty]
light	**valo**	[ʋɑlo]
to turn on	**sytyttää**	[sytyttæ:]
to turn off	**katkaista**	[kɑtkɑjstɑ]
to turn off the light	**sammuttaa valo**	[sɑmmuttɑ: ʋɑlo]
to burn out (vi)	**lamppu on palanut**	[lɑmppu on pɑlɑnut]
short circuit	**oikosulku**	[ojkosulku]
broken wire	**katkeama**	[kɑtkeɑmɑ]
contact	**kontakti**	[kontɑkti]
light switch	**katkaisin**	[kɑtkɑjsin]
socket outlet	**pistorasia**	[pistorɑsiɑ]
plug	**pistoke**	[pistoke]
extension lead	**pistoliitin**	[pistoli:itin]
fuse	**suojalaite**	[suojɑlɑjte]
cable, wire	**johdin**	[øhdin]
wiring	**johde**	[øhde]
ampere	**ampeeri**	[ɑmpe:ri]
amperage	**virran voimakkuus**	[ʋirrɑn ʋojmɑkku:s]
volt	**voltti**	[ʋoltti]
voltage	**jännite**	[jæŋite]
electrical device	**sähkölaite**	[sæhkølɑjte]
indicator	**indikaattori**	[indikɑ:ttori]
electrician	**sähkömies**	[sæhkømies]
to solder (vt)	**juottaa**	[juottɑ:]
soldering iron	**juotin**	[juotin]
electric current	**virta**	[ʋirtɑ]

168. Tools

tool, instrument	**työkalu**	[tyøkɑlu]
tools	**työkalut**	[tyøkɑlut]
equipment (factory ~)	**varusteet**	[ʋɑruste:t]
hammer	**vasara**	[ʋɑsɑrɑ]
screwdriver	**ruuvitaltta**	[ru:ʋitɑlttɑ]
axe	**kirves**	[kirʋes]

saw	**saha**	[saha]
to saw (vt)	**sahata**	[sahata]
plane (tool)	**höylä**	[høyʎæ]
to plane (vt)	**höylätä**	[høyʎætæ]
soldering iron	**juotin**	[juotin]
to solder (vt)	**juottaa**	[juotta:]
file (for metal)	**viila**	[ʋi:ila]
carpenter pincers	**pihdit**	[pihdit]
combination pliers	**laakapihdit**	[la:kapihdit]
chisel	**taltta**	[taltta]
drill bit	**pora**	[pora]
electric drill	**porakone**	[porakone]
to drill (vi, vt)	**porata**	[porata]
knife	**veitsi**	[ʋejtsi]
pocket knife	**taskuveitsi**	[taskuʋejtsi]
folding (knife, etc.)	**kokoonpantava**	[koko:npantaʋa]
blade	**terä**	[teræ]
sharp (blade, etc.)	**terävä**	[teræʋæ]
blunt (adj)	**tylsä**	[tylsæ]
to become blunt	**tylsyttyä**	[tylsyttyæ]
to sharpen (vt)	**teroittaa**	[terojtta:]
bolt	**pultti**	[pultti]
nut	**mutteri**	[mutteri]
thread (of a screw)	**kierre**	[kierre]
wood screw	**ruuvi**	[ru:ʋi]
nail	**naula**	[naula]
nailhead	**kanta**	[kanta]
ruler (for measuring)	**viivoitin**	[ʋi:iʋojtin]
tape measure	**mittanauha**	[mittanauha]
spirit level	**taso**	[taso]
magnifying glass	**suurennuslasi**	[su:reŋuslasi]
measuring instrument	**mittauslaite**	[mittauslajte]
to measure (vt)	**mitata**	[mitata]
scale (of thermometer, etc.)	**asteikko**	[astejkko]
readings	**lukema**	[lukema]
compressor	**kompressori**	[kompressori]
microscope	**mikroskooppi**	[mikrosko:ppi]
pump (e.g. water ~)	**pumppu**	[pumppu]
robot	**robotti**	[robotti]
laser	**laser**	[laser]
spanner	**ruuviavain**	[ru:ʋiaʋajn]
adhesive tape	**teippi**	[tejppi]
glue	**liima**	[li:ima]
emery paper	**hiomapaperi**	[hiomapaperi]
spring	**jousi**	[øusi]

magnet	**magneetti**	[magne:tti]
gloves	**käsineet**	[kæsine:t]
rope	**nuora**	[nuora]
cord	**punos**	[punos]
wire (e.g. telephone ~)	**johdin**	[øhdin]
cable	**kaapeli**	[ka:peli]
sledgehammer	**moukari**	[moukari]
crowbar	**rautakanki**	[rautakaŋki]
ladder	**tikapuut**	[tikapu:t]
stepladder	**tikkaat**	[tikka:t]
to screw (tighten)	**kiertää**	[kærtæ:]
to unscrew, untwist (vt)	**kiertää auki**	[kiertæ: auki]
to tighten (vt)	**puristaa**	[purista:]
to glue, to stick	**liimata**	[li:imata]
to cut (vt)	**leikata**	[lejkata]
malfunction (fault)	**vika**	[ʋika]
repair (mending)	**korjaus**	[korʰjaus]
to repair, to mend (vt)	**korjata**	[korʰjata]
to adjust (machine, etc.)	**säädellä**	[sæ:deʎæ]
to check (to examine)	**tarkastaa**	[tarkasta:]
checking	**tarkastus**	[tarkastus]
readings	**lukema**	[lukema]
reliable (machine)	**varma**	[ʋarma]
complicated (adj)	**monimutkainen**	[monimutkajnen]
to rust (vi)	**ruostua**	[ruostua]
rusty (adj)	**ruosteinen**	[ruostejnen]
rust	**ruoste**	[ruoste]

Transport

169. Aeroplane

aeroplane	**lentokone**	[lentokone]
air ticket	**lentolippu**	[lentolippu]
airline	**lentoyhtiö**	[lentoyhtiø]
airport	**lentoasema**	[lentoasema]
supersonic (adj)	**äänen nopeuden ylittävä**	[æ:nen nopeuden ylittæʋæ]
captain	**lentokoneen päällikkö**	[lentokone:n pæ:llikkø]
crew	**miehistö**	[mæhisto]
pilot	**lentäjä**	[lentæjæ]
stewardess	**lentoemäntä**	[lentoemæntæ]
navigator	**perämies**	[peræmies]
wings	**siivet**	[si:iʋet]
tail	**pyrstö**	[pyrstø]
cockpit	**hytti**	[hytti]
engine	**moottori**	[mo:ttori]
undercarriage	**laskuteline**	[laskuteline]
turbine	**turbiini**	[turbi:ini]
propeller	**propelli**	[propelli]
black box	**musta laatikko**	[musta la:tikko]
control column	**ruoriratas**	[ruoriratas]
fuel	**polttoaine**	[polttoajne]
safety card	**ohje**	[ohʰje]
oxygen mask	**happinaamari**	[happina:mari]
uniform	**univormu**	[uniʋormu]
lifejacket	**pelastusliivi**	[pelastusli:iʋi]
parachute	**laskuvarjo**	[lasku ʋarʰø]
takeoff	**ilmaannousu**	[ilma:ŋousu]
to take off (vi)	**nousta ilmaan**	[nousta ilma:n]
runway	**kiitorata**	[ki:itorata]
visibility	**näkyvyys**	[ɲækyʋy:s]
flight (act of flying)	**lento**	[lento]
altitude	**korkeus**	[korkeus]
air pocket	**ilmakuoppa**	[ilmakuoppa]
seat	**paikka**	[pajkka]
headphones	**kuulokkeet**	[ku:lokke:t]
folding tray	**kääntöpöytä**	[kæ:ntøpøytæ]
airplane window	**ikkuna**	[ikkuna]
aisle	**käytävä**	[kæytæʋæ]

170. Train

train	**juna**	[juna]
suburban train	**sähköjuna**	[sæhkøjuna]
fast train	**pikajuna**	[pikajuna]
diesel locomotive	**moottoriveturi**	[mo:ttoriυeturi]
steam engine	**veturi**	[υeturi]
coach, carriage	**vaunu**	[υaunu]
restaurant car	**ravintolavaunu**	[raυintola υaunu]
rails	**ratakiskot**	[ratakiskot]
railway	**rautatie**	[rautatie]
sleeper (track support)	**ratapölkky**	[ratapølkky]
platform (railway ~)	**asemalaituri**	[asema lajturi]
platform (~ 1, 2, etc.)	**raide**	[rajde]
semaphore	**siipiopastin**	[si:ipi opastin]
station	**asema**	[asema]
train driver	**junankuljettaja**	[yneŋkuʎættaja]
porter (of luggage)	**kantaja**	[kantaja]
train steward	**vaununhoitaja**	[υaunun hojtaja]
passenger	**matkustaja**	[matkustaja]
ticket inspector	**tarkastaja**	[tarkastaja]
corridor (in train)	**käytävä**	[kæytæυæ]
emergency break	**hätäjarru**	[ɦætæjarru]
compartment	**vaununosasto**	[υaunun osasto]
berth	**vuode**	[υuode]
upper berth	**ylävuode**	[yʎæυuode]
lower berth	**alavuode**	[alaυuode]
linen	**vuodevaatteet**	[υuodeυa:tte:t]
ticket	**lippu**	[lippu]
timetable	**aikataulu**	[ajkataulu]
information display	**ilmoitustaulu**	[ilmojtustaulu]
to leave, to depart	**lähteä**	[ʎæhteæ]
departure (of train)	**junan lähtö**	[junan ʎæhtø]
to arrive (ab. train)	**saapua**	[sa:pua]
arrival	**saapuminen**	[sa:puminen]
to arrive by train	**tulla junalla**	[tulla junalla]
to get on the train	**nousta junaan**	[nousta juna:n]
to get off the train	**nousta junasta**	[nousta junasta]
train crash	**onnettomuus**	[oŋettomu:s]
steam engine	**veturi**	[υeturi]
stoker, fireman	**lämmittäjä**	[ʎæmmittæjæ]
firebox	**lämmitys**	[ʎæmmitys]
coal	**hiili**	[hi:ili]

171. Ship

ship	**laiva**	[lajʋɑ]
vessel	**alus**	[ɑlus]
steamship	**höyrylaiva**	[højrylajʋɑ]
riverboat	**jokilaiva**	[økilajʋɑ]
ocean liner	**risteilijä**	[ristejlijæ]
cruiser	**risteilijä**	[ristejlijæ]
yacht	**pursi**	[pursi]
tugboat	**hinausköysi**	[hinɑuskøysi]
barge	**proomu**	[pro:mu]
ferry	**lautta**	[lɑuttɑ]
sailing ship	**purjealus**	[purʰjeɑlus]
brigantine	**merirosvot**	[merirosʋot]
ice breaker	**jäänmurtaja**	[jæ:nmurtɑjɑ]
submarine	**sukellusvene**	[sukellusʋene]
boat (flat-bottomed ~)	**jolla**	[ølla]
dinghy	**vene**	[ʋene]
lifeboat	**pelastusvene**	[pelɑstus ʋene]
motorboat	**moottorivene**	[mo:ttoriʋene]
captain	**kapteeni**	[kɑpte:ni]
seaman	**matruusi**	[mɑtru:si]
sailor	**merimies**	[merimies]
crew	**miehistö**	[mæhisto]
boatswain	**pursimies**	[pursimies]
ship's boy	**laivapoika**	[lajʋɑ pojkɑ]
cook	**kokki**	[kokki]
ship's doctor	**laivalääkäri**	[lajʋɑ læ:kæri]
deck	**kansi**	[kɑnsi]
mast	**masto**	[mɑsto]
sail	**purje**	[purʰje]
hold	**ruuma**	[ru:mɑ]
bow (prow)	**keula**	[keulɑ]
stern	**perä**	[peræ]
oar	**airo**	[ɑjro]
propeller	**potkuri**	[potkuri]
cabin	**hytti**	[hytti]
wardroom	**upseerimessi**	[upse:ri messi]
engine room	**konehuone**	[konehuone]
bridge	**komentosilta**	[komentosiltɑ]
radio room	**radiohuone**	[rɑdiohuone]
wave (radio)	**aalto**	[ɑ:lto]
logbook	**laivapäiväkirja**	[lajʋɑ pæjʋækirʰjɑ]
spyglass	**kaukoputki**	[kɑukoputki]
bell	**kello**	[kello]

flag	**lippu**	[lippu]
rope (mooring ~)	**köysi**	[køysi]
knot (bowline, etc.)	**solmu**	[solmu]
handrail	**käsipuu**	[kæsipu:]
gangway	**portaat**	[porta:t]
anchor	**ankkuri**	[aŋkkuri]
to weigh anchor	**nostaa ankkuri**	[nosta: aŋkkuri]
to drop anchor	**heittää ankkuri**	[hejttæ: aŋkkuri]
anchor chain	**ankkuriketju**	[aŋkkuriketju]
port (harbour)	**satama**	[satama]
wharf, quay	**laituri**	[lajturi]
to berth (moor)	**laskea laituriin**	[laskea lajturi:in]
to cast off	**irtautua**	[irtautua]
trip, voyage	**matka**	[matka]
cruise (sea trip)	**laivamatka**	[lajʋamatka]
course (route)	**kurssi**	[kurssi]
route (itinerary)	**reitti**	[rejtti]
fairway	**väylä**	[ʋæyʎæ]
shallows (shoal)	**matalikko**	[matalikko]
to run aground	**ajautua matalikolle**	[ajautua matalikolle]
storm	**myrsky**	[myrsky]
signal	**merkki**	[merkki]
to sink (vi)	**upota**	[upota]
SOS	**SOS**	[sos]
ring buoy	**pelastusrengas**	[pelastus reŋas]

172. Airport

airport	**lentoasema**	[lentoasema]
aeroplane	**lentokone**	[lentokone]
airline	**lentoyhtiö**	[lentoyhtiø]
air-traffic controller	**valvoja**	[ʋalʋoja]
departure	**lentoonlähtö**	[lento:nʎæhtø]
arrival	**tulo**	[tulo]
to arrive (by plane)	**lentää**	[lentæ:]
departure time	**lähtöaika**	[ʎæhtø ajka]
arrival time	**saapumisaika**	[sa:pumis ajka]
to be delayed	**myöhästyä**	[myøɦæstyæ]
flight delay	**lennon viivytys**	[leŋon ʋi:iʋytys]
information board	**tiedotustaulu**	[tiedotus taulu]
information	**tiedotus**	[tiedotus]
to announce (vt)	**ilmoittaa**	[ilmojtta:]
flight (e.g. next ~)	**lento**	[lento]
customs	**tulli**	[tulli]

customs officer	**tullimies**	[tullimies]
customs declaration	**tullausilmoitus**	[tullaus ilmojtus]
to fill in the declaration	**täyttää tullausilmoitus**	[tæyttæ: tullaus ilmojtus]
passport control	**passintarkastus**	[passin tarkastus]
luggage	**matkatavarat**	[matkataʋarat]
hand luggage	**käsimatkatavara**	[kæsimatkataʋara]
Lost Luggage Desk	**matkatavaroiden etsintä**	[matkataʋarojden etsintæ]
luggage trolley	**matkatavarakärryt**	[matkataʋarat kærryt]
landing	**lasku**	[lasku]
landing strip	**laskurata**	[laskurata]
to land (vi)	**laskeutua**	[laskeutua]
airstairs	**portaat**	[porta:t]
check-in	**rekisteröinti**	[rekisterøinti]
check-in desk	**rekisteröintitiski**	[rekisterøinti tiski]
to check-in (vi)	**ilmoittautua**	[ilmojttautua]
boarding pass	**lippu**	[lippu]
departure gate	**lentokoneen pääsy**	[lentokone:n pæ:sy]
transit	**kauttakulku**	[kauttakulku]
to wait (vt)	**odottaa**	[odotta:]
departure lounge	**odotussali**	[odotussali]
to see off	**saattaa**	[sa:tta:]
to say goodbye	**hyvästellä**	[hyʋæsteʎæ]

173. Bicycle. Motorcycle

bicycle	**polkupyörä**	[polkupyøræ]
scooter	**skootteri**	[sko:tteri]
motorbike	**moottoripyörä**	[mo:ttori pyøræ]
to go by bicycle	**pyöräillä**	[pyøræjʎæ]
handlebars	**ohjaustanko**	[ohʰjaus taŋko]
pedal	**poljin**	[polʰjın]
brakes	**jarrut**	[jarrut]
saddle	**satula**	[satula]
pump	**pumppu**	[pumppu]
luggage rack	**tavarateline**	[taʋarateline]
front lamp	**lyhty**	[lyhty]
helmet	**kypärä**	[kypæræ]
wheel	**pyörä**	[pyøræ]
mudguard	**siipi**	[si:ipi]
rim	**kehä**	[keɦæ]
spoke	**puola**	[puola]

Cars

174. Types of cars

car	**auto**	[auto]
sports car	**urheiluauto**	[urhejlu auto]
limousine	**limusiini**	[limousi:ine]
off-road vehicle	**maastoauto**	[ma:sto auto]
convertible	**kabrioletti**	[kabrioletti]
minibus	**pikkubussi**	[pikkubussi]
ambulance	**ambulanssi**	[ambulanssi]
snowplough	**lumiaura**	[lumiaura]
lorry	**kuorma-auto**	[kuorma auto]
road tanker	**bensiinisäiliöauto**	[bensi:ini sæjliø auto]
van (small truck)	**kuomuauto**	[kuomu auto]
road tractor	**veturi**	[ʋeturi]
trailer	**perävaunu**	[peræiʋaunu]
comfortable (adj)	**mukava**	[mukaʋa]
second hand (adj)	**käytetty**	[kæutetty]

175. Cars. Bodywork

bonnet	**suojuskoppa**	[suojuskoppa]
wing	**lokasuojat**	[lokasuojat]
roof	**katto**	[katto]
windscreen	**tuulilasi**	[tu:lilasi]
rear-view mirror	**taustapeili**	[taustapejli]
windscreen washer	**tuulilasinpesin**	[tu:lilasin pesin]
windscreen wipers	**tuulilasinpyyhkimet**	[tu:lilasin py:hkimet]
side window	**sivulasi**	[siʋulasi]
window lift	**lasinosturi**	[lasinosturi]
aerial	**antenni**	[anteŋi]
sun roof	**luukku**	[lu:kku]
bumper	**puskuri**	[puskuri]
boot	**tavaratila**	[taʋaratila]
door	**ovi**	[oʋi]
door handle	**ripa**	[ripa]
door lock	**lukko**	[lukko]
number plate	**numero**	[numero]
silencer	**vaimennin**	[ʋajmeŋin]

petrol tank	**bensiinitankki**	[bensi:ini tɑŋkki]
exhaust pipe	**pakoputki**	[pɑkoputki]
accelerator	**kaasu**	[kɑ:su]
pedal	**poljin**	[polʰjɪn]
accelerator pedal	**kaasupoljin**	[kɑ:supolʰjɪn]
brake	**jarru**	[jɑrru]
brake pedal	**jarrupoljin**	[jɑrrupolʰjɪn]
to slow down (to brake)	**jarruttaa**	[jɑrruttɑ:]
handbrake	**käsijarru**	[kæsijɑrru]
clutch	**kytkin**	[kytkin]
clutch pedal	**kytkinpoljin**	[kytkin polʰjɪn]
clutch plate	**kytkinlevy**	[kytkin leʋy]
shock absorber	**iskunvaimennin**	[iskunʋɑjmeŋin]
wheel	**rengas**	[reŋɑs]
spare tyre	**vararengas**	[ʋɑrɑreŋɑs]
wheel cover (hubcap)	**vanne**	[ʋɑŋe]
driving wheels	**vetorenkaat**	[ʋetoreŋkɑ:t]
front-wheel drive (as adj)	**etuveto-**	[etuʋeto]
rear-wheel drive (as adj)	**takaveto-**	[tɑkɑʋeto]
all-wheel drive (as adj)	**täysveto-**	[tæysʋeto]
gearbox	**vaihdelaatikko**	[ʋɑjhdelɑ:tikko]
automatic (adj)	**automaattinen**	[ɑutomɑ:ttinen]
mechanical (adj)	**mekaaninen**	[mekɑ:ninen]
gear lever	**vaihdetanko**	[ʋɑjhdetɑŋko]
headlight	**etulyhty**	[etulyhty]
headlights	**lyhdyt**	[lyhdyt]
dipped headlights	**lähivalot**	[ʎæhiʋɑlot]
full headlights	**kaukovalot**	[kɑukoʋɑlot]
brake light	**pysäköintivalo**	[pysækøintiʋɑlo]
sidelights	**perävalot**	[peræʋɑlot]
hazard lights	**hätävilkut**	[ɦætæʋilkut]
fog lights	**sumuvalot**	[sumuʋɑlot]
turn indicator	**kääntymisvalo**	[kæ:ntymisʋɑlo]
reversing light	**taaksepäin käynti**	[tɑ:ksepæjn kæuntti]

176. Cars. Passenger compartment

car inside	**salonki**	[sɑloŋki]
leather (as adj)	**nahka-**	[nɑhkɑ]
velour (as adj)	**veluuri-**	[ʋelu:ri]
upholstery	**päällys**	[pæ:llys]
instrument (gage)	**koje**	[koje]
dashboard	**kojelauta**	[kojelɑutɑ]
speedometer	**nopeusmittari**	[nopeusmittɑri]

needle (pointer)	**osoitin**	[osojtin]
mileometer	**matkamittari**	[matkamittari]
indicator (sensor)	**indikaattori**	[indika:ttori]
level	**taso**	[taso]
warning light	**lamppu**	[lamppu]
steering wheel	**ratti**	[ratti]
horn	**torvi**	[toruі]
button	**näppäin**	[ɲæppæjn]
switch	**kytkin**	[kytkin]
seat	**istuin**	[istujn]
seat back	**selkänoja**	[selkænoja]
headrest	**päänalunen**	[pæ:n alunen]
seat belt	**turvavyö**	[turʋaʋyø]
to fasten the belt	**kiinnittää turvavyö**	[ki:iŋittæ: turʋaʋyø]
adjustment (of seats)	**säännöstely**	[sæ:ŋøstely]
airbag	**turvatyyny**	[turʋa ty:ny]
air-conditioner	**ilmastointilaite**	[ilmastojntilajte]
radio	**radio**	[radio]
CD player	**CD-levysoitin**	[sede leʋysojtin]
to turn on	**avata**	[aʋata]
aerial	**antenni**	[anteŋi]
glove box	**hylly**	[hylly]
ashtray	**tuhkakuppi**	[tuhkakuppi]

177. Cars. Engine

engine, motor	**moottori**	[mo:ttori]
diesel (as adj)	**diesel-**	[dieseʎ]
petrol (as adj)	**bensiini-**	[bensi:ini]
engine volume	**moottorin tilavuus**	[mo:ttorin tilaʋu:s]
power	**teho**	[teho]
horsepower	**hevosvoima**	[heʋosʋojma]
piston	**mäntä**	[mæntæ]
cylinder	**sylinteri**	[sylinteri]
valve	**läppä**	[ʎæppæ]
injector	**injektori**	[inʰjektori]
generator	**generaattori**	[genera:ttori]
carburettor	**kaasutin**	[ka:sutin]
engine oil	**koneöljy**	[kone ølʰy]
radiator	**jäähdytin**	[jæ:hdytin]
coolant	**jäähdytysneste**	[jæ:hdytys neste]
cooling fan	**tuuletin**	[tu:letin]
battery (accumulator)	**akku**	[akku]
starter	**käynnistin**	[kæyŋistin]
ignition	**sytytys**	[sytytys]
sparking plug	**sytytystulppa**	[sytytys tulppa]

terminal (of battery)	**liitin**	[li:itin]
positive terminal	**plus**	[plus]
negative terminal	**miinus**	[mi:inus]
fuse	**varoke**	[ʋaroke]
air filter	**ilmasuodatin**	[ilma suodatin]
oil filter	**öljysuodatin**	[øl^{h}y suodatin]
fuel filter	**polttoainesuodatin**	[polttoajne suodatin]

178. Cars. Crash. Repair

car accident	**vaurio**	[ʋaurio]
road accident	**kolari**	[kolari]
to run into ...	**törmätä**	[tørmætæ]
to have an accident	**särkyä**	[særkyæ]
damage	**vaurio**	[ʋaurio]
intact (adj)	**ehjä**	[eh^{h}jæ]
to break down (vi)	**mennä rikki**	[meŋæ rikki]
towrope	**hinausvaijeri**	[hinaus ʋaijeri]
puncture	**reikä**	[rejkæ]
to have a puncture	**päästää ilma**	[pæ:stæ: ilma]
to pump up	**pumpata**	[pumpata]
pressure	**paine**	[pajne]
to check (to examine)	**tarkastaa**	[tarkasta:]
repair	**korjaus**	[kor^{h}jaus]
auto repair shop	**korjaamo**	[kor^{h}ja:mo]
spare part	**varaosa**	[ʋaraosa]
part	**osa**	[osa]
bolt	**pultti**	[pultti]
screw bolt	**ruuvi**	[ru:ʋi]
nut	**mutteri**	[mutteri]
washer	**pesin**	[pesin]
bearing	**laakeri**	[la:keri]
tube	**putki**	[putki]
gasket, washer	**välike**	[ʋælike]
cable, wire	**johdin**	[øhdin]
jack	**tunkki**	[tuŋkki]
spanner	**ruuviavain**	[ru:ʋiaʋajn]
hammer	**vasara**	[ʋasara]
pump	**pumppu**	[pumppu]
screwdriver	**ruuvitaltta**	[ru:ʋitaltta]
fire extinguisher	**sammutin**	[sammutin]
warning triangle	**heijastin**	[hejastin]
to stall (vi)	**sammua**	[sammua]
stalling	**sammutus**	[sammutus]
to be broken	**olla rikki**	[olla rikki]

to overheat (vi)	**kuumeta liikaa**	[ku:meta li:ika:]
to freeze up (pipes, etc.)	**jäätyä**	[jæ:tyæ]
to burst (vi, ab. tube)	**haljeta**	[halʰjeta]
pressure	**paine**	[pajne]
level	**taso**	[taso]
slack (~ belt)	**heikko**	[hejkko]
dent	**lommo**	[lommo]
abnormal noise (motor)	**kolina**	[kolina]
crack	**halkeama**	[halkeama]
scratch	**naarmu**	[na:rmu]

179. Cars. Road

road	**tie**	[tie]
motorway	**liikennetie**	[li:ikeŋetie]
highway	**maantie**	[ma:ntie]
direction (way)	**suunta**	[su:nta]
distance	**välimatka**	[ʋælimatka]
bridge	**silta**	[silta]
car park	**parkkipaikka**	[parkki pajkka]
square	**aukio**	[aukio]
road junction	**liittymä**	[li:ittymæ]
tunnel	**tunneli**	[tuŋeli]
petrol station	**bensiiniasema**	[bensi:ini asema]
car park	**parkkipaikka**	[parkki pajkka]
petrol pump	**bensiinipumppu**	[bensi:ini pumppu]
auto repair shop	**autotalli**	[autotalli]
to fill up	**tankata**	[taŋkata]
fuel	**polttoaine**	[polttoajne]
jerrycan	**kanisteri**	[kanisteri]
asphalt	**asfaltti**	[asfaltti]
road markings	**merkintä**	[merkintæ]
kerb	**reunakiveys**	[reunakiʋeus]
guardrail	**suojakaide**	[suojakajde]
ditch	**oja**	[oja]
roadside	**piennar**	[pæŋar]
lamppost	**pylväs**	[pylʋæs]
to drive (a car)	**ajaa**	[aja:]
to turn (~ to the left)	**kääntää**	[kæ:ntæ:]
to make a U-turn	**tehdä u-käännös**	[tehdæ u:kæ:ŋøs]
reverse	**peruutus**	[peru:tus]
to honk (vi)	**antaa äänimerkki**	[anta: æ:nimerkki]
honk (sound)	**äänimerkki**	[æ:nimerkki]
to get stuck	**juuttua**	[ju:ttua]
to spin (in mud)	**jumiutua**	[jumiutua]
to cut, to turn off	**sammuttaa**	[sammutta:]
speed	**nopeus**	[nopeus]

to exceed the speed limit	**ajaa ylinopeutta**	[ɑjɑ: ylinopeuttɑ]
to give a ticket	**sakottaa**	[sɑkottɑ:]
traffic lights	**liikennevalot**	[li:ikeŋeʋɑlot]
driving licence	**ajokortti**	[ɑøkortti]
level crossing	**ylitys**	[ylitys]
crossroads	**risteys**	[risteys]
zebra crossing	**suojatie**	[suojɑtæ]
bend, curve	**mutka**	[mutkɑ]
pedestrian precinct	**liikenteeltä suljettu alue**	[li:ikente:ltæ sul^{h}jettu ɑlue]

180. Signs

Highway Code	**liikennesäännöt**	[li:ikeŋe sæ:ŋøt]
traffic sign	**liikennemerkki**	[li:ikeŋe merkki]
overtaking	**ohitus**	[ohitus]
curve	**käännös**	[kæ:ŋøs]
U-turn	**U-käännös**	[u:kæ:ŋøs]
roundabout	**Liikenneympyrä**	[li:ikeŋe ympyrɑ]
No entry	**Kielletty ajosuunta**	[kielletty ɑøsu:ntɑ]
All vehicles prohibited	**Ajoneuvolla ajo kielletty**	[ɑønøuʋollɑ ɑø kielletty]
No overtaking	**Ohituskielto**	[ohituskielto]
No parking	**Pysäköinti kielletty**	[pysækøinti kielletty]
No stopping	**Pysäyttäminen kielletty**	[pysæjttɑminen kielletty]
dangerous curve	**jyrkkä mutka**	[yrkkæ mutkɑ]
steep descent	**jyrkkä alamäki**	[yrkkæ ɑlɑmæki]
one-way traffic	**Yksisuuntainen katu**	[yksi su:ntɑjnen kɑtu]
zebra crossing	**suojatie**	[suojɑtæ]
slippery road	**Liukas ajorata**	[liukɑs ɑørɑtɑ]
GIVE WAY	**Kärkikolmio**	[kærkikolmio]

PEOPLE. LIFE EVENTS

Life events

181. Holidays. Event

celebration, holiday	**juhla**	[juhlɑ]
national day	**kansallisjuhla**	[kɑnsɑllis juhlɑ]
public holiday	**juhlapäivä**	[juhlɑpæjʋæ]
to fete (celebrate)	**juhlia**	[juhliɑ]
event (happening)	**tapahtuma**	[tɑpɑhtumɑ]
event (organized activity)	**tilaisuus**	[tilɑjsu:s]
banquet (party)	**banketti**	[bɑŋketti]
reception (formal party)	**vastaanotto**	[ʋɑstɑ:notto]
feast	**pidot**	[pidot]
anniversary	**vuosipäivä**	[ʋuosipæjʋæ]
jubilee	**vuosipäivä**	[ʋuosipæjʋæ]
to celebrate (vt)	**pitää**	[pitæ:]
New Year	**Uusivuosi**	[u:siʋuosi]
Happy New Year!	**Hyvää uutta vuotta!**	[hyʋæ: u:ttɑ ʋuottɑ]
Christmas	**Joulu**	[øulu]
Merry Christmas!	**Hyvää joulua!**	[hyʋæ: øuluɑ]
Christmas tree	**joulukuusi**	[øuluku:si]
fireworks	**ilotulitus**	[ilotulitus]
wedding	**häät**	[hæ:t]
groom	**sulhanen**	[sulhɑnen]
bride	**morsian**	[morsiɑn]
to invite (vt)	**kutsua**	[kutsuɑ]
invitation card	**kutsu**	[kutsu]
guest	**vieras**	[ʋierɑs]
to visit (go to see)	**käydä kylässä**	[kɑ:ydɑ: kylɑ:ssɑ:]
to greet the guests	**ottaa vieraita vastaan**	[ottɑ: ʋierɑjtɑ ʋɑstɑ:n]
gift, present	**lahja**	[lɑhʰjɑ]
to give (sth as present)	**lahjoittaa**	[lɑhʰøjttɑ:]
to receive gifts	**saada lahjat**	[sɑ:dɑ lɑhʰjɑt]
bouquet (of flowers)	**kukkakimppu**	[kukkɑkimppu]
greetings (New Year ~)	**onnittelu**	[oŋittelu]
to congratulate (vt)	**onnitella**	[oŋitellɑ]
greetings card	**onnittelukortti**	[oŋittelukortti]
to send a postcard	**lähettää kortti**	[ʎæhettæ: kortti]

to get a postcard	**saada kortti**	[sa:da kortti]
toast	**maljapuhe**	[mal^{h}japuhe]
to offer (a drink, etc.)	**kestitä**	[kestitæ]
champagne	**samppanja**	[samppan^{h}ja]
to have fun	**huvitella**	[huʋitella]
fun, merriment	**ilo, hilpeys**	[ilo], [hilbeus]
joy (emotion)	**ilo**	[ilo]
dance	**tanssi**	[tanssi]
to dance (vi, vt)	**tanssia**	[tanssia]
waltz	**valssi**	[ʋalssi]
tango	**tango**	[taŋo]

182. Funerals. Burial

cemetery	**hautausmaa**	[hautausma:]
grave, tomb	**hauta**	[hauta]
cross	**risti**	[risti]
gravestone	**hautamuistomerkki**	[hautamujsto merkki]
fence	**aita**	[ajta]
chapel	**kappeli**	[kappeli]
death	**kuolema**	[kuolema]
to die (vi)	**kuolla**	[kuolla]
the deceased	**vainaja**	[ʋajnaja]
mourning	**suru**	[suru]
to bury (vt)	**haudata**	[haudata]
undertakers	**hautaustoimisto**	[hautaus tojmisto]
funeral	**hautajaiset**	[hautajajset]
wreath	**seppele**	[seppele]
coffin	**ruumisarkku**	[ru:misarkku]
hearse	**ruumisvaunut**	[ru:misʋaunut]
shroud	**kuolinvaate**	[kuolinʋa:te]
cremation urn	**uurna**	[u:rna]
crematorium	**krematorio**	[krematorio]
obituary	**muistokirjoitus**	[mujstokir^{h}øjtus]
to cry (weep)	**itkeä**	[itkeæ]
to sob (vi)	**nyyhkyttää**	[ny:hkyttæ:]

183. War. Soldiers

platoon	**joukkue**	[øukkue]
company	**komppania**	[komppania]
regiment	**rykmentti**	[rykmentti]
army	**armeija**	[a:rmeja]
division	**divisioona**	[diʋisio:na]

detachment	**joukko**	[øukko]
host (army)	**armeija**	[ɑ:rmejɑ]
soldier	**sotilas**	[sotilɑs]
officer	**upseeri**	[upse:ri]
private	**rivimies**	[riʋimies]
sergeant	**kersantti**	[kersɑntti]
lieutenant	**luutnantti**	[lu:tnɑntti]
captain	**kapteeni**	[kɑpte:ni]
major	**majuri**	[mɑjuri]
colonel	**eversti**	[eʋersti]
general	**kenraali**	[kenrɑ:li]
sailor	**merimies**	[merimies]
captain	**kapteeni**	[kɑpte:ni]
boatswain	**pursimies**	[pursimies]
artilleryman	**tykkimies**	[tykkimies]
paratrooper	**desantti**	[desɑntti]
pilot	**lentäjä**	[lentæjæ]
navigator	**perämies**	[peræmies]
mechanic	**konemestari**	[konemestɑri]
pioneer (sapper)	**pioneeri**	[pione:ri]
parachutist	**laskuvarjohyppääjä**	[lɑskuʋɑr^{h}øhyppæ:jæ]
scout	**tiedustelija**	[tiedustelijɑ]
sniper	**tarkka-ampuja**	[tɑrkkɑ ɑmpujɑ]
patrol (group)	**partio**	[pɑrtio]
to patrol (vt)	**partioida**	[pɑrtiojdɑ]
sentry, guard	**vartiomies**	[ʋɑrtiomies]
warrior	**soturi**	[soturi]
hero	**sankari**	[sɑŋkɑri]
heroine	**sankaritar**	[sɑŋkɑritɑr]
patriot	**isänmaanystävä**	[isænmɑ:nystæʋæ]
traitor	**petturi**	[petturi]
deserter	**karkuri**	[kɑrkuri]
to desert (vi)	**karata**	[kɑrɑtɑ]
mercenary	**palkkasoturi**	[pɑlkkɑsoturi]
recruit	**alokas**	[ɑlokɑs]
volunteer	**vapaaehtoinen**	[ʋɑpɑ: ehtojnen]
dead	**kaatunut**	[kɑ:tunut]
wounded (n)	**haavoittunut**	[hɑ:ʋojttunut]
prisoner of war	**vanki**	[ʋɑŋki]

184. War. Military actions. Part 1

war	**sota**	[sotɑ]
to be at war	**sotia**	[sotiɑ]

civil war	**kansalaissota**	[kansalajs sota]
treacherously (adv)	**petollisesti**	[petollisesti]
declaration of war	**julistus**	[julistus]
to declare (~ war)	**julistaa**	[julista:]
aggression	**vihaisuus**	[ʋihajsu:s]
to attack (invade)	**hyökätä**	[hyøkætæ]
to invade (vt)	**vallata**	[ʋallata]
invader	**valloittaja**	[ʋallojttaja]
conqueror	**valloittaja**	[ʋallojttaja]
defence	**puolustus**	[puolustus]
to defend (a country, etc.)	**puolustaa**	[puolusta:]
to defend oneself	**puolustautua**	[puolustautua]
enemy	**vihollinen**	[ʋihollinen]
foe, adversary	**vastustaja**	[ʋastustaja]
enemy (as adj)	**vihollisen**	[ʋihollisen]
strategy	**strategia**	[strategia]
tactics	**taktiikka**	[takti:ikka]
order	**käsky**	[kæsky]
command (order)	**komento**	[komento]
to order (vt)	**käskeä**	[kæskeæ]
mission	**tehtävä**	[tehtæʋæ]
secret (adj)	**salainen**	[salajnen]
battle, combat	**taistelu**	[tajstelu]
attack	**hyökkäys**	[hyøkkæys]
storming (assault)	**rynnäkkö**	[ryŋækkø]
to storm (vt)	**rynnätä**	[ryŋætæ]
siege (to be under ~)	**piiritys**	[pi:iritys]
offensive (n)	**hyökkäys**	[hyøkkæys]
to go on the offensive	**hyökätä**	[hyøkætæ]
retreat	**perääntyminen**	[peræ:ntyminen]
to retreat (vi)	**perääntyä**	[peræ:ntyæ]
encirclement	**saarto**	[sa:rto]
to encircle (vt)	**saarrostaa**	[sa:rrosta:]
bombing (by aircraft)	**pommitus**	[pommitus]
to drop a bomb	**heittää pommi**	[hejttæ: pommi]
to bomb (vt)	**pommittaa**	[pommitta:]
explosion	**räjähdys**	[ræjæhdys]
shot	**laukaus**	[laukaus]
to fire a shot	**laukaista**	[laukajsta]
shooting	**ammunta**	[ammunta]
to take aim (at ...)	**tähdätä**	[tæhdætæ]
to point (a gun)	**suunnata**	[su:ŋata]
to hit (the target)	**osua**	[osua]
to sink (~ a ship)	**upottaa**	[upotta:]

hole (in a ship)	**aukko**	[aukko]
to founder, to sink (vi)	**painua pohjaan**	[pajnua pohʰja:n]
front (at war)	**rintama**	[rintama]
rear (homefront)	**selusta**	[selusta]
evacuation	**evakuointi**	[eʋakuojnti]
to evacuate (vt)	**evakuoida**	[eʋakuojda]
trench	**taisteluhauta**	[tajsteluhauta]
barbed wire	**piikkilanka**	[pi:ikkilaŋka]
barrier (anti tank ~)	**este**	[este]
watchtower	**torni**	[torni]
hospital	**sotilassairaala**	[sotilas sajra:la]
to wound (vt)	**haavoittaa**	[ha:ʋojtta:]
wound	**haava**	[ha:ʋa]
wounded (n)	**haavoittunut**	[ha:ʋojttunut]
to be injured	**haavoittua**	[ha:ʋojttua]
serious (wound)	**vaikea**	[ʋajkea]

185. War. Military actions. Part 2

captivity	**sotavankeus**	[sotaʋaŋkeus]
to take captive	**ottaa vangiksi**	[otta: ʋaŋiksi]
to be in captivity	**olla sotavankeudessa**	[olla sotaʋaŋkeudessa]
to be taken prisoner	**joutua sotavankeuteen**	[øutua sotaʋaŋkeute:n]
concentration camp	**keskitysleiri**	[keskityslejri]
prisoner of war	**vanki**	[ʋaŋki]
to escape (vi)	**karata**	[karata]
to betray (vt)	**pettää**	[pettæ:]
betrayer	**pettäjä**	[pettæjæ]
betrayal	**petos**	[petos]
to execute (shoot)	**ampua**	[ampua]
execution (shooting)	**ampuminen**	[ampuminen]
equipment (uniform, etc.)	**vaatetus**	[ʋa:tetus]
shoulder board	**olkain**	[olkajn]
gas mask	**kaasunaamari**	[ka:suna:mari]
radio transmitter	**radiopuhelin**	[radiopuhelin]
cipher, code	**salakirjoitus**	[salakirʰøjtus]
conspiracy	**salatoiminta**	[salatojminta]
password	**tunnussana**	[tuŋussana]
land mine	**miina**	[mi:ina]
to mine (road, etc.)	**miinoittaa**	[mi:inojtta:]
minefield	**miinakenttä**	[mi:inakenttæ]
air-raid warning	**ilmahälytys**	[ilmaɦælytys]
alarm (warning)	**hälytys**	[ɦælytys]
signal	**signaali**	[signa:li]

signal flare	**signaaliohjus**	[signa:li ohʰjus]
headquarters	**esikunta**	[esikunta]
reconnaissance	**tiedustelu**	[tiedustelu]
situation	**tilanne**	[tilaŋe]
report	**raportti**	[raportti]
ambush	**väijytys**	[ʋæytys]
reinforcement (of army)	**lisävoimat**	[lisæʋojmat]
target	**maali**	[ma:li]
training area	**ampuma-ala**	[ampuma ala]
military exercise	**manööverit**	[manø:ʋerit]
panic	**pakokauhu**	[pakokauhu]
devastation	**rappio**	[rappio]
destruction, ruins	**hävitykset**	[ɦæʋitykset]
to destroy (vt)	**hävittää**	[ɦæʋittæ:]
to survive (vi, vt)	**jäädä eloon**	[jæ:dæ elo:n]
to disarm (vt)	**riisua aseista**	[ri:isua asejsta]
to handle (~ a gun)	**käyttää**	[kæyttæ:]
Attention!	**Asento!**	[asento]
At ease!	**Lepo!**	[lepo]
feat (of courage)	**urotyö**	[urotyø]
oath (vow)	**vala**	[ʋala]
to swear (an oath)	**vannoa**	[ʋaŋoa]
decoration (medal, etc.)	**palkinto**	[palkinto]
to award (give medal to)	**palkita**	[palkita]
medal	**mitali**	[mitali]
order (e.g. ~ of Merit)	**kunniamerkki**	[kuŋia merkki]
victory	**voitto**	[ʋojtto]
defeat	**tappio**	[tappio]
armistice	**välirauha**	[ʋæli rauha]
banner (standard)	**lippu**	[lippu]
glory (honour, fame)	**maine**	[majne]
parade	**paraati**	[para:ti]
to march (on parade)	**marssia**	[marssia]

186. Weapons

weapons	**ase**	[ase]
firearm	**ampuma-ase**	[ampuma ase]
cold weapons (knives, etc.)	**teräase**	[teræase]
chemical weapons	**kemiallinen ase**	[kemiallinen ase]
nuclear (adj)	**ydin-**	[ydin]
nuclear weapons	**ydinase**	[ydinase]
bomb	**pommi**	[pommi]
atomic bomb	**ydinpommi**	[ydinpommi]

pistol (gun)	**pistooli**	[pisto:li]
rifle	**pyssy**	[pyssy]
submachine gun	**konepistooli**	[konepisto:li]
machine gun	**konekivääri**	[konekiʋæ:ri]
muzzle	**suu**	[su:]
barrel	**piippu**	[pi:ippu]
calibre	**kaliiperi**	[kɑli:iperi]
trigger	**hana**	[hɑnɑ]
sight (aiming device)	**tähtäin**	[tæhtæjn]
magazine	**lipas**	[lipɑs]
butt (of rifle)	**perä**	[peræ]
hand grenade	**kranaatti**	[krɑnɑ:tti]
explosive	**räjähdysaine**	[ræjæhdysɑjne]
bullet	**luoti**	[luoti]
cartridge	**patruuna**	[pɑtru:nɑ]
charge	**lataus**	[lɑtɑus]
ammunition	**ampumatarvikkeet**	[ɑmpumɑ tɑrʋikke:t]
bomber (aircraft)	**pommikone**	[pommikone]
fighter	**hävittäjä**	[ɦæʋittæjæ]
helicopter	**helikopteri**	[helikopteri]
anti-aircraft gun	**ilmatorjuntatykki**	[ilmɑtor^{h}juntɑ tykki]
tank	**panssarivaunu**	[pɑnssɑriʋɑunu]
tank gun	**tykki**	[tykki]
artillery	**tykistö**	[tykistø]
cannon	**tykki**	[tykki]
to lay (a gun)	**suunnata**	[su:ŋɑtɑ]
shell (projectile)	**ammus**	[ɑmmus]
mortar bomb	**kranaatti**	[krɑnɑ:tti]
mortar	**kranaatinheitin**	[krɑnɑ:tinhejtin]
splinter (of shell)	**sirpale**	[sirpɑle]
submarine	**sukellusvene**	[sukellusʋene]
torpedo	**torpedo**	[torpedo]
missile	**raketti**	[rɑketti]
to load (gun)	**ladata**	[lɑdɑtɑ]
to shoot (vi)	**ampua**	[ɑmpuɑ]
to take aim (at ...)	**tähdätä**	[tæhdætæ]
bayonet	**pistin**	[pistin]
epee	**miekka**	[miekkɑ]
sabre (e.g. cavalry ~)	**sapeli**	[sɑpeli]
spear (weapon)	**keihäs**	[kejɦæs]
bow	**jousi**	[øusi]
arrow	**nuoli**	[nuoli]
musket	**musketti**	[musketti]
crossbow	**jalkajousi**	[jɑlkɑøusi]

187. Ancient people

primitive (prehistoric)	**alkukantainen**	[alkukantajnen]
prehistoric (adj)	**esihistoriallinen**	[esihistoriallinen]
ancient (~ civilization)	**muinainen**	[mujnajnen]
Stone Age	**kivikausi**	[kiυikausi]
Bronze Age	**pronssikausi**	[pronssikausi]
Ice Age	**jääkausi**	[jæ:kausi]
tribe	**heimo**	[hejmo]
cannibal	**ihmissyöjä**	[ihmissyøjæ]
hunter	**metsästäjä**	[metsæstæjæ]
to hunt (vi, vt)	**metsästää**	[metsæstæ:]
mammoth	**mammutti**	[mammutti]
cave	**luola**	[luola]
fire	**tuli**	[tuli]
campfire	**nuotio**	[nuotio]
rock painting	**kalliopiirros**	[kalliopi:irros]
tool (e.g. stone axe)	**työväline**	[tyøυæline]
spear	**keihäs**	[kejɦæs]
stone axe	**kivikirves**	[kiυikirυes]
to be at war	**sotia**	[sotia]
to domesticate (vt)	**kesyttää**	[kesyttæ:]
idol	**epäjumala**	[epæjumala]
to worship (vt)	**palvoa**	[palυoa]
superstition	**taikausko**	[tajkausko]
evolution	**evoluutio**	[eυolu:tio]
development	**kehitys**	[kehitys]
disappearance	**katoaminen**	[katoaminen]
to adapt oneself	**sopeutua**	[sopeutua]
archaeology	**arkeologia**	[arkeologia]
archaeologist	**arkeologi**	[arkeologi]
archaeological (adj)	**muinaistieteellinen**	[mujnajs tiete:llinen]
excavation site	**kaivaukset**	[kajυaukset]
excavations	**kaivaukset**	[kajυaukset]
find (object)	**löytö**	[løytø]
fragment	**katkelma**	[katkelma]

188. Middle Ages

people (population)	**kansa**	[kansa]
peoples	**kansat**	[kansat]
tribe	**heimo**	[hejmo]
tribes	**heimot**	[hejmot]
barbarians	**barbaarit**	[barba:rit]
Gauls	**gallialaiset**	[gallialajset]

Goths	**gootit**	[go:tit]
Slavs	**slaavit**	[slɑ:ʋit]
Vikings	**viikingit**	[ʋi:kiŋit]
Romans	**roomalaiset**	[ro:mɑlɑjset]
Roman (adj)	**roomalainen**	[ro:mɑlɑjnen]
Byzantines	**bysanttilaiset**	[bysɑnttilɑjset]
Byzantium	**Bysantti**	[bysɑntti]
Byzantine (adj)	**bysanttilainen**	[bysɑnttilɑjnen]
emperor	**keisari**	[kejsɑri]
leader, chief	**päällikkö**	[pæ:likkø]
powerful (~ king)	**voimakas**	[ʋojmɑkɑs]
king	**kuningas**	[kuniŋɑs]
ruler (sovereign)	**hallitsija**	[hɑllitsijɑ]
knight	**ritari**	[ritɑri]
knightly (adj)	**ritari-**	[ritɑri]
feudal lord	**feodaaliherra**	[feodɑ:li herrɑ]
feudal (adj)	**feodaali-**	[feodɑ:li]
vassal	**vasalli**	[ʋɑsɑlli]
duke	**herttua**	[herttuɑ]
earl	**kreivi**	[krejʋi]
baron	**paroni**	[pɑroni]
bishop	**piispa**	[pi:ispɑ]
armour	**rautavaateet**	[rɑutɑʋɑ:tte:t]
shield	**kilpi**	[kilpi]
sword	**miekka**	[miekkɑ]
visor	**visiiri**	[ʋisi:iri]
chain armour	**teräspaita**	[teræspɑjtɑ]
crusade	**ristiretki**	[ristiretki]
crusader	**ristiretkeläinen**	[ristiretkeʎæjnen]
territory	**alue**	[ɑlue]
to attack (invade)	**hyökätä**	[hyøkætæ]
to conquer (vt)	**valloittaa**	[ʋɑllojttɑ:]
to occupy (invade)	**siepata**	[siepɑtɑ]
siege (to be under ~)	**piiritys**	[pi:iritys]
besieged (adj)	**piiritetty**	[pi:iritetty]
to besiege (vt)	**piirittää**	[pi:irittæ:]
inquisition	**inkvisitio**	[iŋkʋisitio]
inquisitor	**inkvisiittori**	[iŋkʋisi:ittori]
torture	**kidutus**	[kidutus]
cruel (adj)	**julma**	[julmɑ]
heretic	**harhaoppinen**	[hɑrhɑoppinen]
heresy	**harhaoppi**	[hɑrhɑoppi]
seafaring	**merenkulku**	[mereŋkulku]
pirate	**merirosvo**	[merirosʋo]
piracy	**merirosvous**	[merirosʋous]

boarding (attack)	**hyökkäys**	[hyøkkæys]
loot, booty	**saalis**	[sɑ:lis]
treasures	**aarteet**	[ɑ:rte:t]
discovery	**avaus**	[ɑʋɑus]
to discover (new land, etc.)	**avata**	[ɑʋɑtɑ]
expedition	**retki**	[retki]
musketeer	**muskettisoturi**	[muskettisoturi]
cardinal	**kardinaali**	[kɑrdinɑ:li]
heraldry	**heraldiikka**	[herɑldi:ikkɑ]
heraldic (adj)	**heraldinen**	[herɑldinen]

189. Leader. Chief. Authorities

king	**kuningas**	[kuniŋɑs]
queen	**kuningatar**	[kuniŋɑtɑr]
royal (adj)	**kuningas-**	[kuniŋɑs]
kingdom	**kuningaskunta**	[kuniŋɑskuntɑ]
prince	**prinssi**	[prinssi]
princess	**prinsessa**	[prinsessɑ]
president	**presidentti**	[presidentti]
vice-president	**varapresidentti**	[ʋɑrɑ presidentti]
senator	**senaattori**	[senɑ:ttori]
monarch	**monarkki**	[monɑrkki]
ruler (sovereign)	**hallitsija**	[hɑllitsijɑ]
dictator	**diktaattori**	[diktɑ:ttori]
tyrant	**tyranni**	[tyrɑŋi]
magnate	**magnaatti**	[mɑgnɑ:tti]
director	**johtaja**	[øhtɑjɑ]
chief	**esimies**	[esimies]
manager (director)	**johtaja**	[øhtɑjɑ]
boss	**pomo**	[pomo]
owner	**omistaja**	[omistɑjɑ]
leader	**johtaja**	[øhtɑjɑ]
head (~ of delegation)	**johtaja**	[øhtɑjɑ]
authorities	**viranomaiset**	[ʋirɑnomɑjset]
superiors	**päällystö**	[pæ:llystø]
governor	**kuvernööri**	[kuʋernø:ri]
consul	**konsuli**	[konsuli]
diplomat	**diplomaatti**	[diplomɑ:tti]
mayor	**kaupunginjohtaja**	[kɑupuŋin øhtɑjɑ]
sheriff	**seriffi**	[seriffi]
emperor	**keisari**	[kejsɑri]
tsar, czar	**tsaari**	[tsɑ:ri]
Pharaoh	**farao**	[fɑrɑo]
khan	**kaani**	[kɑ:ni]

190. Road. Way. Directions

road	**tie**	[tie]
way (direction)	**tie**	[tie]
highway	**maantie**	[mɑ:ntie]
motorway	**liikennetie**	[li:ikeŋetie]
trunk road	**kansallistie**	[kɑnsɑllistie]
main road	**päätie**	[pæ:tie]
dirt road	**kylätie**	[kyʎætie]
pathway	**polku**	[polku]
footpath	**polku**	[polku]
Where?	**Missä?**	[missæ]
Where (to)?	**Mihin?**	[mihin]
Where ... from?	**Mistä?**	[mistæ]
direction (way)	**suunta**	[su:ntɑ]
to point (~ the way)	**osoittaa**	[osojttɑ:]
to the left	**vasemmalle**	[ʋɑsemɑlle]
to the right	**oikealle**	[ojkeɑlle]
straight ahead (adv)	**suoraan**	[suorɑ:n]
back (e.g. to turn ~)	**takaisin**	[tɑkɑjsin]
bend, curve	**mutka**	[mutkɑ]
to turn (~ to the left)	**kääntää**	[kæ:ntæ:]
to make a U-turn	**tehdä u-käännös**	[tehdæ u:kæ:ŋøs]
to be visible	**näkyä**	[ɲækyæ]
to appear (come into view)	**ilmestyä**	[ilmestyæ]
stop, halt (in journey)	**pysäytys**	[pysæytys]
to rest, to halt (vi)	**levätä**	[leʋætæ]
rest (pause)	**lepo**	[lepo]
to lose one's way	**eksyä**	[eksyæ]
to lead to ... (ab. road)	**viedä**	[ʋiedæ]
to arrive at ...	**tulla kohti**	[tullɑ kohti]
stretch (of road)	**osa**	[osɑ]
asphalt	**asfaltti**	[ɑsfɑltti]
kerb	**bordyyri**	[bordy:ri]
ditch	**oja**	[ojɑ]
manhole	**luukku**	[lu:kku]
roadside	**piennar**	[pæŋɑr]
pit, pothole	**kuoppa**	[kuoppɑ]
to go (on foot)	**mennä**	[meŋæ]
to overtake (vt)	**ohittaa**	[ohittɑ:]
step (footstep)	**askel**	[ɑskel]
on foot (adv)	**jalkaisin**	[jɑlkɑjsin]

to block (road)	**estää pääsy**	[estæ: pæ:sy]
boom barrier	**puomi**	[puomi]
dead end	**umpikuja**	[umpikuja]

191. Breaking the law. Criminals. Part 1

bandit	**rosvo**	[rosʋo]
crime	**rikos**	[rikos]
criminal (person)	**rikollinen**	[rikollinen]
thief	**varas**	[ʋaras]
to steal (vi, vt)	**varastella**	[ʋarastella]
stealing, theft	**varkaus**	[ʋarkaus]
to kidnap (vt)	**ryöstää ihmisen**	[ryøstæ: ihmisen]
kidnapping	**ihmisryöstö**	[ihmisryøstø]
kidnapper	**ihmisryöstäjä**	[ihmisryøstæjæ]
ransom	**lunastus**	[lunastus]
to demand ransom	**vaatia lunastus**	[ʋa:tia lunastus]
to rob (vt)	**ryöstää**	[ryøstæ:]
robbery	**ryöstö**	[ryøstø]
robber	**ryöstäjä**	[ryøstæjæ]
to extort (vt)	**kiristää**	[kiristæ:]
extortionist	**kiristäjä**	[kiristæjæ]
extortion	**kiristys**	[kiristys]
to murder, to kill	**murhata**	[murhata]
murder	**murha**	[murha]
murderer	**murhaaja**	[murha:ja]
gunshot	**laukaus**	[laukaus]
to fire a shot	**laukaista**	[laukajsta]
to shoot down	**ampua**	[ampua]
to shoot (vi)	**ampua**	[ampua]
shooting	**ammunta**	[ammunta]
incident (fight, etc.)	**tapahtuma**	[tapahtuma]
fight, brawl	**tappelu**	[tappelu]
victim	**uhri**	[uhri]
to damage (vt)	**vaurioittaa**	[ʋauriojtta:]
damage	**vahinko**	[ʋahiŋko]
dead body	**ruumis**	[ru:mis]
grave (~ crime)	**törkeä**	[tørkeæ]
to attack (vt)	**hyökätä**	[hyøkætæ]
to beat (dog, person)	**lyödä**	[lyødæ]
to beat up	**piestä**	[piestæ]
to take (snatch)	**ottaa pois**	[otta: pojs]
to stab to death	**teurastaa**	[teurasta:]
to maim (vt)	**runnella**	[ruŋella]

to wound (vt)	**haavoittaa**	[hɑ:ʋojttɑ:]
blackmail	**kiristys**	[kiristys]
to blackmail (vt)	**kiristää**	[kiristæ:]
blackmailer	**kiristäjä**	[kiristæjæ]
protection racket	**kiristys**	[kiristys]
racketeer	**kiristäjä**	[kiristæjæ]
gangster	**gangsteri**	[gɑŋsteri]
mafia	**mafia**	[mɑfiɑ]
pickpocket	**taskuvaras**	[tɑskuʋɑrɑs]
burglar	**murtovaras**	[murtoʋɑrɑs]
smuggling	**salakuljetus**	[sɑlɑkulʰjetus]
smuggler	**salakuljettaja**	[sɑlɑkulʰjettɑjɑ]
forgery	**väärennös**	[ʋæ:reŋøs]
to forge (counterfeit)	**väärentää**	[ʋæ:rentæ:]
fake (forged)	**väärennetty**	[ʋæ:reŋetty]

192. Breaking the law. Criminals. Part 2

rape	**raiskaus**	[rɑjskɑus]
to rape (vt)	**raiskata**	[rɑjskɑtɑ]
rapist	**raiskaaja**	[rɑjskɑ:jɑ]
maniac	**maanikko**	[mɑ:nikko]
prostitute (fem.)	**prostituoitu**	[prostituojtu]
prostitution	**prostituutio**	[prostitu:tio]
pimp	**sutenööri**	[sutenø:ri]
drug addict	**narkomaani**	[nɑrkomɑ:ni]
drug dealer	**huumekauppias**	[hu:me kɑuppiɑs]
to blow up (bomb)	**räjäyttää**	[ræjæyttæ:]
explosion	**räjähdys**	[ræjæhdys]
to set fire	**sytyttää**	[sytyttæ:]
incendiary (arsonist)	**palon sytyttäjä**	[pɑlon sytyttæjæ]
terrorism	**terrorismi**	[terrorismi]
terrorist	**terroristi**	[terroristi]
hostage	**panttivanki**	[pɑntti ʋɑŋki]
to swindle (vt)	**pettää**	[pettæ:]
swindle	**petos**	[petos]
swindler	**huijari**	[huijɑri]
to bribe (vt)	**lahjoa**	[lɑhʰøɑ]
bribery	**lahjonta**	[lɑhʰøntɑ]
bribe	**lahjus**	[lɑhʰjus]
poison	**myrkky**	[myrkky]
to poison (vt)	**myrkyttää**	[myrkyttæ:]
to poison oneself	**myrkyttää itsensä**	[myrkyttæ: itsensɑ]
suicide (act)	**itsemurha**	[itsemurhɑ]

suicide (person)	**itsemurhaaja**	[itsemurha:ja]
to threaten (vt)	**uhata**	[uhata]
threat	**uhkaus**	[uhkaus]
to make an attempt	**tehdä murhayritys**	[tehdæ murhayritys]
attempt (attack)	**murhayritys**	[murhayritys]
to steal (a car)	**viedä**	[ʋiedæ]
to hijack (a plane)	**kaapata**	[ka:pata]
revenge	**kosto**	[kosto]
to avenge (vt)	**kostaa**	[kosta:]
to torture (vt)	**kiduttaa**	[kidutta:]
torture	**kidutus**	[kidutus]
to torment (vt)	**piinata**	[pi:inata]
pirate	**merirosvo**	[merirosʋo]
hooligan	**huligaani**	[huliga:ni]
armed (adj)	**aseellinen**	[ase:llinen]
violence	**väkivalta**	[ʋækiʋalta]
spying (n)	**vakoilu**	[ʋakojlu]
to spy (vi)	**vakoilla**	[ʋakojlla]

193. Police. Law. Part 1

justice	**oikeudenmukaisuus**	[ojkeudenmukajsu:s]
court (court room)	**oikeus**	[ojkeus]
judge	**tuomari**	[tuomari]
jurors	**valamiehistö**	[ʋalamiehistø]
jury trial	**valamiesoikeus**	[ʋalamiesojkeus]
to judge (vt)	**käsitellä oikeudessa**	[kæsiteʎæ ojkeudessa]
lawyer, barrister	**asianajaja**	[asianajaja]
accused	**syytetty**	[sy:tetty]
dock	**syytettyjen penkki**	[sy:tettyjen peŋkki]
charge	**syyte**	[sy:te]
accused	**syytetty**	[sy:tetty]
sentence	**tuomio**	[tuomio]
to sentence (vt)	**tuomita**	[tuomita]
guilty (culprit)	**syypää**	[sy:pæ:]
to punish (vt)	**rangaista**	[raŋajsta]
punishment	**rangaistus**	[raŋajstus]
fine (penalty)	**sakko**	[sakko]
life imprisonment	**elinkautinen vankeustuomio**	[eliŋkautinen ʋaŋkeustuomio]
death penalty	**kuolemanrangaistus**	[kuoleman raŋajstus]
electric chair	**sähkötuoli**	[sæhkøtuoli]
gallows	**hirsipuu**	[hirsipu:]

to execute (vt)	**teloittaa**	[telojtta:]
execution	**teloitus**	[telojtus]
prison, jail	**vankila**	[ʋaŋkila]
cell	**selli**	[selli]
escort	**saattovartio**	[sa:ttoʋartio]
prison officer	**valvoja**	[ʋalʋoja]
prisoner	**vanki**	[ʋaŋki]
handcuffs	**käsiraudat**	[kæsiraudat]
to handcuff (vt)	**panna käsiraudat**	[paŋa kæsiraudat]
prison break	**karkaus**	[karkaus]
to break out (vi)	**karata**	[karata]
to disappear (vi)	**kadota**	[kadota]
to release (from prison)	**päästää vapaaksi**	[pæ:stæ: ʋapa:ksi]
amnesty	**armahdus**	[armahdus]
police	**poliisi**	[poli:isi]
policeman	**poliisi**	[poli:isi]
police station	**poliisiasema**	[poli:isi asema]
truncheon	**kumipamppu**	[kumipamppu]
loudspeaker	**megafoni**	[megafoni]
patrol car	**vartioauto**	[ʋartio auto]
siren	**sireeni**	[sire:ni]
to turn on the siren	**käynnistää sireeni**	[kæyŋistæ: sire:ni]
siren call	**sireenin ulvonta**	[sire:nin ulʋonta]
crime scene	**tapahtumapaikka**	[tapahtuma pajkka]
witness	**todistaja**	[todistaja]
freedom	**vapaus**	[ʋapaus]
accomplice	**rikoskumppani**	[rikos kumppani]
to flee (vi)	**piileksiä**	[pi:ileksiæ]
trace (to leave a ~)	**jälki**	[jælki]

194. Police. Law. Part 2

search (for a criminal)	**etsintä**	[etsintæ]
to look for ...	**etsiä**	[etsiæ]
suspicion	**epäily**	[epæjly]
suspicious (suspect)	**epäilyttävä**	[epæjlyttæʋæ]
to stop (cause to halt)	**pysäyttää**	[pysæyttæ:]
to detain (keep in custody)	**pidättää**	[pidættæ:]
case (lawsuit)	**asia**	[asia]
investigation	**tutkinta**	[tutkinta]
detective	**etsivä**	[etsiʋæ]
investigator	**rikostutkija**	[rikos tutkija]
version	**versio**	[ʋersio]
motive	**syy**	[sy:]
interrogation	**kuulustelu**	[ku:lustelu]

to interrogate (vt) **kuulustella** [ku:lustellɑ]
to question (vt) **kuulustella** [ku:lustellɑ]
checking (police ~) **tarkastus** [tɑrkɑstus]

round-up **ratsia** [rɑtsiɑ]
search (~ warrant) **etsintä** [etsintæ]
chase (pursuit) **takaa-ajo** [tɑkɑ: ɑø]
to pursue, to chase **takaa-ajaja** [tɑkɑ: ɑjɑjæ]
to track (a criminal) **vakoilla** [ʋɑkojllɑ]

arrest **vangitseminen** [ʋɑŋitseminen]
to arrest (sb) **vangita** [ʋɑŋitɑ]
to catch (thief, etc.) **ottaa kiinni** [ottɑ: ki:iŋi]
capture **kiinniotto** [ki:iŋiotto]

document **asiakirja** [ɑsiɑkirʰæ]
proof (evidence) **todiste** [todiste]
to prove (vt) **todistaa** [todistɑ:]
footprint **jälki** [jælki]
fingerprints **sormenjäljet** [sormenjælʰjet]
piece of evidence **todiste** [todiste]

alibi **alibi** [ɑlibi]
innocent (not guilty) **syytön** [sy:tøn]
injustice (unjust act) **epäoikeudenmukaisuus** [epæojkeuden mukɑjsu:s]
unjust, unfair (adj) **epäoikeudenmukainen** [epæojkeuden mukɑjnen]

crime (adj) **rikosuutiset** [rikosu:tiset]
to confiscate (vt) **takavarikoida** [tɑkɑʋɑrikojdɑ]
drug (illegal substance) **huume** [hu:me]
weapon, gun **ase** [ɑse]
to disarm (vt) **riisua aseista** [ri:isuɑ ɑsejstɑ]
to order (command) **käskeä** [kæskeæ]
to disappear (vi) **kadota** [kɑdotɑ]

law **laki** [lɑki]
legal (adj) **laillinen** [lɑ:jlinen]
illegal (adj) **laiton** [lɑjton]

responsibility **vastuu** [ʋɑstu:]
responsible (adj) **vastuunalainen** [ʋɑstu:nɑlɑjnen]

NATURE

The Earth. Part 1

195. Outer space

cosmos	**avaruus**	[avaru:s]
space (as adj)	**avaruus-**	[avaru:s]
outer space	**avaruus**	[avaru:s]
world	**maailma**	[ma:ilma]
universe	**maailmankaikkeus**	[ma:ilman kajkkeus]
galaxy	**galaksi**	[galaksi]
star	**tähti**	[tæhti]
constellation	**tähtikuvio**	[tæhtikuvio]
planet	**planeetta**	[plane:tta]
satellite	**satelliitti**	[satelli:itti]
meteorite	**meteoriitti**	[meteori:itti]
comet	**pyrstötähti**	[pyrstøtæhti]
asteroid	**asteroidi**	[asterojdi]
orbit	**kiertorata**	[kiertorata]
to rotate (vi)	**kiertää**	[kærtæ:]
atmosphere	**ilmakehä**	[ilmakeɦæ]
the Sun	**Aurinko**	[auriŋko]
solar system	**Aurinkokunta**	[auriŋko kunta]
solar eclipse	**auringonpimennys**	[auriŋon pimeŋys]
the Earth	**Maa**	[ma:]
the Moon	**Kuu**	[ku:]
Mars	**Mars**	[mars]
Venus	**Venus**	[venus]
Jupiter	**Jupiter**	[jupiter]
Saturn	**Saturnus**	[saturnus]
Mercury	**Merkurius**	[merkurius]
Uranus	**Uranus**	[uranus]
Neptune	**Neptunus**	[neptunus]
Pluto	**Pluto**	[pluto]
Milky Way	**Linnunrata**	[liŋunrata]
Great Bear	**Otava**	[otava]
North Star	**Pohjantähti**	[poh[h]jantæhti]
Martian	**marsilainen**	[marsilajnen]
extraterrestrial	**avaruusolio**	[avaru:soʎ[j]o]

alien	**humanoidi**	[humanojdi]
flying saucer	**lentävä lautanen**	[lentæʋæ lautanen]
spaceship	**avaruusalus**	[aʋaru:salus]
space station	**avaruusasema**	[aʋaru:sasema]
blast-off	**startti**	[startti]
engine	**moottori**	[mo:ttori]
nozzle	**suutin**	[su:tin]
fuel	**polttoaine**	[polttoajne]
cockpit, flight deck	**hytti**	[hytti]
aerial	**antenni**	[anteŋi]
porthole	**ikkuna**	[ikkuna]
solar battery	**aurinkokennosto**	[auriŋkokeŋosto]
spacesuit	**avaruuspuku**	[aʋaru:spuku]
weightlessness	**painottomuus**	[pajnottomu:s]
oxygen	**happi**	[happi]
docking (in space)	**telakointi**	[telakojnti]
to dock (vi, vt)	**tehdä telakointi**	[tehdæ telakojnti]
observatory	**observatorio**	[obserʋatorio]
telescope	**teleskooppi**	[telesko:ppi]
to observe (vt)	**seurata**	[seurata]
to explore (vt)	**tutkia**	[tutkia]

196. The Earth

the Earth	**Maa**	[ma:]
globe (the Earth)	**maapallo**	[ma:pallo]
planet	**planeetta**	[plane:tta]
atmosphere	**ilmakehä**	[ilmakeɦæ]
geography	**maantiede**	[ma:ntiede]
nature	**luonto**	[luonto]
globe (table ~)	**karttapallo**	[karttapallo]
map	**kartta**	[kartta]
atlas	**atlas**	[atlas]
Europe	**Eurooppa**	[euro:ppa]
Asia	**Aasia**	[a:sia]
Africa	**Afrikka**	[afrikka]
Australia	**Australia**	[australia]
America	**Amerikka**	[amerikka]
North America	**Pohjois-Amerikka**	[pohʰøjs amerikka]
South America	**Etelä-Amerikka**	[eteʎæ amerikka]
Antarctica	**Etelämanner**	[eteʎæmaŋer]
the Arctic	**Arktis**	[arktis]

197. Cardinal directions

north	**pohjola**	[poh^{h}øla]
to the north	**pohjoiseen**	[poh^{h}øjse:n]
in the north	**pohjoisessa**	[poh^{h}øjsessa]
northern (adj)	**pohjoinen**	[poh^{h}øjnen]
south	**etelä**	[eteʎæ]
to the south	**etelään**	[etelæ:n]
in the south	**etelässä**	[eteʎæssæ]
southern (adj)	**eteläinen**	[eteʎæjnen]
west	**länsi**	[ʎænsi]
to the west	**länteen**	[ʎænte:n]
in the west	**lännessä**	[ʎæŋessæ]
western (adj)	**läntinen**	[ʎæntinen]
east	**itä**	[itæ]
to the east	**itään**	[itæ:n]
in the east	**idässä**	[idæssæ]
eastern (adj)	**itäinen**	[itæjnen]

198. Sea. Ocean

sea	**meri**	[meri]
ocean	**valtameri**	[ʋaltameri]
gulf (bay)	**lahti**	[lahti]
straits	**salmi**	[salmi]
dry land	**maa**	[ma:]
continent (mainland)	**manner**	[maŋer]
island	**saari**	[sa:ri]
peninsula	**niemimaa**	[niemima:]
archipelago	**saaristo**	[sa:risto]
bay	**poukama**	[poukama]
harbour	**satama**	[satama]
lagoon	**laguuni**	[lagu:ni]
cape	**niemi**	[niemi]
atoll	**atolli**	[atolli]
reef	**riutta**	[riutta]
coral	**koralli**	[koralli]
coral reef	**koralliriutta**	[koralli riutta]
deep (adj)	**syvä**	[syʋæ]
depth (deep water)	**syvyys**	[syʋy:s]
abyss	**kuilu**	[kujlu]
trench (e.g. Mariana ~)	**vajoama**	[ʋaøama]
current, stream	**virta**	[ʋirta]
to surround (bathe)	**huuhdella**	[hu:hdella]
shore	**merenranta**	[merenranta]

coast	**rannikko**	[raŋikko]
high tide	**vuoksi**	[ʋuoksi]
low tide	**pakovesi**	[pakoʋesi]
sandbank	**matalikko**	[matalikko]
bottom	**pohja**	[poh^{h}ja]
wave	**aalto**	[a:lto]
crest (~ of a wave)	**aallonharja**	[a:llonhar^{h}ja]
froth (foam)	**vaahto**	[ʋa:hto]
storm	**myrsky**	[myrsky]
hurricane	**hirmumyrsky**	[hirmumyrsky]
tsunami	**tsunami**	[ʦunami]
calm (dead ~)	**tyyni**	[ty:yni]
quiet, calm (adj)	**rauhallinen**	[rauhallinen]
pole	**napa**	[napa]
polar (adj)	**napa**	[napa]
latitude	**leveys**	[leʋeys]
longitude	**pituus**	[pitu:s]
parallel	**leveyspiiri**	[leʋeyspi:iri]
equator	**päiväntasaaja**	[pæjʋæntasa:ja]
sky	**taivas**	[tajʋas]
horizon	**taivaanranta**	[tajʋa:nranta]
air	**ilma**	[ilma]
lighthouse	**majakka**	[majakka]
to dive (vi)	**sukeltaa**	[sukelta:]
to sink (ab. boat)	**upota**	[upota]
treasures	**aarteet**	[a:rte:t]

199. Seas & Oceans names

Atlantic Ocean	**Atlantin valtameri**	[atlantin ʋalta meri]
Indian Ocean	**Intian valtameri**	[intian ʋalta meri]
Pacific Ocean	**Tyynimeri**	[ty:ni meri]
Arctic Ocean	**Pohjoinen jäämeri**	[poh^{h}øjnen jæ: meri]
Black Sea	**Mustameri**	[musta meri]
Red Sea	**Punainenmeri**	[punajnen meri]
Yellow Sea	**Keltainenmeri**	[keltajnen meri]
White Sea	**Vienanmeri**	[ʋjenanmeri]
Caspian Sea	**Kaspianmeri**	[kaspian meri]
Dead Sea	**Kuollutmeri**	[kuollut meri]
Mediterranean Sea	**Välimeri**	[ʋæli meri]
Aegean Sea	**Egeanmeri**	[egean meri]
Adriatic Sea	**Adrianmeri**	[adrian meri]
Arabian Sea	**Arabianmeri**	[arabian meri]
Sea of Japan	**Japaninmeri**	[japanin meri]

Bering Sea	**Beringinmeri**	[beriŋin meri]
South China Sea	**Etelä-Kiinan meri**	[eteʎæ ki:inɑn meri]
Coral Sea	**Korallimeri**	[korɑlli meri]
Tasman Sea	**Tasmaninmeri**	[tɑsmɑnin meri]
Caribbean Sea	**Karibianmeri**	[kɑribiɑn meri]
Barents Sea	**Barentsinmeri**	[bɑrentsin meri]
Kara Sea	**Karanmeri**	[kɑrɑn meri]
North Sea	**Pohjanmeri**	[pohʰjɑn meri]
Baltic Sea	**Itämeri**	[itæ meri]
Norwegian Sea	**Norjanmeri**	[norʰjɑn meri]

200. Mountains

mountain	**vuori**	[ʋuori]
mountain range	**vuorijono**	[ʋuoriøno]
mountain ridge	**vuorenharjanne**	[ʋuoren hɑrʰjɑŋe]
summit, top	**huippu**	[hujppu]
peak	**vuorenhuippu**	[ʋuorenhujppu]
foot (of mountain)	**juuri**	[ju:ri]
slope (mountainside)	**rinne**	[riŋe]
volcano	**tulivuori**	[tuliʋuori]
active volcano	**toimiva tulivuori**	[tojmiʋɑ tuliʋuori]
dormant volcano	**sammunut tulivuori**	[sɑmmunut tuliʋuori]
eruption	**purkaus**	[purkɑus]
crater	**kraatteri**	[krɑ:teri]
magma	**magma**	[mɑgmɑ]
lava	**laava**	[lɑ:ʋɑ]
molten (~ lava)	**hehkuva**	[hehkuʋɑ]
canyon	**rotko**	[rotko]
gorge	**rotko**	[rotko]
crevice	**halkeama**	[hɑlkeɑmɑ]
pass, col	**sola**	[solɑ]
plateau	**ylätasanko**	[yʎætɑsɑŋko]
cliff	**kallio**	[kɑllio]
hill	**mäki**	[mæki]
glacier	**jäätikkö**	[jæ:tikkø]
waterfall	**vesiputous**	[ʋesiputous]
geyser	**geisir**	[gejsir]
lake	**järvi**	[jærʋi]
plain	**tasanko**	[tɑsɑŋko]
landscape	**maisema**	[mɑjsemɑ]
echo	**kaiku**	[kɑjku]
alpinist	**vuorikiipeilijä**	[ʋuoriki:ipejlijæ]
rock climber	**vuorikiipeilijä**	[ʋuoriki:ipejlijæ]

to conquer (in climbing)	**valloittaa**	[ʋallojtta:]
climb (an easy ~)	**nousu**	[nousu]

201. Mountains names

Alps	**Alpit**	[alpit]
Mont Blanc	**Mont Blanc**	[mont blaŋk]
Pyrenees	**Pyreneet**	[pyrine:t]
Carpathians	**Karpaatit**	[karpa:tit]
Ural Mountains	**Ural**	[ural]
Caucasus	**Kaukasus**	[kaukasus]
Elbrus	**Elbrus**	[elbrus]
Altai	**Altai**	[altaj]
Tien Shan	**Tianshan**	[tian ʃan]
Pamir Mountains	**Pamir**	[pamir]
Himalayas	**Himalaja**	[himalaja]
Everest	**Mount Everest**	[maunt eʋerest]
Andes	**Andit**	[andit]
Kilimanjaro	**Kilimanjaro**	[kiliman^{h}jaro]

202. Rivers

river	**joki**	[øki]
spring (natural source)	**lähde**	[ʎæhde]
riverbed	**uoma**	[uoma]
basin	**joen vesistö**	[øen ʋesistø]
to flow into …	**laskea**	[laskea]
tributary	**sivujoki**	[siʋuøki]
bank (of river)	**ranta**	[ranta]
current, stream	**virta**	[ʋirta]
downstream (adv)	**myötävirtaan**	[myøtæʋirta:n]
upstream (adv)	**ylävirtaan**	[yʎæʋirta:n]
inundation	**tulva**	[tulʋa]
flooding	**kevättulva**	[keʋættulʋa]
to overflow (vi)	**tulvia**	[tulʋia]
to flood (vt)	**tulvia**	[tulʋia]
shallows (shoal)	**matalikko**	[matalikko]
rapids	**koski**	[koski]
dam	**pato**	[pato]
canal	**kanava**	[kanaʋa]
reservoir (artificial lake)	**vedensäiliö**	[ʋedensæjliø]
sluice, lock	**sulku**	[sulku]
water body (pond, etc.)	**vesistö**	[ʋesistø]
swamp, bog	**suo**	[suo]

marsh	**hete**	[hete]
whirlpool	**pyörre**	[pyørre]
stream (brook)	**puro**	[puro]
drinking (ab. water)	**juoma-**	[yoma]
fresh (~ water)	**makea**	[makea]
ice	**jää**	[jæ:]
to ice over	**jäätyä**	[jæ:tyæ]

203. Rivers names

Seine	**Seine**	[sejne]
Loire	**Loire**	[lojre]
Thames	**Thames**	[thames]
Rhine	**Rein**	[rejn]
Danube	**Tonava**	[tonaʋa]
Volga	**Volga**	[ʋolga]
Don	**Don**	[don]
Lena	**Lena**	[lena]
Yellow River	**Keltainenjoki**	[keltajnenøki]
Yangtze	**Jangtse**	[jaŋdse]
Mekong	**Mekong**	[mekoŋ]
Ganges	**Ganges**	[gaŋes]
Nile	**Niili**	[ni:ili]
Congo	**Kongo**	[koŋo]
Okavango	**Okavango**	[okaʋaŋo]
Zambezi	**Sambesi**	[sambesi]
Limpopo	**Limpopojoki**	[limpopoøki]
Mississippi River	**Mississippi**	[mississippi]

204. Forest

forest	**metsä**	[metsæ]
forest (as adj)	**metsä-**	[metsæ]
thick forest	**tiheikkö**	[tihejkkø]
grove	**lehto**	[lehto]
clearing	**aho**	[aho]
thicket	**tiheikkö**	[tihejkkø]
scrubland	**pensaikko**	[pensajkko]
footpath	**polku**	[polku]
gully	**rotko**	[rotko]
tree	**puu**	[pu:]
leaf	**lehti**	[lehti]

leaves	**lehdistö**	[lehdistø]
falling leaves	**lehdenlähtö**	[lehdenʎæhtø]
to fall (ab. leaves)	**karista**	[karista]
top (of the tree)	**latva**	[latʋa]
branch	**oksa**	[oksa]
bough	**oksa**	[oksa]
bud (on shrub, tree)	**silmu**	[silmu]
needle (of pine tree)	**neulanen**	[neulanen]
fir cone	**käpy**	[kæpy]
hollow (in a tree)	**ontelo**	[ontelo]
nest	**pesä**	[pesæ]
burrow (animal hole)	**kolo**	[kolo]
trunk	**runko**	[ruŋko]
root	**juuri**	[ju:ri]
bark	**kuori**	[kuori]
moss	**sammal**	[sammal]
to uproot (vt)	**juuria**	[ju:ria]
to chop down	**hakata**	[hakata]
to deforest (vt)	**hakata**	[hakata]
tree stump	**kanto**	[kanto]
campfire	**nuotio**	[nuotio]
forest fire	**palo**	[palo]
to extinguish (vt)	**sammuttaa**	[sammutta:]
forest ranger	**metsänvartija**	[metsænʋartija]
protection	**suojelu**	[suojelu]
to protect (~ nature)	**suojella**	[suojella]
poacher	**salametsästäjä**	[salametsæstæjæ]
trap (e.g. bear ~)	**raudat**	[raudat]
to pick (mushrooms)	**sienestää**	[sienestæ:]
to pick (berries)	**marjastaa**	[marʰjasta:]
to lose one's way	**eksyä**	[eksyæ]

205. Natural resources

natural resources	**luonnonvarat**	[luoŋonʋarat]
minerals	**mineraalit**	[minera:lit]
deposits	**esiintymä**	[esi:intymæ]
field (e.g. oilfield)	**esiintymä**	[esi:intymæ]
to mine (extract)	**louhia**	[louhia]
mining (extraction)	**kaivostoiminta**	[kajʋostojminta]
ore	**malmi**	[malmi]
mine (e.g. for coal)	**kaivos**	[kajʋos]
mine shaft, pit	**kaivos**	[kajʋos]
miner	**kaivosmies**	[kajʋosmies]
gas	**kaasu**	[ka:su]
gas pipeline	**kaasujohto**	[ka:suøhto]

oil (petroleum)	**öljy**	[ølʰy]
oil pipeline	**öljyjohto**	[ølʰy øhto]
oil rig	**öljynporausreikä**	[ølʰyn poraus rejkæ]
derrick	**öljynporaustorni**	[ølʰyn poraus torni]
tanker	**tankkilaiva**	[taŋkki lajʋa]
sand	**hiekka**	[hiekka]
limestone	**kalkkikivi**	[kalkkikiʋi]
gravel	**sora**	[sora]
peat	**turve**	[turʋe]
clay	**savi**	[saʋi]
coal	**hiili**	[hi:ili]
iron	**rauta**	[rauta]
gold	**kulta**	[kulta]
silver	**hopea**	[hopea]
nickel	**nikkeli**	[nikkeli]
copper	**kupari**	[kupari]
zinc	**sinkki**	[siŋkki]
manganese	**mangaani**	[maŋa:ni]
mercury	**elohopea**	[elo hopea]
lead	**lyijy**	[lyiy]
mineral	**mineraali**	[minera:li]
crystal	**kristalli**	[kristalli]
marble	**marmori**	[marmori]
uranium	**uraani**	[ura:ni]

The Earth. Part 2

206. Weather

weather	**sää**	[sæ:]
weather forecast	**sääennuste**	[sæ:eŋuste]
temperature	**lämpötila**	[ʎæmpøtila]
thermometer	**lämpömittari**	[ʎæmpømittari]
barometer	**ilmapuntari**	[ilmapuntari]
humidity	**kosteus**	[kosteus]
heat (of summer)	**helle**	[helle]
hot (torrid)	**kuuma**	[ku:ma]
it's hot	**on kuumaa**	[on ku:ma:]
it's warm	**on lämmintä**	[on ʎæmmintæ]
warm (moderately hot)	**lämmin**	[ʎæmmin]
it's cold	**on kylmää**	[on kylmæ:]
cold (adj)	**kylmä**	[kylmæ]
sun	**aurinko**	[auriŋko]
to shine (vi)	**paistaa**	[pajsta:]
sunny (day)	**aurinkoinen**	[auriŋkojnen]
to come up (vi)	**nousta**	[nousta]
to set (vi)	**laskea**	[laskea]
cloud	**pilvi**	[piʋi]
cloudy (adj)	**pilvinen**	[piʋinen]
rain cloud	**pilvi**	[piʋi]
somber (gloomy)	**pilvinen**	[piʋinen]
rain	**sade**	[sade]
it's raining	**sataa vettä**	[sata: ʋettæ]
rainy (day)	**sateinen**	[satejnen]
to drizzle (vi)	**vihmoa**	[ʋihmoa]
pouring rain	**kaatosade**	[ka:tosade]
downpour	**rankka sade**	[raŋkkasade]
heavy (e.g. ~ rain)	**rankka**	[raŋkka]
puddle	**lätäkkö**	[ʎætækkø]
to get wet (in rain)	**kastua**	[kastua]
fog (mist)	**sumu**	[sumu]
foggy	**sumuinen**	[sumujnen]
snow	**lumi**	[lumi]
it's snowing	**sataa lunta**	[sata: lunta]

207. Severe weather. Natural disasters

thunderstorm	**ukkonen**	[ukkonen]
lightning (~ strike)	**salama**	[salama]
to flash (vi)	**kimaltaa**	[kimalta:]
thunder	**ukkonen**	[ukkonen]
to thunder (vi)	**jyristä**	[yristæ]
it's thundering	**ukkonen jyrisee**	[ukkonen yrise:]
hail	**raesade**	[raesade]
it's hailing	**sataa rakeita**	[sata: rakejta]
to flood (vt)	**upottaa**	[upotta:]
flood, inundation	**tulva**	[tulʋa]
earthquake	**maanjäristys**	[ma:njaristys]
tremor, quake	**maantärähdys**	[ma:ntæræhdys]
epicentre	**keskus**	[keskus]
eruption	**purkaus**	[purkaus]
lava	**laava**	[la:ʋa]
twister	**pyörre**	[pyørre]
tornado	**tornado**	[tornado]
typhoon	**pyörremyrsky**	[pyørremyrsky]
hurricane	**hirmumyrsky**	[hirmumyrsky]
storm	**myrsky**	[myrsky]
tsunami	**tsunami**	[t͡sunami]
cyclone	**sykloni**	[sykloni]
bad weather	**koiran ilma**	[kojran ilma]
fire (accident)	**palo**	[palo]
disaster	**katastrofi**	[katastrofi]
meteorite	**meteoriitti**	[meteori:itti]
avalanche	**lumivyöry**	[lumiʋyøry]
snowslide	**lumivyöry**	[lumiʋyøry]
blizzard	**pyry**	[pyry]
snowstorm	**pyry**	[pyry]

208. Noises. Sounds

quiet, silence	**hiljaisuus**	[hilʲjajsu:s]
sound	**ääni**	[æ:ni]
noise	**melu**	[melu]
to make noise	**meluta**	[meluta]
noisy (adj)	**meluisa**	[melujsa]
loudly (to speak, etc.)	**äänekkäästi**	[æ:nekkæ:sti]
loud (voice, etc.)	**äänekäs**	[æ:nekæs]
constant (continuous)	**vakinainen**	[ʋakinajnen]

shout (n)	**huuto**	[hu:to]
to shout (vi)	**huutaa**	[hu:tɑ:]
whisper	**kuiskaus**	[kujskɑus]
to whisper (vi, vt)	**kuiskata**	[kujskɑtɑ]
barking (of dog)	**haukunta**	[hɑukuntɑ]
to bark (vi)	**haukkua**	[hɑukkuɑ]
groan (of pain)	**vaikerrus**	[ʋɑjkerrus]
to groan (vi)	**vaikertaa**	[ʋɑjkertɑ:]
cough	**yskä**	[yskæ]
to cough (vi)	**yskiä**	[yskiæ]
whistle	**vihellys**	[ʋihellys]
to whistle (vi)	**viheltää**	[ʋiheltæ:]
knock (at the door)	**koputus**	[koputus]
to knock (at the door)	**koputtaa**	[koputtɑ:]
to crack (vi)	**ritistä**	[ritistæ]
crack (plank, etc.)	**ryske**	[ryske]
siren	**sireeni**	[sire:ni]
whistle (factory's ~)	**puhallus**	[puhɑllus]
to whistle (ship, train)	**puhaltaa**	[puhɑltɑ:]
honk (signal)	**signaali**	[signɑ:li]
to honk (vi)	**tuutata**	[tu:tɑtɑ]

209. Winter

winter (n)	**talvi**	[tɑlʋi]
winter (as adj)	**talvinen**	[tɑlʋinen]
in winter	**talvella**	[tɑlʋellɑ]
snow	**lumi**	[lumi]
it's snowing	**sataa lunta**	[sɑtɑ: luntɑ]
snowfall	**lumikuuro**	[lumiku:ro]
snowdrift	**lumikinos**	[lumikinos]
snowflake	**lumihiutale**	[lumihiutɑle]
snowball	**lumipallo**	[lumipɑllo]
snowman	**lumiukko**	[lumiukko]
icicle	**jääpuikko**	[jæ:pujkko]
December	**joulukuu**	[øuluku:]
January	**tammikuu**	[tɑmmiku:]
February	**helmikuu**	[helmiku:]
heavy frost	**pakkanen**	[pɑkkɑnen]
frosty (weather, air)	**pakkas-**	[pɑkkɑs]
below zero (adv)	**nollan alapuolella**	[nollɑn ɑlɑpuolellɑ]
first frost	**halla**	[hɑllɑ]
hoarfrost	**huurre**	[hu:rre]
cold (cold weather)	**kylmyys**	[kylmy:s]

it's cold	**on kylmää**	[on kylmæ:]
fur coat	**turkki**	[turkki]
mittens	**lapaset**	[lɑpɑset]
to fall ill	**sairastua**	[sɑjrɑstuɑ]
cold (illness)	**vilustus**	[ʋilustus]
to catch a cold	**vilustua**	[ʋilustuɑ]
ice	**jää**	[jæ:]
black ice	**iljanne**	[il^{h}jɑŋe]
to ice over	**jäätyä**	[jæ:tyæ]
ice floe	**jäälohkare**	[jæ:lohkɑre]
skis	**sukset**	[sukset]
skier	**hiihtäjä**	[hi:ihtæjæ]
to ski (vi)	**hiihdellä**	[hi:ihdeʎæ]
to skate (vi)	**luistella**	[luistellɑ]

Fauna

210. Mammals. Predators

predator	**peto**	[peto]
tiger	**tiikeri**	[ti:ikeri]
lion	**leijona**	[leiøna]
wolf	**susi**	[susi]
fox	**kettu**	[kettu]
jaguar	**jaguaari**	[jagua:ri]
leopard	**leopardi**	[leopardi]
cheetah	**gepardi**	[gepardi]
black panther	**pantteri**	[pantteri]
puma	**puuma**	[pu:ma]
snow leopard	**lumileopardi**	[lumi leopardi]
lynx	**ilves**	[ilʋes]
coyote	**kojootti**	[koø:tti]
jackal	**sakaali**	[saka:li]
hyena	**hyeena**	[hye:na]

211. Wild animals

animal	**eläin**	[eʎæjn]
beast (animal)	**eläin**	[eʎæjn]
squirrel	**orava**	[oraʋa]
hedgehog	**siili**	[si:ili]
hare	**jänis**	[jænis]
rabbit	**kaniini**	[kani:ini]
badger	**mäyrä**	[mæuræ]
raccoon	**pesukarhu**	[pesukarhu]
hamster	**hamsteri**	[hamsteri]
marmot	**murmeli**	[murmeli]
mole	**maamyyrä**	[ma:my:ræ]
mouse	**hiiri**	[hi:iri]
rat	**rotta**	[rotta]
bat	**lepakko**	[lepakko]
ermine	**kärppä**	[kærppæ]
sable	**soopeli**	[so:peli]
marten	**näätä**	[næ:tæ]
weasel	**lumikko**	[lumikko]
mink	**minkki**	[miŋkki]

beaver	**majava**	[mɑjɑʋɑ]
otter	**saukko**	[sɑukko]
horse	**hevonen**	[heʋonen]
moose	**hirvi**	[hirʋi]
deer	**poro**	[poro]
camel	**kameli**	[kɑmeli]
bison	**biisoni**	[bi:isoni]
aurochs	**visentti**	[ʋisentti]
buffalo	**puhveli**	[puhʋeli]
zebra	**seepra**	[se:prɑ]
antelope	**antilooppi**	[ɑntilo:ppi]
roe deer	**metsäkauris**	[met͡sæ kɑuris]
fallow deer	**kuusipeura**	[ku:si peurɑ]
chamois	**gemssi**	[gemssi]
wild boar	**villisika**	[ʋilli sikɑ]
whale	**valas**	[ʋɑlɑs]
seal	**hylje**	[hylʰje]
walrus	**mursu**	[mursu]
fur seal	**merikarhu**	[merikɑrhu]
dolphin	**delfiini**	[delfi:ini]
bear	**karhu**	[kɑrhu]
polar bear	**jääkarhu**	[jæ:kɑrhu]
panda	**panda**	[pɑndɑ]
monkey	**apina**	[ɑpinɑ]
chimpanzee	**simpanssi**	[simpɑnssi]
orangutan	**oranki**	[orɑŋki]
gorilla	**gorilla**	[gorillɑ]
macaque	**makaki**	[mɑkɑki]
gibbon	**gibboni**	[gibboni]
elephant	**norsu**	[norsu]
rhinoceros	**sarvikuono**	[sɑrʋikuono]
giraffe	**kirahvi**	[kirɑhʋi]
hippopotamus	**virtahepo**	[ʋirtɑ hepo]
kangaroo	**kenguru**	[keŋuru]
koala (bear)	**pussikarhu**	[pussikɑrhu]
mongoose	**faaraorotta**	[fɑ:rɑorottɑ]
chinchilla	**sinsilla**	[sinsillɑ]
skunk	**haisunäätä**	[hɑjsunæ:tæ]
porcupine	**piikkisika**	[pi:ikkisikɑ]

212. Domestic animals

cat	**kissa**	[kissɑ]
tomcat	**kollikissa**	[kollikissɑ]
dog	**koira**	[kojrɑ]

horse	**hevonen**	[heʋonen]
stallion	**ori**	[ori]
mare	**tamma**	[tɑmmɑ]
cow	**lehmä**	[lehmæ]
bull	**sonni**	[soŋi]
ox	**härkä**	[ɦærkæ]
sheep	**lammas**	[lɑmmɑs]
ram	**pässi**	[pæssi]
goat	**vuohi**	[ʋuohi]
billy goat, he-goat	**pukki**	[pukki]
donkey	**aasi**	[ɑ:si]
mule	**muuli**	[mu:li]
pig	**sika**	[sikɑ]
piglet	**porsas**	[porsɑs]
rabbit	**kaniini**	[kɑni:ini]
hen (chicken)	**kana**	[kɑnɑ]
cock	**kukko**	[kukko]
duck	**ankka**	[ɑŋkkɑ]
drake	**urosankka**	[urosɑŋkkɑ]
goose	**hanhi**	[hɑnhi]
stag turkey	**uroskalkkuna**	[uroskɑlkkunɑ]
turkey (hen)	**naaraskalkkuna**	[nɑ:rɑskɑlkkunɑ]
domestic animals	**kotieläimet**	[kotieʎæjmet]
tame (e.g. ~ hamster)	**kesy**	[kesy]
to tame (vt)	**kesyttää**	[kesyttæ:]
to breed (vt)	**kasvattaa**	[kɑsʋɑttɑ:]
farm	**farmi**	[fɑrmi]
poultry	**siipikarja**	[si:ipikɑr^hjɑ]
cattle	**karja**	[kɑr^hjɑ]
herd (cattle)	**lauma**	[lɑumɑ]
stable	**hevostalli**	[heʋostɑlli]
pigsty	**sikala**	[sikɑlɑ]
cowshed	**navetta**	[nɑʋettɑ]
rabbit hutch	**kanikoppi**	[kɑnikoppi]
hen house	**kanala**	[kɑnɑlɑ]

213. Dogs. Dog breeds

dog	**koira**	[kojrɑ]
sheepdog	**paimenkoira**	[pɑjmeŋkojrɑ]
poodle	**villakoira**	[ʋillɑkojrɑ]
dachshund	**mäyräkoira**	[mæurækojrɑ]
bulldog	**bulldoggi**	[bulldoggi]
boxer	**bokseri**	[bokseri]

mastiff	**mastiffi**	[mastiffi]
rottweiler	**rottweiler**	[rottuajler]
Doberman	**dobermanni**	[dobermaŋi]
basset	**basset**	[basset]
bobtail	**bobtail, lampuri**	[bobtejl], [ʎæmpuri]
Dalmatian	**dalmatiankoira**	[dalmatianikojra]
cocker spaniel	**cockerspanieli**	[kokker spanieli]
Newfoundland	**newfoundlandinkoira**	[ɲjyfaundlandin kojra]
Saint Bernard	**bernhardinkoira**	[bernhardin kojra]
husky	**siperianhusky**	[siperian husky]
Chow Chow	**kiinanpystykorva**	[ki:inanpysty korua]
spitz	**kääpiöpystykorva**	[kæ:piøpysty korua]
pug	**mopsi**	[mopsi]

214. Sounds made by animals

barking (n)	**haukunta**	[haukunta]
to bark (vi)	**haukkua**	[haukkua]
to miaow (vi)	**naukua**	[naukua]
to purr (vi)	**kehrätä**	[kehrætæ]
to moo (vi)	**ammua**	[ammua]
to bellow (bull)	**ulvoa**	[uluoa]
to growl (vi)	**möristä**	[møristæ]
howl (n)	**ulvonta**	[uluonta]
to howl (vi)	**ulvoa**	[uluoa]
to whine (vi)	**inistä**	[inistæ]
to bleat (sheep)	**määkiä**	[mæ:kiæ]
to oink, to grunt (pig)	**röhkiä**	[røhkiæ]
to squeal (vi)	**vinkua**	[uiŋkua]
to croak (vi)	**kurnuttaa**	[kurnutta:]
to buzz (insect)	**surista**	[surista]
to stridulate (vi)	**sirittää**	[sirittæ:]

215. Young animals

cub	**pentu**	[pentu]
kitten	**kissanpentu**	[kissan pentu]
baby mouse	**hiirenpoika**	[hi:iren pojka]
pup, puppy	**koiranpentu**	[kojran pentu]
leveret	**jäniksenpoika**	[jæniksen pojka]
baby rabbit	**kaniininpoikanen**	[kani:inin pojkanen]
wolf cub	**sudenpentu**	[suden pentu]
fox cub	**ketunpentu**	[ketun pentu]
bear cub	**karhunpentu**	[karhun pentu]

lion cub	**leijonanpentu**	[leiønan pentu]
tiger cub	**tiikerinpentu**	[ti:ikerin pentu]
elephant calf	**norsunpoikanen**	[norsun pojkanen]
piglet	**porsas**	[porsas]
calf (young cow, bull)	**vasikka**	[ʋasikka]
kid (young goat)	**kili**	[kili]
lamb	**karitsa**	[karitsa]
fawn (deer)	**poronvasa**	[poron ʋasa]
young camel	**kamelin varsa**	[kamelin ʋarsa]
baby snake	**käärmeenpoikanen**	[kæ:rme:n pojkanen]
baby frog	**sammakonpoikanen**	[sammakon pojkanen]
nestling	**linnunpoika**	[liŋun pojka]
chick (of chicken)	**kananpoika**	[kanan pojka]
duckling	**ankanpoikanen**	[aŋkan pojkanen]

216. Birds

bird	**lintu**	[lintu]
pigeon	**kyyhky**	[ky:hky]
sparrow	**varpunen**	[ʋarpunen]
tit	**tiainen**	[tiajnen]
magpie	**harakka**	[harakka]
raven	**korppi**	[korppi]
crow	**varis**	[ʋaris]
jackdaw	**naakka**	[na:kka]
rook	**mustavaris**	[musta ʋaris]
duck	**ankka**	[aŋkka]
goose	**hanhi**	[hanhi]
pheasant	**fasaani**	[fasa:ni]
eagle	**kotka**	[kotka]
hawk	**haukka**	[haukka]
falcon	**haukka**	[haukka]
vulture	**korppikotka**	[korppikotka]
condor	**kondori**	[kondori]
swan	**joutsen**	[øutsen]
crane	**kurki**	[kurki]
stork	**haikara**	[hajkara]
parrot	**papukaija**	[papukaija]
hummingbird	**kolibri**	[kolibri]
peacock	**riikinkukko**	[ri:ikiŋkukko]
ostrich	**strutsi**	[strutsi]
heron	**haikara**	[hajkara]
flamingo	**flamingo**	[flamiŋo]
pelican	**pelikaani**	[pelika:ni]
nightingale	**satakieli**	[satakieli]

swallow	**pääskynen**	[pæ:skynen]
thrush	**rastas**	[rastas]
song thrush	**laulurastas**	[laulurastas]
blackbird	**mustarastas**	[mustarastas]
swift	**tervapääsky**	[teruapæ:sky]
lark	**leivonen**	[lejuonen]
quail	**viiriäinen**	[ui:iriæjnen]
woodpecker	**tikka**	[tikka]
cuckoo	**käki**	[kæki]
owl	**pöllö**	[pøllø]
eagle owl	**huuhkaja**	[hu:hkaja]
wood grouse	**metso**	[metso]
black grouse	**teeri**	[te:ri]
partridge	**riekko**	[riekko]
starling	**kottarainen**	[kottarajnen]
canary	**kanarianlintu**	[kanarianlintu]
hazel grouse	**pyy**	[py:]
chaffinch	**peipponen**	[pejpponen]
bullfinch	**punatulkku**	[punatulkku]
seagull	**lokki**	[lokki]
albatross	**albatrossi**	[albatrossi]
penguin	**pingviini**	[piŋui:ini]

217. Birds. Singing and sounds

to sing (vi)	**laulaa**	[laula:]
to call (animal, bird)	**huutaa**	[hu:ta:]
to crow (cock)	**kiekua**	[kiekua]
cock-a-doodle-doo	**kukkokiekuu**	[kukkokieku:]
to cluck (hen)	**kotkottaa**	[kotkotta:]
to caw (vi)	**raakkua**	[ra:kkua]
to quack (duck)	**rääkättää**	[ræ:kættæ:]
to cheep (vi)	**piipittää**	[pi:ipittæ:]
to chirp, to twitter	**sirkuttaa**	[sirkutta:]

218. Fish. Marine animals

bream	**lahna**	[lahna]
carp	**karppi**	[karppi]
perch	**ahven**	[ahuen]
catfish	**monni**	[moŋi]
pike	**hauki**	[hauki]
salmon	**lohi**	[lohi]
sturgeon	**sampi**	[sampi]
herring	**silli**	[silli]
Atlantic salmon	**merilohi**	[merilohi]

mackerel	**makrilli**	[makrilli]
flatfish	**kampela**	[kampela]
zander, pike perch	**kuha**	[kuha]
cod	**turska**	[turska]
tuna	**tonnikala**	[toŋikala]
trout	**lohi**	[lohi]
eel	**ankerias**	[aŋkerias]
electric ray	**sähkörausku**	[sæhkørausku]
moray eel	**mureena**	[mure:na]
piranha	**punapiraija**	[puna piraija]
shark	**hai**	[haj]
dolphin	**delfiini**	[delfi:ini]
whale	**valas**	[ʋalas]
crab	**taskurapu**	[taskurapu]
jellyfish	**meduusa**	[medu:sa]
octopus	**meritursas**	[meritursas]
starfish	**meritähti**	[meritæhti]
sea urchin	**merisiili**	[merisi:ili]
seahorse	**merihevonen**	[meriheʋonen]
oyster	**osteri**	[osteri]
prawn	**katkarapu**	[katkarapu]
lobster	**hummeri**	[hummeri]
spiny lobster	**langusti**	[laŋusti]

219. Amphibians. Reptiles

snake	**käärme**	[kæ:rme]
venomous (snake)	**myrkyllinen**	[myrkyllinen]
viper	**kyy**	[ky:]
cobra	**silmälasikäärme**	[silmælasi kæ:rme]
python	**python**	[python]
boa	**jättiläiskäärme**	[jættiʎæjs kæ:rme]
grass snake	**turhakäärme**	[turha kæ:rme]
rattle snake	**kalkkarokäärme**	[kalkkaro kæ:rme]
anaconda	**anakonda**	[anakonda]
lizard	**sisilisko**	[sisilisko]
iguana	**iguaani**	[igua:ni]
monitor lizard	**varaani**	[ʋara:ni]
salamander	**salamanteri**	[salamanteri]
chameleon	**kameleontti**	[kameleontti]
scorpion	**skorpioni**	[skorpioni]
turtle	**kilpikonna**	[kilpikoŋa]
frog	**sammakko**	[sammakko]
toad	**konna**	[koŋa]
crocodile	**krokotiili**	[krokoti:ili]

220. Insects

insect	**hyönteinen**	[hyøntejnen]
butterfly	**perhonen**	[perhonen]
ant	**muurahainen**	[mu:rahajnen]
fly	**kärpänen**	[kærpænen]
mosquito	**hyttynen**	[hyttynen]
beetle	**kovakuoriainen**	[kovakuoriajnen]
wasp	**ampiainen**	[ampiajnen]
bee	**mehiläinen**	[mehiʎæjnen]
bumblebee	**kimalainen**	[kimalajnen]
gadfly	**kiiliäinen**	[ki:liæjnen]
spider	**hämähäkki**	[ɦæmæɦækki]
spider's web	**hämähäkinseitti**	[ɦæmæɦækinsejtti]
dragonfly	**sudenkorento**	[sudeŋkorento]
grasshopper	**hepokatti**	[hepokatti]
moth (night butterfly)	**perho**	[perho]
cockroach	**torakka**	[torakka]
tick	**punkki**	[puŋkki]
flea	**kirppu**	[kirppu]
midge	**mäkärä**	[mækæræ]
locust	**kulkusirkka**	[kulkusirkka]
snail	**etana**	[etana]
cricket	**sirkka**	[sirkka]
firefly	**kiiltomato**	[ki:ltomato]
ladybird	**leppäkerttu**	[leppækerttu]
cockchafer	**turilas**	[turilas]
leech	**juotikas**	[juotikas]
caterpillar	**toukka**	[toukka]
earthworm	**mato**	[mato]
larva	**toukka**	[toukka]

221. Animals. Body parts

beak	**nokka**	[nokka]
wings	**siivet**	[si:iuet]
foot (of bird)	**käpälä**	[kæpæʎæ]
feathering	**höyhenpeite**	[høyhenpejte]
feather	**höyhen**	[høyhen]
crest	**töyhtö**	[tøyhtø]
gill	**kidukset**	[kidukset]
spawn	**kaviaari**	[kauia:ri]
larva	**toukka**	[toukka]
fin	**evä**	[euæ]
scales (of fish, reptile)	**suomukset**	[suomukset]
fang (of wolf, etc.)	**torahammas**	[torahammas]

paw (e.g. cat's ~)	**käpälä**	[kæpæʎæ]
muzzle (snout)	**kuono**	[kuono]
mouth (of cat, dog)	**kita**	[kitɑ]
tail	**häntä**	[ɦæntæ]
whiskers	**viikset**	[ʋi:ikset]
hoof	**kavio**	[kɑʋio]
horn	**sarvi**	[sɑrʋi]
carapace	**panssari**	[pɑnssɑri]
shell (of mollusc)	**simpukka**	[simpukkɑ]
eggshell	**kuori**	[kuori]
hair (e.g. dog's ~)	**karva**	[kɑrʋɑ]
pelt	**vuota**	[ʋuotɑ]

222. Actions of animals

to fly (vi)	**lentää**	[lentæ:]
to make circles	**kaarrella**	[kɑ:rrellɑ]
to fly away	**lentää**	[lentæ:]
to flap (~ the wings)	**räpyttää**	[ræpyttæ:]
to peck (vi)	**nokkia**	[nokkiɑ]
to sit on (vt)	**hautoa munat**	[hɑutoɑ munɑt]
to hatch out (vi)	**kuoriutua**	[kuoriutuɑ]
to build the nest	**rakentaa**	[rɑkentɑ:]
to slither, to crawl	**ryömiä**	[ryømiæ]
to sting, to bite (insect)	**pistää**	[pistæ:]
to bite (ab. animal)	**purra**	[purrɑ]
to sniff (vt)	**nuuskia**	[nu:skiɑ]
to bark (vi)	**haukkua**	[hɑukkuɑ]
to hiss (snake)	**sihistä**	[sihistæ]
to scare (vt)	**pelottaa**	[pelottɑ:]
to attack (vt)	**hyökätä**	[hyøkætæ]
to gnaw (bone, etc.)	**jyrsiä**	[yrsiæ]
to scratch (with claws)	**raapia**	[rɑ:piɑ]
to hide (vi)	**piileskellä**	[pi:ileskeʎæ]
to play (kittens, etc.)	**leikkiä**	[lejkkiæ]
to hunt (vi, vt)	**metsästää**	[metsæstæ:]
to hibernate (vi)	**olla horroksessa**	[ollɑ horroksessɑ]
to become extinct	**kuolla sukupuuttoon**	[kuollɑ sukupu:tto:n]

223. Animals. Habitats

habitat	**elinympäristö**	[elinympæristø]
migration	**muuttoliike**	[mu:ttoli:ike]
mountain	**vuori**	[ʋuori]

reef	**riutta**	[riutta]
cliff	**kallio**	[kallio]
forest	**metsä**	[metsæ]
jungle	**viidakko**	[ʋi:idakko]
savanna	**savanni**	[saʋaŋi]
tundra	**tundra**	[tundra]
steppe	**aro**	[aro]
desert	**aavikko**	[a:ʋikko]
oasis	**keidas**	[kejdas]
sea	**meri**	[meri]
lake	**järvi**	[jærʋi]
ocean	**valtameri**	[ʋaltameri]
swamp	**suo**	[suo]
freshwater (adj)	**makeavetinen**	[makeaʋetinen]
pond	**lammikko**	[lammikko]
river	**joki**	[øki]
den	**karhunpesä**	[karhun pesæ]
nest	**pesä**	[pesæ]
hollow (in a tree)	**ontelo**	[ontelo]
burrow (animal hole)	**kolo**	[kolo]
anthill	**muurahaiskeko**	[mu:rahajs keko]

224. Animal care

zoo	**eläintarha**	[eʎæjntarha]
nature reserve	**rauhoitusalue**	[rauhojtusalue]
breeder, breed club	**tarha**	[tarha]
open-air cage	**kotelo**	[kotelo]
cage	**häkki**	[ɦækki]
kennel	**koppi**	[koppi]
dovecot	**kyyhkyslakka**	[ky:hkyslakka]
aquarium	**akvaario**	[akʋa:rio]
dolphinarium	**delfinaario**	[delfina:rio]
to breed (animals)	**kasvattaa**	[kasʋatta:]
brood, litter	**jälkeläiset**	[jælkeʎæjset]
to tame (vt)	**kesyttää**	[kesyttæ:]
feed (for animal)	**ruoka**	[ruoka]
to feed (vt)	**ruokkia**	[ruokkia]
to train (animals)	**kouluttaa**	[koulutta:]
pet shop	**eläinkauppa**	[eʎæjŋkauppa]
muzzle (for dog)	**kuonokoppa**	[kuonokoppa]
collar	**kaulapanta**	[kaulapanta]
name (of animal)	**nimi**	[nimi]
pedigree (of dog)	**sukutaulu**	[sukutaulu]

225. Animals. Miscellaneous

pack (wolves)	**lauma**	[lauma]
flock (birds)	**parvi**	[parʋi]
shoal (fish)	**kalaparvi**	[kala parʋi]
herd of horses	**lauma**	[lauma]
male (n)	**uros**	[uros]
female	**naaras**	[na:ras]
hungry (adj)	**nälkäinen**	[ɲælkæjnen]
wild (adj)	**villi**	[ʋilli]
dangerous (adj)	**vaarallinen**	[ʋa:ralinen]

226. Horses

horse	**hevonen**	[heʋonen]
breed (race)	**rotu**	[rotu]
foal (of horse)	**varsa**	[ʋarsa]
mare	**tamma**	[tamma]
mustang	**mustangi**	[mustaŋi]
pony (small horse)	**poni**	[poni]
draught horse	**kuormahevonen**	[kuormaheʋonen]
mane	**harja**	[harʰja]
tail	**häntä**	[ɦæntæ]
hoof	**kavio**	[kaʋio]
horseshoe	**hevosenkenkä**	[heʋoseŋkeŋkæ]
to shoe (vt)	**kengittää**	[keŋittæ:]
blacksmith	**seppä**	[seppæ]
saddle	**satula**	[satula]
stirrup	**jalustin**	[jalustin]
bridle	**suitset**	[suitset]
reins	**ohjakset**	[ohʰjakset]
whip (for riding)	**ruoska**	[ruoska]
rider	**ratsastaja**	[ratsastaja]
to break in (horse)	**murtautua**	[murtautua]
to saddle (vt)	**satuloida**	[satulojda]
to mount a horse	**nousta satulaan**	[nousta satula:n]
gallop	**laukka**	[laukka]
to gallop (vi)	**ajaa laukkaa**	[aja: laukka:]
trot (n)	**ravi**	[raʋi]
at a trot (adv)	**ravia**	[raʋia]
racehorse	**ratsu**	[ratsu]
races	**ratsastuskilpailut**	[ratsastus kilpajlut]
stable	**hevostalli**	[heʋostalli]

to feed (vt)	**ruokkia**	[ruokkiɑ]
hay	**heinä**	[hejɲæ]
to water (animals)	**juottaa**	[juottɑ:]
to wash (horse)	**puhdistaa**	[puhdistɑ:]
to hobble (vt)	**kammitsoida**	[kɑmmitsojdɑ]
to graze (vi)	**olla laitumella**	[ollɑ lɑjtumellɑ]
to neigh (vi)	**hirnua**	[hirnuɑ]
to jib, to kick out	**potkia**	[potkiɑ]

Flora

227. Trees

tree	**puu**	[pu:]
deciduous (adj)	**lehti-**	[lehti]
coniferous (adj)	**havu-**	[haʋu]
evergreen (adj)	**ikivihreä**	[ikiʋihrea]
apple tree	**omenapuu**	[omenapu:]
pear tree	**päärynäpuu**	[pæ:ryɲæpu:]
sweet cherry tree	**linnunkirsikkapuu**	[liŋun kirsikkapu:]
sour cherry tree	**hapankirsikkapuu**	[hapan kirsikkapu:]
plum tree	**luumupuu**	[lu:mupu:]
birch	**koivu**	[kojʋu]
oak	**tammi**	[tammi]
linden tree	**lehmus**	[lehmus]
aspen	**haapa**	[ha:pa]
maple	**vaahtera**	[ʋa:htera]
spruce	**kuusi**	[ku:si]
pine	**mänty**	[mænty]
larch	**lehtikuusi**	[lehtiku:si]
fir	**jalokuusi**	[jaloku:si]
cedar	**setri**	[setri]
poplar	**poppeli**	[poppeli]
rowan	**pihlaja**	[pihlaja]
willow	**paju**	[paju]
alder	**leppä**	[leppæ]
beech	**pyökki**	[pyøkki]
elm	**jalava**	[jalaʋa]
ash (tree)	**saarni**	[sa:rni]
chestnut	**kastanja**	[kastan'ja]
magnolia	**magnolia**	[magnolia]
palm tree	**palmu**	[palmu]
cypress	**sypressi**	[sypressi]
mangrove	**mangrovepuu**	[maŋroʋepu:]
baobab	**apinanleipäpuu**	[apinan lejpæpu:]
eucalyptus	**eukalyptus**	[eukalyptus]
sequoia	**punapuu**	[punapu:]

228. Shrubs

bush	**pensas**	[pensas]
shrub	**pensaikko**	[pensajkko]

grapevine	**viinirypäleet**	[ʋi:inirypæle:t]
vineyard	**viinitarha**	[ʋi:initarha]
raspberry bush	**vadelma**	[ʋadelma]
redcurrant bush	**punaherukka**	[punaherukka]
gooseberry bush	**karviaismarja**	[karʋiajsmarʰja]
acacia	**akasia**	[akasia]
barberry	**happomarja**	[happomarʰja]
jasmine	**jasmiini**	[jasmi:ini]
juniper	**kataja**	[kataja]
rosebush	**ruusupensas**	[ru:supensas]
dog rose	**villiruusu**	[ʋilliru:su]

229. Mushrooms

mushroom	**sieni**	[sieni]
edible mushroom	**ruokasieni**	[ruokasieni]
toadstool	**myrkkysieni**	[myrkkysieni]
cap (of mushroom)	**lakki**	[lakki]
stipe (of mushroom)	**jalka**	[jalka]
cep, penny bun	**herkkutatti**	[herkkutatti]
orange-cap boletus	**punikkitatti**	[punikkitatti]
birch bolete	**lehmäntatti**	[lehmæntatti]
chanterelle	**keltavahvero**	[keltaʋahʋero]
russula	**hapero**	[hapero]
morel	**huhtasieni**	[huhtasieni]
fly agaric	**kärpässieni**	[kærpæssieni]
death cap	**myrkkysieni**	[myrkkysieni]

230. Fruits. Berries

fruit	**hedelmä**	[hedelmæ]
fruits	**hedelmät**	[hedelmæt]
apple	**omena**	[omena]
pear	**päärynä**	[pæ:ryɲæ]
plum	**luumu**	[lu:mu]
strawberry	**mansikka**	[mansikka]
sour cherry	**hapankirsikka**	[hapan kirsikka]
sweet cherry	**linnunkirsikka**	[liŋun kirsikka]
grape	**viinirypäleet**	[ʋi:inirypæle:t]
raspberry	**vadelma**	[ʋadelma]
blackcurrant	**mustaherukka**	[mustaherukka]
redcurrant	**punaiset viinimarjat**	[punajset ʋi:inimarʰjat]
gooseberry	**karviaiset**	[karʋiajset]
cranberry	**karpalo**	[karpalo]
orange	**appelsiini**	[appelsi:ini]

tangerine	**mandariini**	[mandari:ini]
pineapple	**ananas**	[ananas]
banana	**banaani**	[bana:ni]
date	**taateli**	[ta:teli]
lemon	**sitruuna**	[sitru:na]
apricot	**aprikoosi**	[apriko:si]
peach	**persikka**	[persikka]
kiwi	**kiivi**	[ki:iʋi]
grapefruit	**greippi**	[grejppi]
berry	**marja**	[marʰja]
berries	**marjat**	[marʰjat]
cowberry	**puolukka**	[puolukka]
wild strawberry	**mansikka**	[mansikka]
bilberry	**mustikka**	[mustikka]

231. Flowers. Plants

flower	**kukka**	[kukka]
bouquet (of flowers)	**kukkakimppu**	[kukkakimppu]
rose (flower)	**ruusu**	[ru:su]
tulip	**tulppani**	[tulppani]
carnation	**neilikka**	[nejlikka]
gladiolus	**miekkalilja**	[miekkalilija]
cornflower	**kaunokki**	[kaunokki]
bluebell	**kellokukka**	[kelloikukka]
dandelion	**voikukka**	[ʋojkukka]
camomile	**päivänkakkara**	[pæjʋæn kakkara]
aloe	**aaloe**	[a:loe]
cactus	**kaktus**	[kaktus]
rubber plant, ficus	**fiikus**	[fi:ikus]
lily	**lilja**	[lilʰja]
geranium	**kurjenpolvi**	[kurʰjenpolʋi]
hyacinth	**hyasintti**	[hyasintti]
mimosa	**mimoosa**	[mimo:sa]
narcissus	**narsissi**	[narsissi]
nasturtium	**krassi**	[krassi]
orchid	**orkidea**	[orkidea]
peony	**pioni**	[pioni]
violet	**orvokki**	[orʋokki]
pansy	**keto-orvokki**	[keto orʋokki]
forget-me-not	**lemmikki**	[lemmikki]
daisy	**kaunokainen**	[kaunokajnen]
poppy	**unikko**	[unikko]
hemp	**hamppu**	[hamppu]

mint	**minttu**	[minttu]
lily of the valley	**kielo**	[kielo]
snowdrop	**lumikello**	[lumikello]
nettle	**nokkonen**	[nokkonen]
sorrel	**hierakka**	[hierɑkkɑ]
water lily	**lumme**	[lumme]
fern	**saniainen**	[sɑniɑjnen]
lichen	**jäkälä**	[jækæʎæ]
tropical glasshouse	**ansari**	[ɑnsɑri]
grass lawn	**nurmikko**	[nurmikko]
flowerbed	**kukkapenkki**	[kukkɑ peŋkki]
plant	**kasvi**	[kɑsʋi]
grass	**ruoho**	[ruoho]
blade of grass	**heinänkorsi**	[hejɲæŋkorsi]
leaf	**lehti**	[lehti]
petal	**terälehti**	[teræ lehti]
stem	**varsi**	[ʋɑrsi]
tuber	**mukula**	[mukulɑ]
young plant (shoot)	**itu**	[itu]
thorn	**piikki**	[pi:ikki]
to blossom (vi)	**kukkia**	[kukkiɑ]
to fade, to wither	**kuihtua**	[kujhtuɑ]
smell (odour)	**tuoksu**	[tuoksu]
to cut (flowers)	**leikata**	[lejkɑtɑ]
to pick (a flower)	**repiä**	[repiæ]

232. Cereals, grains

grain	**vilja**	[ʋilʰjɑ]
cereals (plants)	**viljat**	[ʋilʰjɑt]
ear (of barley, etc.)	**tähkä**	[tæhkæ]
wheat	**vehnä**	[ʋehɲæ]
rye	**ruis**	[rujs]
oats	**kaura**	[kɑurɑ]
millet	**hirssi**	[hirssi]
barley	**ohra**	[ohrɑ]
maize	**maissi**	[mɑjssi]
rice	**riisi**	[ri:isi]
buckwheat	**tattari**	[tɑttɑri]
pea	**herne**	[herne]
kidney bean	**pavut**	[pɑʋut]
soya	**soijapapu**	[soijɑpɑpu]
lentil	**kylvövirvilä**	[kylʋøʋirʋiʎæ]
beans (broad ~)	**pavut**	[pɑʋut]

233. Vegetables. Greens

vegetables	**vihannekset**	[ʋihaŋekset]
greens	**kasvikset**	[kasʋikset]
tomato	**tomaatti**	[toma:tti]
cucumber	**kurkku**	[kurkku]
carrot	**porkkana**	[porkkana]
potato	**peruna**	[peruna]
onion	**sipuli**	[sipuli]
garlic	**valkosipuli**	[ʋalko sipuli]
cabbage	**kaali**	[ka:li]
cauliflower	**kukkakaali**	[kukkaka:li]
Brussels sprouts	**brysselinkaali**	[brysseliŋka:li]
beetroot	**punajuuri**	[punaju:ri]
aubergine	**munakoiso**	[munakojso]
marrow	**kesäkurpitsa**	[kesækurpitsa]
pumpkin	**kurpitsa**	[kurpitsa]
turnip	**nauris**	[nauris]
parsley	**persilja**	[persilʰæ]
dill	**tilli**	[tilli]
lettuce	**salaatti**	[sala:tti]
celery	**selleri**	[selleri]
asparagus	**parsa**	[parsa]
spinach	**pinaatti**	[pina:tti]
pea	**herne**	[herne]
beans	**pavut**	[paʋut]
maize	**maissi**	[majssi]
kidney bean	**pavut**	[paʋut]
bell pepper	**paprika**	[paprika]
radish	**retiisi**	[reti:isi]
artichoke	**artisokka**	[artisokka]

REGIONAL GEOGRAPHY

Countries. Nationalities

234. Western Europe

Europe	**Eurooppa**	[euro:ppɑ]
European Union	**Euroopan unioni**	[euro:pɑn unioni]
European (n)	**eurooppalainen**	[euro:ppɑlɑjnen]
European (adj)	**eurooppalainen**	[euro:ppɑlɑjnen]
Austria	**Itävalta**	[itæʋɑltɑ]
Austrian (masc.)	**itävaltalainen**	[itæʋɑltɑjnen]
Austrian (fem.)	**itävaltalainen**	[itæʋɑltɑjnen]
Austrian (adj)	**itävaltainen**	[itæʋɑltɑjnen]
Great Britain	**Iso-Britannia**	[isobritɑŋiɑ]
England	**Englanti**	[eŋlɑnti]
British (masc.)	**englantilainen**	[eŋlɑntilɑjnen]
British (fem.)	**englantilainen**	[eŋlɑntilɑjnen]
English, British (adj)	**englantilainen**	[eŋlɑntilɑjnen]
Belgium	**Belgia**	[belgiɑ]
Belgian (masc.)	**belgialainen**	[belgiɑlɑjnen]
Belgian (fem.)	**belgialainen**	[belgiɑlɑjnen]
Belgian (adj)	**belgialainen**	[belgiɑlɑjnen]
Germany	**Saksa**	[sɑksɑ]
German (masc.)	**saksalainen**	[sɑksɑlɑjnen]
German (fem.)	**saksalainen**	[sɑksɑlɑjnen]
German (adj)	**saksalainen**	[sɑksɑlɑjnen]
Netherlands	**Alankomaat**	[ɑlɑŋkomɑ:t]
Holland	**Hollanti**	[hollɑnti]
Dutchman	**hollantilainen**	[hollɑntilɑjnen]
Dutchwoman	**hollantilainen**	[hollɑntilɑjnen]
Dutch (adj)	**hollantilainen**	[hollɑntilɑjnen]
Greece	**Kreikka**	[krejkkɑ]
Greek (masc.)	**kreikkalainen**	[krejkkɑlɑjnen]
Greek (fem.)	**kreikkalainen**	[krejkkɑlɑjnen]
Greek (adj)	**kreikkalainen**	[krejkkɑlɑjnen]
Denmark	**Tanska**	[tɑnskɑ]
Dane (masc.)	**tanskalainen**	[tɑnskɑlɑjnen]
Dane (fem.)	**tanskalainen**	[tɑnskɑlɑjnen]
Danish (adj)	**tanskalainen**	[tɑnskɑlɑjnen]
Ireland	**Irlanti**	[irlɑnti]
Irishman	**irlantilainen**	[irlɑntilɑjnen]

Irishwoman	**irlantilainen**	[irlantilajnen]
Irish (adj)	**irlantilainen**	[irlantilajnen]
Iceland	**Islanti**	[islanti]
Icelander (masc.)	**islantilainen**	[islantilajnen]
Icelander (fem.)	**islantilainen**	[islantilajnen]
Icelandic (adj)	**islantilainen**	[islantilajnen]
Spain	**Espanja**	[espanʰja]
Spaniard (masc.)	**espanjalainen**	[espanʰjalajnen]
Spaniard (fem.)	**espanjalainen**	[espanʰjalajnen]
Spanish (adj)	**espanjalainen**	[espanʰjalajnen]
Italy	**Italia**	[italia]
Italian (masc.)	**italialainen**	[italialajnen]
Italian (fem.)	**italialainen**	[italialajnen]
Italian (adj)	**italialainen**	[italialajnen]
Cyprus	**Kypros**	[kypros]
Cypriot (masc.)	**kyproslainen**	[kyproslajnen]
Cypriot (fem.)	**kyproslainen**	[kyproslajnen]
Cypriot (adj)	**kyproslainen**	[kyproslajnen]
Malta	**Malta**	[malta]
Maltese (masc.)	**maltalainen**	[maltalajnen]
Maltese (fem.)	**maltalainen**	[maltalajnen]
Maltese (adj)	**maltalainen**	[maltalajnen]
Norway	**Norja**	[norʰja]
Norwegian (masc.)	**norjalainen**	[norʰjalajnen]
Norwegian (fem.)	**norjalainen**	[norʰjalajnen]
Norwegian (adj)	**norjalainen**	[norʰjalajnen]
Portugal	**Portugali**	[portugali]
Portuguese (masc.)	**portugalilainen**	[portugalilajnen]
Portuguese (fem.)	**portugalilainen**	[portugalilajnen]
Portuguese (adj)	**portugalilainen**	[portugalilajnen]
Finland	**Suomi**	[suomi]
Finn (masc.)	**suomalainen**	[suomalajnen]
Finn (fem.)	**suomalainen**	[suomalajnen]
Finnish (adj)	**suomalainen**	[suomalajnen]
France	**Ranska**	[ranska]
Frenchman	**ranskalainen**	[ranskalajnen]
Frenchwoman	**ranskalainen**	[ranskalajnen]
French (adj)	**ranskalainen**	[ranskalajnen]
Sweden	**Ruotsi**	[ruotsi]
Swede (masc.)	**ruotsalainen**	[ruotsalajnen]
Swede (fem.)	**ruotsalainen**	[ruotsalajnen]
Swedish (adj)	**ruotsalainen**	[ruotsalajnen]
Switzerland	**Sveitsi**	[sʋejtsi]
Swiss (masc.)	**sveitsiläinen**	[sʋejtsiʎæjnen]
Swiss (fem.)	**sveitsiläinen**	[sʋejtsiʎæjnen]

Swiss (adj)	**sveitsiläinen**	[sʊejtsiʎæjnen]
Scotland	**Skotlanti**	[skotlɑnti]
Scottish (masc.)	**skotlantilainen**	[skotlɑntilɑjnen]
Scottish (fem.)	**skotlantilainen**	[skotlɑntilɑjnen]
Scottish (adj)	**skotlantilainen**	[skotlɑntilɑjnen]
Vatican	**Vatikaanivaltio**	[ʊɑtikɑ:ni ʊɑltio]
Liechtenstein	**Liechtenstein**	[lihtenʃtɑjn]
Luxembourg	**Luxemburg**	[lyksemburg]
Monaco	**Monaco**	[monɑko]

235. Central and Eastern Europe

Albania	**Albania**	[ɑlbɑniɑ]
Albanian (masc.)	**albanialainen**	[ɑlbɑniɑlɑjnen]
Albanian (fem.)	**albanialainen**	[ɑlbɑniɑlɑjnen]
Albanian (adj)	**albanialainen**	[ɑlbɑniɑlɑjnen]
Bulgaria	**Bulgaria**	[bulgɑriɑ]
Bulgarian (masc.)	**bulgarialainen**	[bulgɑriɑlɑjnen]
Bulgarian (fem.)	**bulgarialainen**	[bulgɑriɑlɑjnen]
Bulgarian (adj)	**bulgarialainen**	[bulgɑriɑlɑjnen]
Hungary	**Unkari**	[uŋkɑri]
Hungarian (masc.)	**unkarilainen**	[uŋkɑrilɑjnen]
Hungarian (fem.)	**unkarilainen**	[uŋkɑrilɑjnen]
Hungarian (adj)	**unkarilainen**	[uŋkɑrilɑjnen]
Latvia	**Latvia**	[lɑtʊiɑ]
Latvian (masc.)	**latvialainen**	[lɑtʊiɑlɑjnen]
Latvian (fem.)	**latvialainen**	[lɑtʊiɑlɑjnen]
Latvian (adj)	**latvialainen**	[lɑtʊiɑlɑjnen]
Lithuania	**Liettua**	[liettuɑ]
Lithuanian (masc.)	**liettualainen**	[liettuɑlɑjnen]
Lithuanian (fem.)	**liettualainen**	[liettuɑlɑjnen]
Lithuanian (adj)	**liettualainen**	[liettuɑlɑjnen]
Poland	**Puola**	[puolɑ]
Pole (masc.)	**puolalainen**	[puolɑlɑjnen]
Pole (fem.)	**puolalainen**	[puolɑlɑjnen]
Polish (adj)	**puolalainen**	[puolɑlɑjnen]
Romania	**Romania**	[romɑniɑ]
Romanian (masc.)	**romanialainen**	[romɑniɑlɑjnen]
Romanian (fem.)	**romanialainen**	[romɑniɑlɑjnen]
Romanian (adj)	**romanialainen**	[romɑniɑlɑjnen]
Serbia	**Serbia**	[serbiɑ]
Serbian (masc.)	**serbialainen**	[serbiɑlɑjnen]
Serbian (fem.)	**serbialainen**	[serbiɑlɑjnen]
Serbian (adj)	**serbialainen**	[serbiɑlɑjnen]
Slovakia	**Slovakia**	[sloʊɑkiɑ]
Slovak (masc.)	**slovakki**	[sloʊɑkki]

Slovak (fem.)	**slovakki**	[slouakki]
Slovak (adj)	**slovakialainen**	[slouakialajnen]
Croatia	**Kroatia**	[kroatia]
Croatian (masc.)	**kroaatti**	[kroa:tti]
Croatian (fem.)	**kroaatti**	[kroa:tti]
Croatian (adj)	**kroatialainen**	[kroatialajnen]
Czech Republic	**Tšekki**	[ʧekki]
Czech (masc.)	**tšekkiläinen**	[ʧekkiʎæjnen]
Czech (fem.)	**tšekkiläinen**	[ʧekkiʎæjnen]
Czech (adj)	**tšekkiläinen**	[ʧekkiʎæjnen]
Estonia	**Viro**	[υiro]
Estonian (masc.)	**virolainen**	[υirolajnen]
Estonian (fem.)	**virolainen**	[υirolajnen]
Estonian (adj)	**virolainen**	[υirolajnen]
Bosnia-Herzegovina	**Bosnia ja Hertsegovina**	[bosnia ja herʦegoυina]
Macedonia	**Makedonia**	[makedonia]
Slovenia	**Slovenia**	[sloυenia]
Montenegro	**Montenegro**	[monte negro]

236. Former USSR countries

Azerbaijan	**Azerbaidžan**	[azerbajʤan]
Azerbaijani (masc.)	**azerbaidžanilainen**	[azerbajʤanialajnen]
Azerbaijani (fem.)	**azerbaidžanilainen**	[azerbajʤanialajnen]
Azerbaijani (adj)	**azerbaidžanilainen**	[azerbajʤanialajnen]
Armenia	**Armenia**	[armeniæ]
Armenian (masc.)	**armenialainen**	[armenialajnen]
Armenian (fem.)	**armenialainen**	[armenialajnen]
Armenian (adj)	**armenialainen**	[armenialajnen]
Belarus	**Valko-Venäjä**	[υalko υeɲæjæ]
Belarusian (masc.)	**valkovenäläinen**	[υalko υeɲæʎæjnen]
Belarusian (fem.)	**valkovenäläinen**	[υalko υeɲæʎæjnen]
Belarusian (adj)	**valkovenäläinen**	[υalko υeɲæʎæjnen]
Georgia	**Gruusia**	[gru:sia]
Georgian (masc.)	**gruusialainen**	[gru:sialajnen]
Georgian (fem.)	**gruusialainen**	[gru:sialajnen]
Georgian (adj)	**gruusialainen**	[gru:sialajnen]
Kazakhstan	**Kazakstan**	[kazakstan]
Kazakh (masc.)	**kazahi**	[kazahi]
Kazakh (fem.)	**kazahi**	[kazahi]
Kazakh (adj)	**kazakstanilainen**	[kazakstanilajnen]
Kirghizia	**Kirgisia**	[kirgisia]
Kirghiz (masc.)	**kirgiisi**	[kirgi:isi]
Kirghiz (fem.)	**kirgiisi**	[kirgi:isi]
Kirghiz (adj)	**kirgisialainen**	[kirgisialajnen]

Moldavia	**Moldova**	[moldoʋɑ]
Moldavian (masc.)	**moldovalainen**	[moldoʋɑlɑjnen]
Moldavian (fem.)	**moldovalainen**	[moldoʋɑlɑjnen]
Moldavian (adj)	**moldovalainen**	[moldoʋɑlɑjnen]
Russia	**Venäjä**	[ʋeɲæjæ]
Russian (masc.)	**venäläinen**	[ʋeɲæʎæjnen]
Russian (fem.)	**venäläinen**	[ʋeɲæʎæjnen]
Russian (adj)	**venäläinen**	[ʋeɲæʎæjnen]
Tajikistan	**Tadžhikistan**	[tɑʤikistɑn]
Tajik (masc.)	**tadžikki**	[tɑʤikki]
Tajik (fem.)	**tadžikki**	[tɑʤikki]
Tajik (adj)	**tadžikkilainen**	[tɑʤikkilɑjnen]
Turkmenistan	**Turkmenistan**	[turkmenistɑn]
Turkmen (masc.)	**turkmeeni**	[turkme:ni]
Turkmen (fem.)	**turkmeeni**	[turkme:ni]
Turkmenian (adj)	**turkmenialainen**	[turkmeniɑlɑjnen]
Uzbekistan	**Uzbekistan**	[uzbekistɑn]
Uzbek (masc.)	**uzbekki**	[uzbekki]
Uzbek (fem.)	**uzbekki**	[uzbekki]
Uzbek (adj)	**uzbekkilainen**	[uzbekkilɑjnen]
Ukraine	**Ukraina**	[ukrɑinɑ]
Ukrainian (masc.)	**ukrainalainen**	[ukrɑinɑlɑjnen]
Ukrainian (fem.)	**ukrainalainen**	[ukrɑinɑlɑjnen]
Ukrainian (adj)	**ukrainalainen**	[ukrɑinɑlɑjnen]

237. Asia

Asia	**Aasia**	[ɑ:siɑ]
Asian (adj)	**aasialainen**	[ɑ:siɑlɑjnen]
Vietnam	**Vietnam**	[ʋjetnɑm]
Vietnamese (masc.)	**vietnamilainen**	[ʋjetnɑmilɑjnen]
Vietnamese (fem.)	**vietnamilainen**	[ʋjetnɑmilɑjnen]
Vietnamese (adj)	**vietnamilainen**	[ʋjetnɑmilɑjnen]
India	**Intia**	[intiɑ]
Indian (masc.)	**intialainen**	[i:ntiɑlɑjnen]
Indian (fem.)	**intialainen**	[i:ntiɑlɑjnen]
Indian (adj)	**intialainen**	[i:ntiɑlɑjnen]
Israel	**Israel**	[israel]
Israeli (masc.)	**israelilainen**	[israelilɑjnen]
Israeli (fem.)	**israelilainen**	[israelilɑjnen]
Israeli (adj)	**israelilainen**	[israelilɑjnen]
Jew (n)	**juutalainen**	[ju:tɑlɑjnen]
Jewess (n)	**juutalainen**	[ju:tɑlɑjnen]
Jewish (adj)	**juutalainen**	[ju:tɑlɑjnen]
China	**Kiina**	[ki:inɑ]

Chinese (masc.)	**kiinalainen**	[ki:inalajnen]
Chinese (fem.)	**kiinalainen**	[ki:inalajnen]
Chinese (adj)	**kiinalainen**	[ki:inalajnen]
Korean (masc.)	**korealainen**	[korealajnen]
Korean (fem.)	**korealainen**	[korealajnen]
Korean (adj)	**korealainen**	[korealajnen]
Lebanon	**Libanon**	[libanon]
Lebanese (masc.)	**libanonilainen**	[libanonilajnen]
Lebanese (fem.)	**libanonilainen**	[libanonilajnen]
Lebanese (adj)	**libanonilainen**	[libanonilajnen]
Mongolia	**Mongolia**	[moŋolia]
Mongolian (masc.)	**mongoli**	[moŋoli]
Mongolian (fem.)	**mongoli**	[moŋoli]
Mongolian (adj)	**mongolilainen**	[moŋolilajnen]
Malaysia	**Malesia**	[malesia]
Malaysian (masc.)	**malaiji**	[malaijı]
Malaysian (fem.)	**malaiji**	[malaijı]
Malaysian (adj)	**malaijilainen**	[malaj:ılajnen]
Pakistan	**Pakistan**	[pakistan]
Pakistani (masc.)	**pakistanilainen**	[pakistanilajnen]
Pakistani (fem.)	**pakistanilainen**	[pakistanilajnen]
Pakistani (adj)	**pakistanilainen**	[pakistanilajnen]
Saudi Arabia	**Saudi-Arabia**	[saudi arabia]
Arab (masc.)	**arabi**	[arabi]
Arab (fem.)	**arabi**	[arabi]
Arabian (adj)	**arabialainen**	[arabialajnen]
Thailand	**Thaimaa**	[thajma:]
Thai (masc.)	**thaimaalainen**	[thajma:lajnen]
Thai (fem.)	**thaimaalainen**	[thajma:lajnen]
Thai (adj)	**thaimaalainen**	[thajma:lajnen]
Taiwan	**Taiwan**	[tajʋan]
Taiwanese (masc.)	**taiwanilainen**	[tajʋanilajnen]
Taiwanese (fem.)	**taiwanilainen**	[tajʋanilajnen]
Taiwanese (adj)	**taiwanilainen**	[tajʋanilajnen]
Turkey	**Turkki**	[turkki]
Turk (masc.)	**turkkilainen**	[turkkilajnen]
Turk (fem.)	**turkkilainen**	[turkkilajnen]
Turkish (adj)	**turkkilainen**	[turkkilajnen]
Japan	**Japani**	[japani]
Japanese (masc.)	**japanilainen**	[japanilajnen]
Japanese (fem.)	**japanilainen**	[japanilajnen]
Japanese (adj)	**japanilainen**	[japanilajnen]
Afghanistan	**Afganistan**	[afganistan]
Bangladesh	**Bangladesh**	[baŋladeʃ]
Indonesia	**Indonesia**	[indonesia]

Jordan	**Jordania**	[ørdania]
Iraq	**Irak**	[irak]
Iran	**Iran**	[iran]
Cambodia	**Kambodža**	[kambodʒa]
Kuwait	**Kuwait**	[kuʋajt]
Laos	**Laos**	[laos]
Myanmar	**Myanmar**	[myanmar]
Nepal	**Nepal**	[nepal]
United Arab Emirates	**Arabiemiirikuntien liitto**	[arabi emi:iri kuntien li:itto]
Syria	**Syyria**	[sy:ria]
Palestine	**Palestiinalaishallinto**	[palesti:inalajs hallinto]
South Korea	**Etelä-Korea**	[eteʎæ korea]
North Korea	**Pohjois-Korea**	[pohʰøjs korea]

238. North America

United States of America	**Yhdysvallat**	[yhdys ʋallat]
American (masc.)	**amerikkalainen**	[amerikkalajnen]
American (fem.)	**amerikkalainen**	[amerikkalajnen]
American (adj)	**amerikkalainen**	[amerikkalajnen]
Canada	**Kanada**	[kanada]
Canadian (masc.)	**kanadalainen**	[kanadalajnen]
Canadian (fem.)	**kanadalainen**	[kanadalajnen]
Canadian (adj)	**kanadalainen**	[kanadalajnen]
Mexico	**Meksiko**	[meksiko]
Mexican (masc.)	**meksikolainen**	[meksikolajnen]
Mexican (fem.)	**meksikolainen**	[meksikolajnen]
Mexican (adj)	**meksikolainen**	[meksikolajnen]

239. Central and South America

Argentina	**Argentiina**	[argenti:ina]
Argentinian (masc.)	**argentiinalainen**	[argenti:inalajnen]
Argentinian (fem.)	**argentiinalainen**	[argenti:inalajnen]
Argentinian (adj)	**argentiinalainen**	[argenti:inalajnen]
Brazil	**Brasilia**	[brasilia]
Brazilian (masc.)	**brasilialainen**	[brasilialajnen]
Brazilian (fem.)	**brasilialainen**	[brasilialajnen]
Brazilian (adj)	**brasilialainen**	[brasilialajnen]
Colombia	**Kolumbia**	[kolumbia]
Colombian (masc.)	**kolumbialainen**	[kolumbialajnen]
Colombian (fem.)	**kolumbialainen**	[kolumbialajnen]
Colombian (adj)	**kolumbialainen**	[kolumbialajnen]
Cuba	**Kuuba**	[ku:ba]
Cuban (masc.)	**kuubalainen**	[ku:balajnen]

Cuban (fem.)	**kuubalainen**	[ku:balajnen]
Cuban (adj)	**kuubalainen**	[ku:balajnen]
Chile	**Chile**	[ʧile]
Chilean (masc.)	**chileläinen**	[ʧileʎæjnen]
Chilean (fem.)	**chileläinen**	[ʧileʎæjnen]
Chilean (adj)	**chileläinen**	[ʧileʎæjnen]
Bolivia	**Bolivia**	[boliʋia]
Venezuela	**Venezuela**	[ʋenezuela]
Paraguay	**Paraguay**	[paraguaj]
Peru	**Peru**	[peru]
Suriname	**Suriname**	[suriname]
Uruguay	**Uruguay**	[uruguaj]
Ecuador	**Ecuador**	[ekuador]
The Bahamas	**Bahama**	[bahama]
Haiti	**Haiti**	[haiti]
Dominican Republic	**Dominikaaninen tasavalta**	[dominika:ninen tasaʋalta]
Panama	**Panama**	[panama]
Jamaica	**Jamaika**	[jamajka]

240. Africa

Egypt	**Egypti**	[egypti]
Egyptian (masc.)	**egyptiläinen**	[egyptiʎæjnen]
Egyptian (fem.)	**egyptiläinen**	[egyptiʎæjnen]
Egyptian (adj)	**egyptiläinen**	[egyptiʎæjnen]
Morocco	**Marokko**	[marokko]
Moroccan (masc.)	**marokkolainen**	[marokkolajnen]
Moroccan (fem.)	**marokkolainen**	[marokkolajnen]
Moroccan (adj)	**marokkolainen**	[marokkolajnen]
Tunisia	**Tunisia**	[tunisia]
Tunisian (masc.)	**tunisialainen**	[tunisialajnen]
Tunisian (fem.)	**tunisialainen**	[tunisialajnen]
Tunisian (adj)	**tunisialainen**	[tunisialajnen]
Ghana	**Ghana**	[gana]
Zanzibar	**Sansibar**	[sansibar]
Kenya	**Kenia**	[kenia]
Libya	**Libya**	[libya]
Madagascar	**Madagaskar**	[madagaskar]
Namibia	**Namibia**	[namibiæ]
Senegal	**Senegal**	[senegal]
Tanzania	**Tansania**	[tansania]
South Africa	**Etelä-Afrikka**	[eteʎæ afrikka]
African (masc.)	**afrikkalainen**	[afrikkalajnen]
African (fem.)	**afrikkalainen**	[afrikkalajnen]
African (adj)	**afrikkalainen**	[afrikkalajnen]

241. Australia. Oceania

Australia	**Australia**	[australia]
Australian (masc.)	**australialainen**	[australialajnen]
Australian (fem.)	**australialainen**	[australialajnen]
Australian (adj)	**australialainen**	[australialajnen]
New Zealand	**Uusi-Seelanti**	[u:si se:lanti]
New Zealander (masc.)	**uusiseelantilainen**	[u:si se:lantilajnen]
New Zealander (fem.)	**uusiseelantilainen**	[u:si se:lantilajnen]
New Zealand (as adj)	**uusiseelantilainen**	[u:si se:lantilajnen]
Tasmania	**Tasmania**	[tasmania]
French Polynesia	**Ranskan Polynesia**	[ranskan polynesia]

242. Cities

Amsterdam	**Amsterdam**	[amsterdam]
Ankara	**Ankara**	[aŋkara]
Athens	**Ateena**	[ate:na]
Baghdad	**Bagdad**	[bagdad]
Bangkok	**Bangkok**	[baŋkok]
Barcelona	**Barcelona**	[barselona]
Beijing	**Peking**	[pekin]
Beirut	**Beirut**	[bejrut]
Berlin	**Berliini**	[berli:ini]
Bombay, Mumbai	**Mumbai**	[mumbaj]
Bonn	**Bonn**	[boŋ]
Bordeaux	**Bordeaux**	[bordo]
Bratislava	**Bratislava**	[bratislaʋa]
Brussels	**Bryssel**	[bryssel]
Bucharest	**Bukarest**	[bukarest]
Budapest	**Budapest**	[budapest]
Cairo	**Kairo**	[kajro]
Calcutta	**Kalkutta**	[kalkutta]
Chicago	**Chicago**	[ʧikago]
Copenhagen	**Kööpenhamina**	[kø:penhamina]
Dar-es-Salaam	**Dar es Salaam**	[dar es sala:m]
Delhi	**Delhi**	[deli]
Dubai	**Dubai**	[dubaj]
Dublin	**Dublin**	[dublin]
Düsseldorf	**Düsseldorf**	[dysseldorf]
Florence	**Firenze**	[firentse]
Frankfurt	**Frankfurt**	[fraŋkfurt]
Geneva	**Geneve**	[geneʋe]
The Hague	**Haag**	[ha:g]
Hamburg	**Hampuri**	[hampuri]

Hanoi	**Hanoi**	[hanoj]
Havana	**Havanna**	[haʋaŋa]
Helsinki	**Helsinki**	[helsiŋki]
Hiroshima	**Hiroshima**	[hiroʃima]
Hong Kong	**Hongkong**	[hoŋkoŋ]
Istanbul	**Istanbul**	[istanbul]
Jerusalem	**Jerusalem**	[jerusalem]
Kiev	**Kiova**	[kioʋa]
Kuala Lumpur	**Kuala Lumpur**	[kuala lumpur]
Lisbon	**Lissabon**	[lissabon]
London	**Lontoo**	[lonto:]
Los Angeles	**Los Angeles**	[los aŋeles]
Lyons	**Lyon**	[lyon]
Madrid	**Madrid**	[madrid]
Marseille	**Marseille**	[marsejlle]
Mexico City	**México**	[meksiko]
Miami	**Miami**	[majami]
Montreal	**Montreal**	[montreal]
Moscow	**Moskova**	[moskoʋa]
Munich	**München**	[mynhen]
Nairobi	**Nairobi**	[najrobi]
Naples	**Napoli**	[napoli]
New York	**New York**	[njy ørk]
Nice	**Nizza**	[nitsa]
Oslo	**Oslo**	[oslo]
Ottawa	**Ottawa**	[ottaʋa]
Paris	**Pariisi**	[pari:isi]
Prague	**Praha**	[praha]
Rio de Janeiro	**Rio de Janeiro**	[rio de janejro]
Rome	**Rooma**	[ro:ma]
Saint Petersburg	**Pietari**	[pietari]
Seoul	**Soul**	[soul]
Shanghai	**Shanghai**	[ʃaŋhaj]
Singapore	**Singapore**	[siŋapore]
Stockholm	**Tukholma**	[tukholma]
Sydney	**Sydney**	[sidnej]
Taipei	**Taipei**	[tajpej]
Tokyo	**Tokio**	[tokio]
Toronto	**Toronto**	[toronto]
Venice	**Venetsia**	[ʋenetsia]
Vienna	**Wien**	[ʋien]
Warsaw	**Varsova**	[ʋarsoʋa]
Washington	**Washington**	[ʋaʃiŋton]

243. Politics. Government. Part 1

politics	**politiikka**	[politi:ikka]
political (adj)	**poliittinen**	[poli:ittinen]

politician	**poliitikko**	[poli:itikko]
state (country)	**valtio**	[ʋaltio]
citizen	**kansalainen**	[kansalajnen]
citizenship	**kansalaisuus**	[kansalajsu:s]
national emblem	**kansallinen vaakuna**	[kansallinen ʋa:kuna]
national anthem	**kansallishymni**	[kansallis hymni]
government	**hallitus**	[hallitus]
head of state	**maan johtaja**	[ma:n øhtaja]
parliament	**parlamentti**	[parlamentti]
party	**puolue**	[puolue]
capitalism	**kapitalismi**	[kapitalismi]
capitalist (adj)	**kapitalistinen**	[kapitalistinen]
socialism	**sosialismi**	[sosialismi]
socialist (adj)	**sosialistinen**	[sosialistinen]
communism	**kommunismi**	[kommunismi]
communist (adj)	**kommunistinen**	[kommunistinen]
communist (n)	**kommunisti**	[kommunisti]
democracy	**demokratia**	[demokratia]
democrat	**demokraatti**	[demokra:tti]
democratic (adj)	**demokraattinen**	[demokra:ttinen]
Democratic party	**demokraattinen puolue**	[demokra:ttinen puolue]
liberal (n)	**liberaali**	[libera:li]
Liberal (adj)	**liberaali**	[libera:li]
conservative (n)	**vanhoillinen**	[ʋanhojllinen]
conservative (adj)	**vanhoillinen**	[ʋanhojllinen]
republic (n)	**tasavalta**	[tasaʋalta]
republican (n)	**republikaani**	[republika:ni]
Republican party	**republikaanipuolue**	[republika:ni puolue]
poll, elections	**vaalit**	[ʋa:lit]
to elect (vt)	**valita**	[ʋalita]
elector, voter	**valitsija**	[ʋalitsija]
election campaign	**vaalikampanja**	[ʋa:li kampan^{h}ja]
voting (n)	**äänestys**	[æ:nestys]
to vote (vi)	**äänestää**	[æ:nestæ:]
suffrage, right to vote	**äänioikeus**	[æ:niojkeus]
candidate	**ehdokas**	[ehdokas]
to be a candidate	**asettua ehdokkaaksi**	[asettua ehdokka:ksi]
campaign	**kampanja**	[kampan^{h}ja]
opposition (as adj)	**oppositio-**	[oppositio]
opposition (n)	**oppositio**	[oppositio]
visit	**vierailu**	[ʋierajlu]
official visit	**virallinen vierailu**	[ʋirallinen ʋierajlu]
international (adj)	**kansainvälinen**	[kansajnʋælinen]

negotiations	**neuvottelut**	[neuʋottelut]
to negotiate (vi)	**käydä neuvotteluja**	[kæydæ neuʋotteluja]

244. Politics. Government. Part 2

society	**yhteiskunta**	[yhtejskunta]
constitution	**perustuslaki**	[perustuslaki]
power (political control)	**valta**	[ʋalta]
corruption	**lahjottavuus**	[lahʰøttaʋu:s]
law (justice)	**laki**	[laki]
legal (legitimate)	**laillinen**	[la:jlinen]
justice (fairness)	**oikeudenmukaisuus**	[ojkeudenmukajsu:s]
just (fair)	**oikeudenmukainen**	[ojkeuden mukajnen]
committee	**komitea**	[komitea]
bill (draft of law)	**lakiehdotus**	[lakiehdotus]
budget	**budjetti**	[budʰjetti]
policy	**politiikka**	[politi:ikka]
reform	**reformi**	[reformi]
radical (adj)	**radikaali**	[radika:li]
power (strength, force)	**voima**	[ʋojma]
powerful (adj)	**voimakas**	[ʋojmakas]
supporter	**puolustaja**	[puolustaja]
influence	**vaikutus**	[ʋajkutus]
regime (e.g. military ~)	**hallinto**	[hallinto]
conflict	**selkkaus**	[selkkaus]
conspiracy (plot)	**salaliitto**	[salali:itto]
provocation	**provokaatio**	[proʋoka:tio]
to overthrow (regime, etc.)	**kukistaa**	[kukista:]
overthrow (of government)	**kukistaminen**	[kukistaminen]
revolution	**vallankumous**	[ʋallan kumous]
coup d'état	**kumous**	[kumous]
military coup	**sotilasvallankaappaus**	[sotilas ʋallan ka:ppaus]
crisis	**kriisi**	[kri:isi]
economic recession	**taantuma**	[ta:ntuma]
demonstrator (protester)	**mielenosoittaja**	[mielenosojttaja]
demonstration	**mielenosoitus**	[mielenosojtus]
martial law	**sotatila**	[sotatila]
military base	**tukikohta**	[tukikohta]
stability	**vakaus**	[ʋakaus]
stable (adj)	**vakaa**	[ʋaka:]
exploitation	**riisto**	[ri:isto]
to exploit (workers)	**riistää**	[ri:istæ:]
racism	**rasismi**	[rasismi]
racist	**rasisti**	[rasisti]

fascism	**fasismi**	[fasismi]
fascist	**fasisti**	[fasisti]

245. Countries. Miscellaneous

foreigner	**ulkomaalainen**	[ulkoma:lajnen]
foreign (adj)	**ulkomainen**	[ulkomajnen]
abroad (adv)	**ulkomailla**	[ulkomajlla]
emigrant	**maastamuuttaja**	[ma:stamu:ttaja]
emigration	**maastamuutto**	[ma:stamu:tto]
to emigrate (vi)	**muuttaa maasta**	[mu:tta: ma:sta]
the West	**länsi**	[ʎænsi]
the East	**itä**	[itæ]
the Far East	**Kaukoitä**	[kaukojtæ]
civilization	**sivilisaatio**	[siʋilisa:tio]
humanity (mankind)	**ihmiskunta**	[ihmiskunta]
world (earth)	**maailma**	[ma:ilma]
peace	**rauha**	[rauha]
worldwide (adj)	**maailman-**	[ma:jlman]
homeland	**synnyinmaa**	[syŋyjnma:]
people (population)	**kansa**	[kansa]
population	**väestö**	[ʋæestø]
people (a lot of ~)	**ihmiset**	[ihmiset]
nation (people)	**kansakunta**	[kansakunta]
generation	**sukupolvi**	[sukupolʋi]
territory (area)	**alue**	[alue]
region	**seutu**	[seutu]
state (part of a country)	**osavaltio**	[osaʋaltio]
tradition	**perinne**	[periŋe]
custom (tradition)	**tapa**	[tapa]
ecology	**ekologia**	[ekologia]
Indian (Native American)	**intiaani**	[intia:ni]
Gipsy (masc.)	**mustalainen**	[mustalajnen]
Gipsy (fem.)	**mustalainen**	[mustalajnen]
Gipsy (adj)	**mustalainen**	[mustalajnen]
empire	**keisarikunta**	[kejsarikunta]
colony	**kolonia**	[kolonia]
slavery	**orjuus**	[or^{h}ju:s]
invasion	**maahanhyökkäys**	[ma:han hyøkkæys]
famine	**nälänhätä**	[na:la:nha:ta:]

246. Major religious groups. Confessions

religion	**uskonto**	[uskonto]
religious (adj)	**uskonnollinen**	[uskoŋollinen]

belief (in God)	**usko**	[usko]
to believe (in God)	**uskoa**	[uskoɑ]
believer	**uskovainen**	[uskoʋɑjnen]
atheism	**ateismi**	[ɑteismi]
atheist	**ateisti**	[ɑteisti]
Christianity	**Kristinusko**	[kristinusko]
Christian (n)	**kristitty**	[kristitty]
Christian (adj)	**kristillinen**	[kristillinen]
Catholicism	**Katolilaisuus**	[kɑtolilɑjsu:s]
Catholic (n)	**katolilainen**	[kɑtolilɑjnen]
Catholic (adj)	**katolinen**	[kɑtolinen]
Protestantism	**Protestanttisuus**	[protestɑnttisu:s]
Protestant Church	**Protestanttinen Kirkko**	[protestɑnttinen kirkko]
Protestant	**protestantti**	[protestɑntti]
Orthodoxy	**Ortodoksisuus**	[ortodoksisu:s]
Orthodox Church	**Ortodoksinen Kirkko**	[ortodoksinen kirkko]
Orthodox	**ortodoksi**	[ortodoksi]
Presbyterianism	**Presbyteriaaninen kirkko**	[presbyteriɑ:nen kirkko]
Presbyterian Church	**Presbyteerikirkko**	[presbyte:ri kirkko]
Presbyterian (n)	**presbyteeri**	[presbyte:ri]
Lutheranism	**Luterilainen Kirkko**	[luterilɑjnen kirkko]
Lutheran	**luterilainen**	[luterilɑjnen]
Baptist Church	**Baptismi**	[bɑptismi]
Baptist	**baptisti**	[bɑptisti]
Anglican Church	**Anglikaaninen Kirkko**	[ɑŋlikɑ:ninen kirkko]
Anglican	**anglikaaninen**	[ɑŋlikɑ:ninen]
Mormonism	**Mormonismi**	[mormonismi]
Mormon	**mormoni**	[mormoni]
Judaism	**Juutalaisuus**	[ju:tɑlɑjsu:s]
Jew	**juutalainen**	[ju:tɑlɑjnen]
Buddhism	**Buddhalaisuus**	[buddhɑlɑjsu:s]
Buddhist	**buddhalainen**	[buddhɑlɑjnen]
Hinduism	**Hindulaisuus**	[hindulɑjsu:s]
Hindu	**hindulainen**	[hindulɑjnen]
Islam	**Islam**	[islɑm]
Muslim (n)	**muslimi**	[muslimi]
Muslim (adj)	**islamilainen**	[islɑmilɑjnen]
Shiism	**Šiialaisuus**	[ʃi:iɑlɑjsu:s]
Shiite (n)	**shiialainen**	[ʃi:iɑlɑjnen]
Sunni (religion)	**Sunnalaisuus**	[suŋɑlɑjsu:s]
Sunnite (n)	**sunnalainen**	[suŋɑlɑjnen]

247. Religions. Priests

priest	**pappi**	[pappi]
the Pope	**Paavi**	[pa:ʋi]
monk, friar	**munkki**	[muŋkki]
nun	**nunna**	[nuŋa]
pastor	**pastori**	[pastori]
abbot	**apotti**	[apotti]
vicar	**kirkkoherra**	[kirkkoherra]
bishop	**piispa**	[pi:ispa]
cardinal	**kardinaali**	[kardina:li]
preacher	**saarnaaja**	[sa:rna:ja]
preaching	**saarna**	[sa:rna]
parishioners	**seurakuntalaiset**	[seurakuntalajset]
believer	**uskovainen**	[uskoʋajnen]
atheist	**ateisti**	[ateisti]

248. Faith. Christianity. Islam

Adam	**Aadam**	[a:dam]
Eve	**Eeva**	[e:ʋa]
God	**Jumala**	[jumala]
the Lord	**Luoja**	[lo:jæ]
the Almighty	**Kaikkivoipa**	[kajkkiʋojpa]
sin	**synti**	[synti]
to sin (vi)	**tehdä syntiä**	[tehdæ syntiæ]
sinner (masc.)	**syntinen**	[syntinen]
sinner (fem.)	**syntinen**	[syntinen]
hell	**helvetti**	[helʋetti]
paradise	**paratiisi**	[parati:isi]
Jesus	**Jeesus**	[je:sus]
Jesus Christ	**Jeesus Kristus**	[je:sus kristus]
the Holy Spirit	**Pyhä henki**	[pyɦæ heŋki]
the Saviour	**Pelastaja**	[pelastaja]
the Virgin Mary	**Jumalanäiti**	[jumalaɲæjti]
the Devil	**perkele**	[perkele]
devil's (adj)	**perkeleen**	[perkele:n]
Satan	**saatana**	[sa:tana]
satanic (adj)	**saatanallinen**	[sa:tanallinen]
angel	**enkeli**	[eŋkeli]
guardian angel	**suojelusenkeli**	[suojeluseŋkeli]
angelic (adj)	**enkelin**	[eŋkelin]

apostle	**apostoli**	[apostoli]
archangel	**arkkienkeli**	[arkkieŋkeli]
the Antichrist	**antikristus**	[antikristus]
Church	**kirkko**	[kirkko]
Bible	**raamattu**	[ra:mattu]
biblical (adj)	**raamatullinen**	[ra:matullinen]
Old Testament	**Vanha testamentti**	[ʋanha testamentti]
New Testament	**Uusi testamentti**	[u:si testamentti]
Gospel	**Evankeliumi**	[eʋaŋkeliumi]
Holy Scripture	**Pyhä Raamattu**	[pyɦæ ra:mattu]
heaven	**Taivas**	[tajʋas]
Commandment	**käsky**	[kæsky]
prophet	**profeetta**	[profe:tta]
prophecy	**profetia**	[profetia]
Allah	**Allah**	[allah]
Mohammed	**Muhammad**	[muhammad]
the Koran	**Koraani**	[kora:ni]
mosque	**moskeija**	[moskeja]
mullah	**mullah**	[mullah]
prayer	**rukous**	[rukous]
to pray (vi, vt)	**rukoilla**	[rukojlla]
pilgrimage	**pyhiinvaellus**	[pyhi:inʋaellus]
pilgrim	**pyhiinvaeltaja**	[pyhi:inʋaeltaja]
Mecca	**Mekka**	[mekka]
church	**kirkko**	[kirkko]
temple	**temppeli**	[temppeli]
cathedral	**tuomiokirkko**	[tuomiokirkko]
Gothic (adj)	**goottilainen**	[go:ttilajnen]
synagogue	**synagoga**	[synagoga]
mosque	**moskeija**	[moskeja]
chapel	**kappeli**	[kappeli]
abbey	**katolinen luostari**	[katolinen luostari]
convent	**nunnaluostari**	[nuŋa luostari]
monastery	**munkkiluostari**	[muŋkki luostari]
bell (in church)	**kello**	[kello]
bell tower	**kellotorni**	[kellotorni]
to ring (ab. bells)	**soittaa**	[sojtta:]
cross	**risti**	[risti]
cupola (roof)	**kupoli**	[kupoli]
icon	**pyhäinkuva**	[pyɦæjŋkuʋa]
soul	**henki**	[heŋki]
fate (destiny)	**kohtalo**	[kohtalo]
evil (n)	**paha**	[paha]
good (n)	**hyvä**	[hyʋæ]
vampire	**vampyyri**	[ʋampy:ri]

witch (sorceress)	**noita**	[nojta]
demon	**demoni**	[demoni]
devil	**piru**	[piru]
spirit	**henki**	[heŋki]
redemption (giving us ~)	**sovitus**	[soʋitus]
to redeem (vt)	**sovittaa**	[soʋitta:]
church service, mass	**jumalanpalvelus**	[jumalanipalʋelus]
to say mass	**toimittaa jumalanpalvelus**	[tojmitta: jumalanpalʋelus]
confession	**rippi**	[rippi]
to confess (vi)	**ripittäytyä**	[ripittæytyæ]
saint (n)	**pyhimys**	[pyhimys]
sacred (holy)	**pyhä**	[pyɦæ]
holy water	**pyhitetty vesi**	[pyhitetty ʋesi]
ritual (n)	**rituaali**	[ritua:li]
ritual (adj)	**rituaalinen**	[ritua:linen]
sacrifice	**uhraus**	[uhraus]
superstition	**taikausko**	[tajkausko]
superstitious (adj)	**taikauskoinen**	[tajkauskojnen]
afterlife	**haudantakainen elämä**	[haudantakajnen eʎæmæ]
eternal life	**ikuinen elämä**	[ikujnen eʎæma]

MISCELLANEOUS

249. Various useful words

background (green ~)	**tausta**	[tausta]
balance (of situation)	**tase**	[tase]
barrier (obstacle)	**este**	[este]
base (basis)	**pohja**	[pohʰja]
beginning	**alku**	[alku]
category	**kategoria**	[kategoria]
cause (reason)	**syy**	[sy:]
choice	**valikoima**	[ʋali kojma]
coincidence	**yhteensattuma**	[yhte:nsattuma]
comfortable (~ chair)	**mukava**	[mukaʋa]
comparison	**vertailu**	[ʋertajlu]
compensation	**korvaus**	[korʋaus]
degree (extent, amount)	**aste**	[aste]
development	**kehitys**	[kehitys]
difference	**erotus**	[erotus]
effect (e.g. of drugs)	**teho**	[teho]
effort (exertion)	**ponnistus**	[poŋistus]
element	**aines**	[ajnes]
end (finish)	**päättyminen**	[pæ:ttyminen]
example (illustration)	**esimerkki**	[esimerkki]
fact	**tosiasia**	[tosiasia]
frequent (adj)	**usea**	[usea]
growth (development)	**kasvu**	[kasʋu]
help	**apu**	[apu]
ideal	**ihanne**	[ihaŋe]
kind (sort, type)	**laji**	[lajı]
labyrinth	**labyrintti**	[labyrintti]
mistake, error	**erehdys**	[erehdys]
moment	**hetki**	[hetki]
object (thing)	**kohde**	[kohde]
obstacle	**este**	[este]
original (original copy)	**alkuperäiskappale**	[alkuperæjskappale]
part (~ of sth)	**osa**	[osa]
particle, small part	**hiukkanen**	[hiukkanen]
pause (break)	**tauko**	[tauko]
position	**asema**	[asema]
principle	**periaate**	[peria:te]
problem	**ongelma**	[oŋelma]

process	**prosessi**	[prosessi]
progress	**edistys**	[edistys]
property (quality)	**ominaisuus**	[ominɑjsu:s]
reaction	**reaktio**	[reɑktio]
risk	**riski**	[riski]
secret	**salaisuus**	[sɑlɑjsu:s]
section (sector)	**osasto**	[osɑsto]
series	**sarja**	[sɑrʰjɑ]
shape (outer form)	**muoto**	[muoto]
situation	**tilanne**	[tilɑŋe]
solution	**ratkaisu**	[rɑtkɑjsu]
standard (adj)	**standardi-**	[stɑndɑrdi]
standard (level of quality)	**standardi**	[stɑndɑrdi]
stop (pause)	**väliaika**	[ʋæliɑjkɑ]
style	**tyyli**	[ty:li]
system	**järjestelmä**	[jærʰjestelmæ]
table (chart)	**taulukko**	[tɑulukko]
tempo, rate	**tempo**	[tempo]
term (word, expression)	**termi**	[termi]
thing (object, item)	**esine**	[esine]
truth	**tosiasia**	[tosiɑsiɑ]
turn (please wait your ~)	**vuoro**	[ʋuoro]
type (sort, kind)	**tyyppi**	[ty:ppi]
urgent (adj)	**pikainen**	[pikɑjnen]
urgently	**pikaisesti**	[pikɑjsesti]
utility (usefulness)	**hyöty**	[hyøty]
variant (alternative)	**toisinto**	[tojsinto]
way (means, method)	**keino**	[kejno]
zone	**vyöhyke**	[ʋyøhyke]

250. Modifiers. Adjectives. Part 1

additional (adj)	**lisä-**	[lisæ]
ancient (~ civilization)	**muinainen**	[mujnɑjnen]
artificial (adj)	**keinotekoinen**	[kejnotekojnen]
back, rear (adj)	**taka-**	[tɑkɑ]
bad (adj)	**huono**	[huono]
beautiful (~ palace)	**ihana**	[ihɑnɑ]
beautiful (person)	**kaunis**	[kɑunis]
big (in size)	**iso**	[iso]
bitter (taste)	**karvas**	[kɑrʋɑs]
blind (sightless)	**sokea**	[sokeɑ]
calm, quiet (adj)	**rauhallinen**	[rɑuhɑllinen]
careless (negligent)	**leväperäinen**	[leʋæperæjnen]
caring (~ father)	**huolehtivainen**	[huolehtiʋɑjnen]
central (adj)	**keskeinen**	[keskejnen]
cheap (adj)	**halpa**	[hɑlpɑ]

cheerful (adj)	**iloinen**	[ilojnen]
children's (adj)	**lasten-**	[lasten]
civil (~ law)	**kansalais-**	[kansalajs]
clandestine (secret)	**maanalainen**	[ma:nalajnen]
clean (free from dirt)	**puhdas**	[puhdas]
clear (explanation, etc.)	**selvä**	[seluæ]
clever (intelligent)	**älykäs**	[ælykæs]
close (near in space)	**läheinen**	[ʎæhejnen]
closed (adj)	**suljettu**	[sulʰjettu]
cloudless (sky)	**pilvetön**	[piluetøn]
cold (drink, weather)	**kylmä**	[kylmæ]
compatible (adj)	**yhteen sopiva**	[yhte:n sopiua]
contented (adj)	**tyytyväinen**	[ty:tyuæjnen]
continuous (adj)	**pitkäaikainen**	[pitkæ ajkajnen]
continuous (incessant)	**tauoton**	[tauoton]
cool (weather)	**viileä**	[ui:leæ]
dangerous (adj)	**vaarallinen**	[ua:ralinen]
dark (room)	**pimeä**	[pimeæ]
dead (not alive)	**kuollut**	[kuollut]
dense (fog, smoke)	**tiivis**	[ti:iuis]
different (adj)	**eri**	[eri]
difficult (decision)	**vaikea**	[uajkea]
difficult (problem, task)	**monimutkainen**	[monimutkajnen]
dim, faint (light)	**himmeä**	[himmeæ]
dirty (not clean)	**likainen**	[likajnen]
distant (faraway)	**etäinen**	[etæjnen]
distant (in space)	**kaukainen**	[kaukajnen]
dry (climate, clothing)	**kuiva**	[kujua]
easy (not difficult)	**helppo**	[helppo]
empty (glass, room)	**tyhjä**	[tyhʰjæ]
exact (amount)	**tarkka**	[tarkka]
excellent (adj)	**mainio**	[majnio]
excessive (adj)	**liiallinen**	[li:iallinen]
expensive (adj)	**kallis**	[kallis]
exterior (adj)	**ulkonainen**	[ulkonajnen]
fast (quick)	**nopea**	[nopea]
fatty (food)	**rasvainen**	[rasuajnen]
fertile (land, soil)	**hedelmällinen**	[hedelmællinen]
flat (~ panel display)	**litteä**	[litteæ]
flat (e.g. ~ surface)	**tasainen**	[tasajnen]
foreign (adj)	**ulkomainen**	[ulkomajnen]
fragile (china, glass)	**hauras**	[hauras]
free (at no cost)	**ilmainen**	[ilmajnen]
free (unrestricted)	**vapaa**	[uapa:]
fresh (~ water)	**makea**	[makea]
fresh (e.g. ~ bred)	**tuore**	[tuore]
frozen (food)	**jäädytetty**	[jæ:dytetty]

full (completely filled)	**täysi**	[tæysi]
good (book, etc.)	**hyvä**	[hyʋæ]
good (kindhearted)	**hyvä**	[hyʋæ]
grateful (adj)	**kiitollinen**	[ki:itollinen]
happy (adj)	**onnellinen**	[oŋellinen]
hard (not soft)	**kova**	[koʋɑ]
heavy (in weight)	**painava**	[pɑjnɑʋɑ]
hostile (adj)	**vihamielinen**	[ʋihɑ mielinen]
hot (adj)	**kuuma**	[ku:mɑ]
huge (adj)	**valtava**	[ʋɑltɑʋɑ]
humid (adj)	**kostea**	[kosteɑ]
hungry (adj)	**nälkäinen**	[ɲælkæjnen]
ill (sick, unwell)	**sairas**	[sɑjrɑs]
incomprehensible	**epäselvä**	[epæselʋæ]
immobile (adj)	**liikkumaton**	[li:ikkumɑton]
important (adj)	**tärkeä**	[tærkeæ]
impossible (adj)	**mahdoton**	[mɑhdoton]
indispensable (adj)	**välttämätön**	[ʋælttæmætøn]
inexperienced (adj)	**kokematon**	[kokemɑton]
insignificant (adj)	**vähäinen**	[ʋæɦæjnen]
interior (adj)	**sisäinen**	[sisæjnen]
joint (~ decision)	**yhteinen**	[yhtejnen]
last (e.g. ~ week)	**viime**	[ʋi:ime]
last (final)	**viimeinen**	[ʋi:imejnen]
left (e.g. ~ side)	**vasen**	[ʋɑsen]
legal (legitimate)	**laillinen**	[lɑ:jlinen]
light (in weight)	**kevyt**	[keʋyt]
light (pale color)	**vaalea**	[ʋɑ:leɑ]
limited (adj)	**rajoitettu**	[rɑøjtettu]
liquid (fluid)	**nestemäinen**	[nestemæønen]
long (e.g. ~ way)	**pitkä**	[pitkæ]
loud (voice, etc.)	**äänekäs**	[æ:nekæs]
low (voice)	**hiljainen**	[hil^{h}jɑjnen]

251. Modifiers. Adjectives. Part 2

main (principal)	**pää-**	[pæ:]
matt (paint)	**himmeä**	[himmeæ]
meticulous (job)	**huolellinen**	[huolellinen]
mysterious (adj)	**arvoituksellinen**	[ɑrʋojtuksellinen]
narrow (street, etc.)	**kapea**	[kɑpeæ]
native (of country)	**kotoinen**	[kotojnen]
necessary (adj)	**tarpeellinen**	[tɑrpe:llinen]
negative (adj)	**kielteinen**	[kieltejnen]
neighbouring (adj)	**naapuri-**	[nɑ:puri]
nervous (adj)	**hermostunut**	[hermostunut]

new (adj)	**uusi**	[u:si]
next (e.g. ~ week)	**seuraava**	[seurɑ:ʋɑ]
nearby	**lähin**	[ʎæhin]
nice (kind)	**herttainen**	[herttɑjnen]
nice (voice)	**miellyttävä**	[miellyttæʋæ]
normal (adj)	**normaalinen**	[normɑ:linen]
not big (adj)	**pieni**	[pæni]
not clear (adj)	**epäselvä**	[epæselʋæ]
not difficult (adj)	**helppo**	[helppo]
obligatory (adj)	**pakollinen**	[pɑkollinen]
old (house)	**vanha**	[ʋɑnhɑ]
open (adj)	**avoin**	[ɑʋojn]
opposite (adj)	**vastakkainen**	[ʋɑstɑkkɑjnen]
ordinary (usual)	**tavallinen**	[tɑʋɑllinen]
original (unusual)	**alkuperäinen**	[ɑlkuperæjnen]
past (recent)	**mennyt**	[meŋyt]
permanent (adj)	**vakinainen**	[ʋɑkinɑjnen]
personal (adj)	**yksityinen**	[yksityjnen]
polite (adj)	**kohtelias**	[kohteliɑs]
poor (not rich)	**köyhä**	[køyɦæ]
possible (adj)	**mahdollinen**	[mɑhdollinen]
poverty-stricken (adj)	**kurja**	[kur^{h}jɑ]
present (current)	**nykyinen**	[nykyjnen]
principal (main)	**perus-**	[perus]
private (~ jet)	**yksityinen**	[yksityjnen]
probable (adj)	**todennäköinen**	[todeŋækøjnen]
public (open to all)	**yhteiskunnallinen**	[yhtejskuŋɑlinen]
punctual (person)	**täsmällinen**	[tæsmællinen]
quiet (tranquil)	**tyyni**	[ty:yni]
rare (adj)	**harvinainen**	[hɑrʋinɑjnen]
raw (uncooked)	**raaka**	[rɑ:kɑ]
right (not left)	**oikeistolainen**	[ojkejstolɑjnen]
right, correct (adj)	**oikea**	[ojkeɑ]
ripe (fruit)	**kypsä**	[kypsæ]
risky (adj)	**riskialtis**	[riskiɑltis]
sad (~ look)	**surullinen**	[surullinen]
sad (depressing)	**surullinen**	[surullinen]
safe (not dangerous)	**turvallinen**	[turʋɑllinen]
salty (food)	**suolainen**	[suolɑjnen]
satisfied (customer)	**tyytyväinen**	[ty:tyʋæjnen]
second hand (adj)	**käytetty**	[kæutetty]
shallow (water)	**matala**	[mɑtɑlɑ]
sharp (blade, etc.)	**terävä**	[teræʋæ]
short (in length)	**lyhyt**	[lyhyt]
short, short-lived (adj)	**lyhytaikainen**	[lyhytɑjkɑjnen]
short-sighted (adj)	**likinäköinen**	[likiɲækøjnen]
significant (notable)	**merkittävä**	[merkttæʋæ]
similar (adj)	**näköinen**	[ɲækøjnen]

simple (easy)	**yksinkertainen**	[yksiŋkertɑjnen]
slim (person)	**laiha**	[lɑjhɑ]
small (in size)	**pieni**	[pæni]
smooth (surface)	**sileä**	[sileæ]
soft (to touch)	**pehmeä**	[pehmeæ]
solid (~ wall)	**vahva**	[ʋɑhʋɑ]
somber, gloomy (adj)	**synkkä**	[syŋkkæ]
sour (flavour, taste)	**hapan**	[hɑpɑn]
spacious (house, etc.)	**avara**	[ɑʋɑrɑ]
special (adj)	**erikoinen**	[erikojnen]
straight (line, road)	**suora**	[suorɑ]
strong (person)	**voimakas**	[ʋojmɑkɑs]
stupid (foolish)	**tyhmä**	[tyhmæ]
convenient (adj)	**kelvollinen**	[kelʋollinen]
sunny (day)	**aurinkoinen**	[ɑuriŋkojnen]
superb, perfect (adj)	**mainio**	[mɑjnio]
swarthy (adj)	**tummaverinen**	[tummɑʋerinen]
sweet (sugary)	**makea**	[mɑkeɑ]
tanned (adj)	**ruskettunut**	[ruskettunut]
tasty (adj)	**maukas**	[mɑukɑs]
tender (affectionate)	**hellä**	[heʎæ]
the highest (adj)	**korkein**	[korkejn]
the most important	**tärkein**	[tærkejn]
the nearest	**lähin**	[ʎæhin]
the same, equal (adj)	**samanlainen**	[sɑmɑn lɑjnen]
thick (e.g. ~ fog)	**taaja**	[tɑ:jɑ]
thick (wall, slice)	**paksu**	[pɑksu]
tired (exhausted)	**väsynyt**	[ʋæsynyt]
tiring (adj)	**väsyttävä**	[ʋæsyttæʋæ]
too thin (emaciated)	**laiha**	[lɑjhɑ]
transparent (adj)	**läpikuultava**	[ʎæpiku:ltɑʋɑ]
unique (exceptional)	**ainutlaatuinen**	[ɑjnutlɑ:tujnen]
various (adj)	**erilainen**	[erilɑjnen]
warm (moderately hot)	**lämmin**	[ʎæmmin]
wet (e.g. ~ clothes)	**märkä**	[mærkæ]
whole (entire, complete)	**kokonainen**	[kokonɑjnen]
wide (e.g. ~ road)	**leveä**	[leʋeæ]
young (adj)	**nuori**	[nuori]

MAIN 500 VERBS

252. Verbs A-C

to accompany (vt)	**saattaa**	[sa:tta:]
to accuse (vt)	**syyttää**	[sy:ttæ:]
to act (take action)	**menetellä**	[menetеʎæ]
to add (supplement)	**lisätä**	[lisætæ]
to address (speak to)	**kääntyä puoleen**	[kæ:ntyæ puole:n]
to admire (vi)	**ihailla**	[ihajlla]
to advertise (vt)	**mainostaa**	[majnosta:]
to advise (vt)	**neuvoa**	[neuʋoa]
to affirm (vt)	**väittää**	[ʋæjttæ:]
to agree (say yes)	**suostua**	[suostua]
to allow (sb to do sth)	**sallia**	[sallia]
to allude (vi)	**vihjata**	[ʋihʰjata]
to amputate (vt)	**amputoida**	[amputojda]
to make angry	**vihastuttaa**	[ʋihastutta:]
to answer (vi, vt)	**vastata**	[ʋastata]
to apologize (vi)	**pyytää anteeksi**	[py:tæ: ante:ksi]
to appear (come into view)	**ilmestyä**	[ilmestyæ]
to applaud (vi, vt)	**taputtaa käsiä**	[taputta: kæsiæ]
to appoint (assign)	**nimittää**	[nimittæ:]
to approach (come nearer)	**mennä**	[meŋæ]
to arrive (ab. train)	**saapua**	[sa:pua]
to ask (~ sb to do sth)	**pyytää**	[py:tæ:]
to aspire to …	**pyrkiä**	[pyrkiæ]
to assist (help)	**avustaa**	[aʋusta:]
to attack (mil.)	**hyökätä**	[hyøkætæ]
to attain (objectives)	**saavuttaa**	[sa:ʋutta:]
to avenge (vt)	**kostaa**	[kosta:]
to avoid (danger, task)	**välttää**	[ʋælttæ:]
to award (give medal to)	**palkita**	[palkita]
to bath (~ one's baby)	**kylvettää**	[kylʋettæ:]
to battle (vi)	**taistella**	[tajstella]
to be (~ on the table)	**sijaita**	[sijajta]
to be (vi)	**olla**	[olla]
to be afraid	**pelätä**	[peʎætæ]
to be angry (with …)	**vihastua**	[ʋihastua]
to be at war	**sotia**	[sotia]
to be based (on …)	**perustua**	[perustua]

to be bored	**ikävöidä**	[ikæuøjdæ]
to be convinced	**vakuuttua**	[uaku:ttua]
to be enough	**riittää**	[ri:ittæ:]
to be envious	**kadehtia**	[kadehtia]
to be indignant	**olla suutuksissa**	[olla su:tuksissa]
to be interested in ...	**kiinnostua**	[ki:iŋostua]
to be lying down	**maata**	[ma:ta]
to be needed	**tarvita**	[taruita]
to be perplexed	**olla ymmällään**	[olla ymmællæ:n]
to be preserved	**säilyä**	[sæjlyæ]
to be required	**tarvita**	[taruita]
to be surprised	**ihmetellä**	[ihmeteʎæ]
to be worried	**huolestua**	[huolestua]
to beat (dog, person)	**lyödä**	[lyødæ]
to become (e.g. ~ old)	**tulla**	[tulla]
to become pensive	**vaipua ajatuksiinsa**	[uajpua ajatuksi:insa]
to behave (vi)	**käyttäytyä**	[kæyttæytyæ]
to believe (think)	**uskoa**	[uskoa]
to belong to ...	**kuulua**	[ku:lua]
to berth (moor)	**laskea laituriin**	[laskea lajturi:in]
to blind (of flash of light)	**häikäistä**	[ɦæjkæjsta]
to blow (wind)	**puhaltaa**	[puhalta:]
to blush (vi)	**punastua**	[punastua]
to boast (vi)	**kehua**	[kehua]
to borrow (money)	**lainata**	[lajnata]
to break (branch, toy, etc.)	**rikkoa**	[rikkoa]
to snap (vi, ab. rope)	**repeytyä**	[repeytyæ]
to breathe (vi)	**hengittää**	[heŋittæ:]
to bring (sth)	**tuoda**	[tuoda]
to burn (paper, logs)	**polttaa**	[poltta:]
to buy (purchase)	**ostaa**	[osta:]
to call (for help)	**kutsua**	[kuʦua]
to call (with one's voice)	**kutsua**	[kuʦua]
to calm down (vt)	**rauhoittaa**	[rauhojtta:]
can (v aux)	**voida**	[uojda]
to cancel (call off)	**peruuttaa**	[peru:tta:]
to cast off	**irtautua**	[irtautua]
to catch (e.g. ~ a ball)	**ottaa kiinni**	[otta: ki:iŋi]
to catch sight (of ...)	**nähdä**	[ɲæhdæ]
to cause ...	**aiheuttaa**	[ajheutta:]
to change (~ one's opinion)	**muuttaa**	[mu:tta:]
to change (exchange)	**vaihtaa**	[uajhta:]
to charm (vt)	**lumota**	[lumota]
to choose (select)	**valita**	[ualita]
to chop off (with an axe)	**katkaista**	[katkajsta]
to clean (from dirt)	**puhdistaa**	[puhdista:]
to clean (shoes, etc.)	**puhdistaa**	[puhdista:]
to clean (tidy)	**siivota**	[si:iuota]

to close (vt)	**sulkea**	[sulkea]
to comb one's hair	**kammata tukkansa**	[kammata tukkansa]
to come down (the stairs)	**laskeutua**	[laskeutua]
to come in (enter)	**astua sisään**	[astua sisæ:n]
to come out (book)	**ilmestyä**	[ilmestyæ]
to compare (vt)	**verrata**	[ʋerrata]
to compensate (vt)	**korvata**	[korʋata]
to compete (vi)	**kilpailla**	[kilpajlla]
to compile (~ a list)	**laatia**	[la:tia]
to complain (vi, vt)	**valittaa**	[ʋalitta:]
to complicate (vt)	**mutkistaa**	[mutkista:]
to compose (music, etc.)	**säveltää**	[sæʋeltæ:]
to compromise (vt)	**kompromettoida**	[komprometto jda]
to concentrate (vi)	**keskittyä**	[keskittyæ]
to confess (criminal)	**tunnustaa**	[tuŋusta:]
to confuse (mix up)	**sotkea**	[sotkea]
to congratulate (vt)	**onnitella**	[oŋitella]
to consult (doctor, expert)	**neuvotella**	[neuʋotella]
to continue (~ to do sth)	**jatkaa**	[jatka:]
to control (vt)	**tarkastaa**	[tarkasta:]
to convince (vt)	**vakuuttaa**	[ʋaku:tta:]
to cooperate (vi)	**olla yhteistyössä**	[olla yhtejstyøssæ]
to coordinate (vt)	**koordinoida**	[ko:rdinojda]
to correct (an error)	**korjata**	[korʰjata]
to cost (vt)	**maksaa**	[maksa:]
to count (money, etc.)	**laskea**	[laskea]
to count on ...	**luottaa**	[luotta:]
to crack (ceiling, wall)	**halkeilla**	[halkejlla]
to create (vt)	**luoda**	[luoda]
to cry (weep)	**itkeä**	[itkeæ]
to cut off (with a knife)	**leikata**	[lejkata]

253. Verbs D-G

to dare (~ to do sth)	**uskaltaa**	[uskalta:]
to date from ...	**ajoittua**	[aøjttua]
to deceive (vi, vt)	**pettää**	[pettæ:]
to decide (~ to do sth)	**päättää**	[pæ:ttæ:]
to decorate (tree, street)	**koristaa**	[korista:]
to dedicate (book, etc.)	**omistaa**	[omista:]
to defend (a country, etc.)	**puolustaa**	[puolusta:]
to defend oneself	**puolustautua**	[puolustautua]
to demand (request firmly)	**vaatia**	[ʋa:tia]
to denounce (vt)	**antaa ilmi**	[anta: ilmi]
to deny (vt)	**kieltää**	[kjeltæ:]

to depend on ...	**riippua**	[ri:ippuɑ]
to deprive (vt)	**riistää**	[ri:istæ:]
to deserve (vt)	**ansaita**	[ɑnsɑjtɑ]
to design (machine, etc.)	**suunnitella**	[su:ŋitellɑ]
to desire (want, wish)	**haluta**	[hɑlutɑ]
to despise (vt)	**halveksia**	[hɑlʋeksiɑ]
to destroy (documents, etc.)	**hävittää**	[ɦæʋittæ:]
to differ (from sth)	**erota**	[erotɑ]
to dig (tunnel, etc.)	**kaivaa**	[kɑjʋɑ:]
to direct (point the way)	**suunnata**	[su:ŋɑtɑ]
to disappear (vi)	**kadota**	[kɑdotɑ]
to discover (new land, etc.)	**löytää**	[løytæ:]
to discuss (vt)	**käsitellä**	[kæsiteʎæ]
to distribute (leaflets, etc.)	**levittää**	[leʋittæ:]
to disturb (vt)	**häiritä**	[ɦæjritæ]
to dive (vi)	**sukeltaa**	[sukeltɑ:]
to divide (math)	**jakaa**	[jɑkɑ:]
to do (vt)	**tehdä**	[tehdæ]
to do the laundry	**pestä**	[pestæ]
to double (increase)	**kahdentaa**	[kɑhdentɑ:]
to doubt (have doubts)	**epäillä**	[epæjʎæ]
to draw a conclusion	**tehdä johtopäätös**	[tehdæ øhtoipæ:tøs]
to dream (daydream)	**haaveilla**	[hɑ:ʋejllɑ]
to dream (in sleep)	**nähdä unta**	[ɲæhdæ untɑ]
to drink (vi, vt)	**juoda**	[juodɑ]
to drive a car	**ajaa autoa**	[ɑjɑ: ɑutoɑ]
to drive away	**ajaa pois**	[ɑjɑ: pojs]
to drop (let fall)	**pudottaa**	[pudottɑ:]
to drown (ab. person)	**hukkua**	[hukkuɑ]
to dry (clothes, hair)	**kuivata**	[kujʋɑtɑ]
to eat (vi, vt)	**syödä**	[syødæ]
to eavesdrop (vi)	**kuunnella salaa**	[ku:ŋellɑ sɑlɑ:]
to enter (on the list)	**lisätä**	[lisætæ]
to entertain (amuse)	**huvittaa**	[huʋittɑ:]
to equip (fit out)	**varustaa**	[ʋɑrustɑ:]
to examine (proposal)	**käsitellä**	[kæsiteʎæ]
to exchange (sth)	**vaihtaa keskenään**	[ʋɑjhtɑ: keskenæ:n]
to exclude, to expel	**poistaa**	[pojstɑ:]
to excuse (forgive)	**antaa anteeksi**	[ɑntɑ: ɑnte:ksi]
to exist (vi)	**olla olemassa**	[ollɑ olemɑssɑ]
to expect (anticipate)	**odottaa**	[odottɑ:]
to expect (foresee)	**nähdä ennakolta**	[ɲæhdæ eŋɑkoltɑ]
to explain (vt)	**selittää**	[selittæ:]
to express (vt)	**ilmaista**	[ilmɑjstɑ]
to extinguish (a fire)	**sammuttaa**	[sɑmmuttɑ:]

to fall in love (with ...)	**rakastua**	[rakastua]
to fancy (vt)	**pitää**	[pitæ:]
to feed (provide food)	**ruokkia**	[ruokkia]
to fight (against the enemy)	**taistella**	[tajstella]
to fight (vi)	**tapella**	[tapella]
to fill (glass, bottle)	**täyttää**	[tæyttæ:]
to find (~ lost items)	**löytää**	[løytæ:]
to finish (vt)	**lopettaa**	[lopetta:]
to fish (vi)	**kalastaa**	[kalasta:]
to fit (ab. dress, etc.)	**sopia**	[sopia]
to flatter (vt)	**imarrella**	[imarrella]
to fly (bird, plane)	**lentää**	[lentæ:]
to follow ... (come after)	**seurata**	[seurata]
to forbid (vt)	**kieltää**	[kjeltæ:]
to force (compel)	**pakottaa**	[pakotta:]
to forget (vi, vt)	**unohtaa**	[unohta:]
to forgive (pardon)	**antaa anteeksi**	[anta: ante:ksi]
to form (constitute)	**muodostaa**	[muodosta:]
to get dirty (vi)	**tahraantua**	[tahra:ntua]
to get infected (with ...)	**saada tartunta**	[sa:da tartunta]
to get irritated	**ärtyä**	[ærtyæ]
to get married	**mennä naimisiin**	[meŋæ na:jmisi:in]
to get rid of ...	**päästä**	[pæ:stæ]
to get tired	**väsyä**	[ʋæsyæ]
to get up (arise from bed)	**nousta**	[nousta]
to give a hug, to hug (vt)	**syleillä**	[sylejʎæ]
to give in (yield to)	**antaa periksi**	[anta: periksi]
to go (by car, etc.)	**mennä**	[meŋæ]
to go (on foot)	**mennä**	[meŋæ]
to go for a swim	**kylpeä**	[kylpeæ]
to go out (for dinner, etc.)	**lähteä**	[ʎæhteæ]
to go to bed	**mennä nukkumaan**	[meŋæ nukkuma:n]
to greet (vt)	**tervehtiä**	[terʋehtiæ]
to grow (plants)	**kasvattaa**	[kasʋatta:]
to guarantee (vt)	**taata**	[ta:ta]
to guess right	**arvata**	[arʋata]

254. Verbs H-M

to hand out (distribute)	**jakaa**	[jaka:]
to hang (curtains, etc.)	**ripustaa**	[ripusta:]
to have (vt)	**omistaa**	[omista:]
to have a bath	**peseytyä**	[peseytyæ]
to have a try	**koettaa**	[koetta:]
to have breakfast	**syödä aamiaista**	[syødæ a:miajsta]
to have dinner	**illastaa**	[illasta:]

to have fun	**huvitella**	[huʋitellɑ]
to have lunch	**syödä päivällistä**	[syødæ pæjʋællistæ]
to head (group, etc.)	**johtaa**	[øhtɑ:]
to hear (vt)	**kuulla**	[ku:llɑ]
to heat (vt)	**lämmittää**	[ʎæmmittæ:]
to help (vt)	**auttaa**	[ɑuttɑ:]
to hide (vt)	**piilotella**	[pi:ilotellɑ]
to hire (e.g. ~ a boat)	**vuokrata**	[ʋuokrɑtɑ]
to hire (staff)	**palkata**	[pɑlkɑtɑ]
to hope (vi, vt)	**toivoa**	[tojʋoɑ]
to hunt (for food, sport)	**metsästää**	[met͡sæstæ:]
to hurry (vi)	**kiiruhtaa**	[ki:iruhtɑ:]
to hurry (sb)	**kiirehtiä**	[ki:irehtiæ]
to imagine (to picture)	**kuvitella**	[kuʋitellɑ]
to imitate (vt)	**jäljitellä**	[jæljıteʎæ]
to implore (vt)	**rukoilla**	[rukojllɑ]
to import (vt)	**tuoda maahan**	[tuodɑ mɑ:hɑn]
to increase (vi)	**lisääntyä**	[lisæ:ntyæ]
to increase (vt)	**lisätä**	[lisætæ]
to infect (vt)	**tartuttaa**	[tɑrtuttɑ:]
to influence (vt)	**vaikuttaa**	[ʋɑjkuttɑ:]
to inform (~ sb about ...)	**ilmoittaa**	[ilmojttɑ:]
to inform (vt)	**tiedottaa**	[tiedottɑ:]
to inherit (vt)	**periä**	[periæ]
to inquire (about ...)	**tietää**	[tietæ:]
to insist (vi, vt)	**pysyä kannassaan**	[pysyæ kɑŋɑssɑ:n]
to inspire (vt)	**innostaa**	[iŋostɑ:]
to instruct (teach)	**ohjata**	[ohʰjɑtɑ]
to insult (offend)	**loukata**	[loukɑtɑ]
to interest (vt)	**kiinnostaa**	[ki:iŋostɑ:]
to intervene (vi)	**puuttua**	[pu:ttuɑ]
to introduce (present)	**tutustua**	[tutustuɑ]
to invent (machine, etc.)	**keksiä**	[keksiæ]
to invite (vt)	**kutsua**	[kut͡suɑ]
to iron (laundry)	**silittää**	[silittæ:]
to irritate (annoy)	**ärsyttää**	[ærsyttæ:]
to isolate (vt)	**eristää**	[eristæ:]
to join (political party, etc.)	**yhtyä**	[yhtyæ]
to joke (be kidding)	**laskea leikkiä**	[lɑskeɑ lejkkiæ]
to keep (old letters, etc.)	**säilyttää**	[sæjlyttæ:]
to keep silent	**olla vaiti**	[ollɑ ʋɑjti]
to kill (vt)	**murhata**	[murhɑtɑ]
to knock (at the door)	**koputtaa oveen**	[koputtɑ: oʋe:n]
to know (sb)	**tuntea**	[tunteɑ]
to know (sth)	**tietää**	[tietæ:]

to laugh (vi)	**nauraa**	[naura:]
to launch (start up)	**käynnistää**	[kæyŋistæ:]
to leave (~ for Mexico)	**lähteä**	[ʎæhteæ]
to leave (forget)	**unohtaa**	[unohta:]
to leave (spouse)	**jättää**	[jættæ:]
to liberate (city, etc.)	**vapauttaa**	[ʋapautta:]
to lie (tell untruth)	**valehdella**	[ʋalehdella]
to light (campfire, etc.)	**sytyttää**	[sytyttæ:]
to light up (illuminate)	**valaista**	[ʋalajsta]
to limit (vt)	**rajoittaa**	[raøjtta:]
to listen (vi)	**kuunnella**	[ku:ŋella]
to live (~ in France)	**asua**	[asua]
to live (exist)	**elää**	[elæ:]
to load (gun)	**ladata**	[ladata]
to load (vehicle, etc.)	**kuormata**	[kuormata]
to look (I'm just ~ing)	**katsoa**	[kat͡soa]
to look for ... (search)	**etsiä**	[et͡siæ]
to look like (resemble)	**olla näköinen**	[olla ɲækøjnen]
to lose (umbrella, etc.)	**kadottaa**	[kadotta:]
to love (sb)	**rakastaa**	[rakasta:]
to love (sth)	**pitää**	[pitæ:]
to lower (blind, head)	**laskea**	[laskea]
to make (~ dinner)	**laittaa**	[lajtta:]
to make a mistake	**erehtyä**	[erehtyæ]
to make copies	**monistaa**	[monista:]
to make easier	**helpottaa**	[helpotta:]
to make the acquaintance	**tutustua**	[tutustua]
to make use (of ...)	**käyttää**	[kæyttæ:]
to manage, to run	**johtaa**	[øhta:]
to mark (make a mark)	**merkitä**	[merkitæ]
to mean (signify)	**merkitä**	[merkitæ]
to memorize (vt)	**muistaa**	[mujsta:]
to mention (talk about)	**mainita**	[majnita]
to miss (school, etc.)	**olla poissa**	[olla pojssa]
to mix (combine, blend)	**sekoittaa**	[sekojtta:]
to mock (deride)	**pilkata**	[pilkata]
to move (wardrobe, etc.)	**siirtää**	[si:irtæ:]
to multiply (math)	**kertoa**	[kertoa]
must (v aux)	**olla velkaa**	[olla ʋelka:]

255. Verbs N-S

to name, to call (vt)	**nimittää**	[nimittæ:]
to negotiate (vi)	**käydä neuvotteluja**	[kæydæ neuʋotteluja]
to note (write down)	**merkitä**	[merkitæ]
to notice (see)	**huomata**	[huomata]
to obey (vi, vt)	**alistua**	[alistua]

to object (vi, vt)	**väittää vastaan**	[ʋæjttæ: ʋɑstɑ:n]
to observe (see)	**seurata**	[seurɑtɑ]
to offend (vt)	**loukata**	[loukɑtɑ]
to omit (word, phrase)	**jättää**	[jættæ:]
to open (vt)	**avata**	[ɑʋɑtɑ]
to order (in restaurant)	**tilata**	[tilɑtɑ]
to order (mil.)	**käskeä**	[kæskeæ]
to organize (concert, party)	**järjestää**	[jærʰjestæ:]
to overestimate (vt)	**yliarvioida**	[yliɑrʋiojdɑ]
to own (possess)	**omistaa**	[omistɑ:]
to participate (vi)	**osallistua**	[osɑllistuɑ]
to pass (go beyond)	**ajaa ohi**	[ɑjɑ: ohi]
to pay (vi, vt)	**maksaa**	[mɑksɑ:]
to peep, to spy on	**tirkistellä**	[tirkisteʎæ]
to penetrate (vt)	**tunkeutua**	[tuŋkeutuɑ]
to permit (vt)	**antaa lupa**	[ɑntɑ: lupɑ]
to pick (flowers)	**repiä**	[repiæ]
to place (put, set)	**sijoittaa**	[si:ojttɑ:]
to plan (~ to do sth)	**suunnitella**	[su:ŋitellɑ]
to play (actor)	**näytellä**	[ɲæyteʎæ]
to play (children)	**leikkiä**	[lejkkiæ]
to point (~ the way)	**osoittaa**	[osojttɑ:]
to pour (liquid)	**kaataa**	[kɑ:tɑ:]
to pray (vi, vt)	**rukoilla**	[rukojllɑ]
to predominate (vi)	**vallita**	[ʋɑllitɑ]
to prefer (vt)	**katsoa paremmaksi**	[kɑtsoɑ pɑremmɑksi]
to prepare (~ a plan)	**valmistaa**	[ʋɑlmistɑ:]
to present (sb to sb)	**esitellä**	[esiteʎæ]
to preserve (peace, life)	**säilyttää**	[sæjlyttæ:]
to progress (move forward)	**edetä**	[edetæ]
to promise (vt)	**luvata**	[luʋɑtɑ]
to pronounce (vt)	**ääntää**	[æ:ntæ:]
to propose (vt)	**ehdottaa**	[ehdottɑ:]
to protect (e.g. ~ nature)	**suojata**	[suojɑtɑ]
to protest (vi)	**vastustaa**	[ʋɑstustɑ:]
to prove (vt)	**todistaa**	[todistɑ:]
to provoke (vt)	**provosoida**	[proʋosojdɑ]
to pull (~ the rope)	**vetää**	[ʋetæ:]
to punish (vt)	**rangaista**	[rɑŋɑjstɑ]
to push (~ the door)	**sysätä**	[sysætæ]
to put away (vt)	**korjata pois**	[korʰjɑtɑ pojs]
to put in (insert)	**panna**	[pɑŋɑ]
to put in order	**panna järjestykseen**	[pɑŋɑ jærʰjestykse:n]
to put, to place	**panna**	[pɑŋɑ]
to quote (cite)	**siteerata**	[site:rɑtɑ]
to reach (arrive at)	**saavuttaa**	[sɑ:ʋuttɑ:]
to read (vi, vt)	**lukea**	[lukeɑ]

to realise (achieve)	**toteuttaa**	[toteuttɑ:]
to recall (~ one's name)	**muistella**	[mujstellɑ]
to recognize (admit)	**tunnustaa**	[tuŋustɑ:]
to recognize (identify sb)	**tuntea**	[tunteɑ]
to recommend (vt)	**suositella**	[suositellɑ]
to recover (~ from flu)	**parantua**	[pɑrɑntuɑ]
to redo (do again)	**tehdä uudelleen**	[tehdæ u:delle:n]
to reduce (speed, etc.)	**vähentää**	[ʋæhentæ:]
to refuse (~ sb)	**kieltää**	[kjeltæ:]
to regret (be sorry)	**sääliä**	[sæ:liæ]
to remember (vt)	**muistaa**	[mujstɑ:]
to remind of ...	**muistuttaa**	[mujstuttɑ:]
to remove (~ a stain)	**poistaa**	[pojstɑ:]
to remove (~ an obstacle)	**poistaa**	[pojstɑ:]
to rent (sth from sb)	**vuokrata**	[ʋuokrɑtɑ]
to repair (mend)	**korjata**	[kor^hjɑtɑ]
to repeat (say again)	**toistaa**	[tojstɑ:]
to report (make a report)	**selostaa**	[selostɑ:]
to reproach (vt)	**moittia**	[mojttiɑ]
to reserve, to book	**varata**	[ʋɑrɑtɑ]
to restrain (hold back)	**estää**	[estæ:]
to return (come back)	**palata**	[pɑlɑtɑ]
to risk, to take a risk	**ottaa riski**	[ottɑ: riski]
to rub off (erase)	**pyyhkiä**	[py:hkiæ]
to run (move fast)	**juosta**	[juostɑ]
to satisfy (please)	**tyydyttää**	[ty:dyttæ:]
to save (rescue)	**pelastaa**	[pelɑstɑ:]
to say (~ thank you)	**sanoa**	[sɑnoɑ]
to scold (vt)	**haukkua**	[hɑukkuɑ]
to scratch (with claws)	**raapia**	[rɑ:piɑ]
to select (to pick)	**valita**	[ʋɑlitɑ]
to sell (goods)	**myydä**	[my:dæ]
to send (a letter)	**lähettää**	[ʎæhettæ:]
to send back (vt)	**lähettää takaisin**	[ʎæhettæ: tɑkɑjsin]
to sense (danger)	**tuntea**	[tunteɑ]
to sentence (vt)	**tuomita**	[tuomitɑ]
to serve (in restaurant)	**palvella**	[pɑlʋellɑ]
to settle (a conflict)	**ratkaista**	[rɑtkɑjstɑ]
to shake (vt)	**pudistaa**	[pudistɑ:]
to shave (vi)	**ajaa partaa**	[ɑjɑ: pɑrtɑ:]
to shine (vi)	**loistaa**	[lojstɑ:]
to shiver (with cold)	**vapista**	[ʋɑpistɑ]
to shoot (vi)	**ampua**	[ɑmpuɑ]
to shout (vi)	**huutaa**	[hu:tɑ:]
to show (to display)	**näyttää**	[ɲæyttæ:]
to shudder (vi)	**vavahdella**	[ʋɑʋɑhdellɑ]

to sigh (vi)	**huokaista**	[huokajsta]
to sign (document)	**allekirjoittaa**	[allekirʰojtta:]
to signify (mean)	**merkitä**	[merkitæ]
to simplify (vt)	**yksinkertaistaa**	[yksiŋkertajsta:]
to sin (vi)	**tehdä syntiä**	[tehdæ syntiæ]
to sit (be sitting)	**istua**	[istua]
to sit down (vi)	**istuutua**	[istu:tua]
to smash (~ a bug)	**litistää**	[litistæ:]
to smell (have odour)	**tuoksua**	[tuoksua]
to smell (sniff at)	**haistella**	[hajstella]
to smile (vi)	**hymyillä**	[hymyjʎæ]
to solve (problem)	**ratkaista**	[ratkajsta]
to sow (seed, crop)	**kylvää**	[kylʋæ:]
to spill (liquid)	**kaataa**	[ka:ta:]
to spit (vi)	**sylkeä**	[sylkeæ]
to emit (smell)	**levittää**	[leʋittæ:]
to stand (toothache, cold)	**kärsiä**	[kærsiæ]
to start (begin)	**aloittaa**	[alojtta:]
to steal (money, etc.)	**varastaa**	[ʋarasta:]
to stop (cease)	**lakata**	[lakata]
to stop (for pause, etc.)	**pysähtyä**	[pysæhtyæ]
to stop talking	**vaieta**	[ʋajeta]
to strengthen	**vahvistaa**	[ʋahʋista:]
to stroke (caress)	**hyväillä**	[hyʋæjʎæ]
to study (vt)	**oppia**	[oppia]
to suffer (feel pain)	**kärsiä**	[kærsiæ]
to support (cause, idea)	**kannattaa**	[kaŋatta:]
to suppose (assume)	**olettaa**	[oletta:]
to surface (ab. submarine)	**nousta pinnalle**	[nousta piŋalle]
to surprise (amaze)	**ihmetyttää**	[ihmetyttæ:]
to suspect (vt)	**epäillä**	[epæjʎæ]
to swim (vi)	**uida**	[ujda]
to switch on (vt)	**avata**	[aʋata]

256. Verbs T-W

to take (get hold of)	**ottaa**	[otta:]
to take a rest	**levätä**	[leʋætæ]
to take aim (at ...)	**tähdätä**	[tæhdætæ]
to take away	**viedä pois**	[ʋiedæ pojs]
to take off (aeroplane)	**nousta ilmaan**	[nousta ilma:n]
to take off (remove)	**ottaa pois**	[otta: pojs]
to take pictures	**valokuvata**	[ʋalokuʋata]
to talk to ...	**puhua**	[puhua]
to teach (give lessons)	**opettaa**	[opetta:]
to tear off (vt)	**repäistä**	[repæjstæ]

to tell (story, joke)	**kertoa**	[kertoa]
to thank (vt)	**kiittää**	[ki:ittæ:]
to think (believe)	**pitää**	[pitæ:]
to think (vi, vt)	**ajatella**	[ajatella]
to threaten (vt)	**uhata**	[uhata]
to throw (stone)	**heittää**	[hejttæ:]
to tie to ...	**sitoa**	[sitoa]
to tie up (prisoner)	**yhdistää**	[yhdistæ:]
to tire (make tired)	**väsyttää**	[ʋæsyttæ:]
to touch (one's arm, etc.)	**koskea**	[koskea]
to tower (over ...)	**kohota**	[kohota]
to train (animals)	**kouluttaa**	[koulutta:]
to train (vi)	**valmentautua**	[ʋalmentautua]
to train (sb)	**valmentaa**	[ʋalmenta:]
to transform (vt)	**muuntaa**	[mu:nta:]
to translate (vt)	**kääntää**	[kæ:ntæ:]
to treat (patient, illness)	**hoitaa**	[hojta:]
to trust (vt)	**luottaa**	[luotta:]
to try (attempt)	**yrittää**	[yrittæ:]
to turn (~ to the left)	**kääntää**	[kæ:ntæ:]
to turn away (vi)	**kääntyä poispäin**	[kæ:ntyæ pojs pæjn]
to turn off (the light)	**sammuttaa**	[sammutta:]
to turn over (stone, etc.)	**kääntää**	[kæ:ntæ:]
to underestimate (vt)	**aliarvioida**	[aliarʋiojda]
to underline (vt)	**alleviivata**	[alleʋi:iʋata]
to understand (vt)	**ymmärtää**	[ymmærtæ:]
to undertake (vt)	**ryhtyä**	[ryhtyæ]
to unite (vt)	**yhdistää**	[yhdistæ:]
to untie (vt)	**irrottaa**	[irotta:]
to use (phrase, word)	**käyttää**	[kæyttæ:]
to vaccinate (vt)	**rokottaa**	[rokotta:]
to vote (vi)	**äänestää**	[æ:nestæ:]
to wait (vt)	**odottaa**	[odotta:]
to wake (sb)	**herättää**	[herættæ:]
to want (wish, desire)	**haluta**	[haluta]
to warn (of the danger)	**varoittaa**	[ʋarojtta:]
to wash (clean)	**pestä**	[pestæ]
to water (plants)	**kastella**	[kastella]
to wave (the hand)	**hosua**	[hosua]
to weigh (have weight)	**painaa**	[pajna:]
to work (vi)	**työskennellä**	[tyøskeŋeʎæ]
to worry (make anxious)	**huolestuttaa**	[huolestutta:]
to worry (vi)	**olla huolissaan**	[olla huolissa:n]
to wrap (parcel, etc.)	**kääriä**	[kæ:riæ]
to wrestle (sport)	**painia**	[pajnia]

to write (vt)	**kirjoittaa**	[kirʰojtta:]
to write down	**kirjoittaa muistiin**	[kirʰojtta: mujsti:in]

3808961R00142

Printed in Germany
by Amazon Distribution
GmbH, Leipzig